TOPOGRAPHIES OF
WHITENESS

This book is number two in the Series on Critical Race Studies and Multiculturalism in LIS
Rose L. Chou and Annie Pho, Series Editors

Also in this series:

Teaching for Justice: Implementing Social Justice in the LIS Classroom, edited by Nicole A. Cooke and Miriam E. Sweeney

TOPOGRAPHIES OF WHITENESS: MAPPING WHITENESS IN LIBRARY AND INFORMATION SCIENCE

Gina Schlesselman-Tarango, Editor

LIBRARY JUICE PRESS
SACRAMENTO, CA

Published in 2017 by Library Juice Press

Library Juice Press
PO Box 188784
Sacramento, CA 95822

http://libraryjuicepress.com/

This book is printed on acid-free, sustainably-sourced paper.

Library of Congress Cataloging-in-Publication Data

Names: Schlesselman-Tarango, Gina, editor.
Title: Topographies of whiteness : mapping whiteness in library and
  information science / Gina Schlesselman-Tarango, editor.
Description: Sacramento, CA : Library Juice Press, 2017. | Series: Series on
  critical race studies and multiculturalism in LIS ; number 2 | Includes
  bibliographical references and index.
Identifiers: LCCN 2017030858 | ISBN 9781634000222 (acid-free paper)
Subjects: LCSH: Library science--Social aspects--United States. | Library
  science--Social aspects--United States--History. | Librarians--United
  States--Social conditions. | Minority librarians--United States--Social
  conditions. | Whites--Race identity--United States | Whites--United
  States--Social conditions. | United States--Race relations. |
  Anti-racism--United States. | Library science--Social aspects.
Classification: LCC Z716.4 .T65 2017 | DDC 020.973--dc23
LC record available at https://lccn.loc.gov/2017030858

Contents

FOREWORD

Topographies of Whiteness: Mapping Whiteness in Library and Information Science is an exciting contribution to library and information science (LIS) scholarship. It takes a critical approach to the study of race with a specific focus on how whiteness has shaped and continues to impact the field and profession. While scholarship that addresses whiteness is scattered across various scholarly journals, online websites, conference proceedings, professional association newsletters, and other such forums, *Topographies of Whiteness* is the first book-length treatment of whiteness available in the LIS field . . . and it's about time! For those of us who have long desired such a volume, this anthology offers a valuable resource that compiles different approaches to the topic of whiteness for us to reflect upon, critique, and chart new paths forward. The timing couldn't be more appropriate, as we enter uncertain times with the inauguration of a new president and an emboldened white demographic euphemistically calling themselves the "alt-right." Now, more than ever, the naming, interrogating, and challenging of whiteness become imperative work for all of us dedicated to a progressive, democratic ethos and politics in our field.

Topographies of Whiteness does a remarkable job of assembling a diverse group of scholars and practitioners to dissect the often hidden ways that whiteness operates at different strata within LIS. Through diverse methods and frameworks, these chapters, taken all together, reveal how whiteness is not monolithic, and instead highlights its very complexities, contradictions, intersectionalities, and capacities for transformation. In other words, this anthology helps us to understand whiteness through its very multidimensionality.[1]

In their landmark study of racial formation, Michael Omi and Howard Winant remind us that "race is a matter of both social structure and cultural representation."[2] Making the link between the macro and micro is an important intervention in articulating how the different facets of race have become embedded in our society, both consciously and unconsciously, and how transforming one necessarily entails transforming the other. *Topographies of Whiteness* asks us, as readers, to embrace this analytical coupling by collecting a range of essays that tackle both the structural and the representational aspects of whiteness in LIS.

For instance, storytelling, particularly as a methodology employed in the field of critical race theory, becomes a fertile ground to address how the presentation and performance of racial signification become ways to question white normativity. Through personal narratives of experiences dealing with overt and covert forms of racism, the writers included here ask formative questions about how to understand whiteness as a privileged racial category. How do we create a culture of white visibility, when it is often the presumed norm? Or, when it is mentioned, is it presumed to be under attack (i.e., white fragility), lending itself to a false equivalence with the experiences of people of color and other marginalized peoples? In the absence of overt racial signifiers, what types of practices are simply coded as white? At stake here is not just making whiteness visible, but also contextualizing these everyday forms of racialized encounters within what Stuart Hall has called "societies

---

1. For further discussion on the multidimensionality of race, see Clara M. Chu et al., "Race as Multidimensional: The Personal Shaping the Professional in the Library and Information Field," in *Celebrating the James Partridge Award: Essays Toward the Development of a More Diverse, Inclusive, and Equitable Field of Library and Information Science*, Advances in Librarianship 42, ed. Diane L. Barlow and Paul T. Jaeger (Bingley, UK: Emerald Group Publishing, 2016), 155-70.

2. Michael Omi and Howard Winant, *Racial Formation in the United States: From the 1960s to the 1990s* (New York: Routledge, 1994).

structured in dominance."[3] These interactions are always already located within the intersections of race, gender, sexuality, class, age, and ability, and form a part of larger patterns of systemic aggressions (whether they be micro or macro) that reproduce historically established structures of power and privilege in our field.

Hence, a careful investigation into the past likewise becomes an important avenue to explore the construction of whiteness and its contemporary ramifications in LIS, learning from the past to understand the present. This entails investigating the way racial thinking has influenced the establishment of information institutions, as a way for us to understand the construction of whiteness, not just as an amorphous ideology, but one that is systematized through specific forms of infrastructure (policies around types of access, collection development, educational programs, spatial organization, cataloging, etc.). As much as we, as individuals, may like to think of ourselves as anti-racist, we must also acknowledge that we inherit these systems. In so doing, we may unwittingly reproduce the racialized structures already embedded in the institutions that we work in on a daily basis. So the question emerges: how do we challenge the weight of history that continues to haunt our everyday practices? Or, to paraphrase Marx, how do we create change, but not under the conditions of our own choosing?

The present volume fits within the emerging field of what Mandy Henk terms "critical librarianship," one that turns the analytical gaze inward to critique our own practices and discourses.[4] Marx, again, provides a useful measure in recognizing this critical imperative. In a letter to Arnold Ruge, he wrote, "if we have no business with the construction of the future or with organizing it for all time, there can still be no doubt about the task confronting us at present: the *ruthless criticism of the existing order*, ruthless in that it will shrink neither from its own discoveries, nor

---

3. Stuart Hall, "Race, Articulation and Societies Structured in Dominance," in *Sociological Theories: Race and Colonialism*. (Paris: UNESCO, 1980), 305-45.

4. Mandy Henk, "Mandy Henk's Hikuwai Event: What Is Critical Librarianship?," *Library Juice* (blog), April 21, 2016, http://libraryjuicepress.com/blog/?p=5252.

from conflict with the powers that be."[5] As librarians, archivists, and information and cultural heritage workers, we actually are in the "business" of thinking about the organization of materials for posterity. Yet that doesn't negate our own responsibility to also engage in the work of social critique. In fact, Marx's quote reminds us that we often have to pull double duty: constructing and organizing these materials while also criticizing the existing order. This is the hallmark trait of a politically engaged praxis, and indeed, the cornerstone of the LIS profession. Yet the critique of race has long been occluded in theoretical discussions of LIS, despite the fact that it continues to undergird the practices and policies that we enact every day.

This ruthlessness often requires that we embrace that which can make us uncomfortable. Indeed, talking about whiteness can be uncomfortable: no one wants to admit our complicity in structures of oppression. But discussions that tiptoe around whiteness in the name of so-called "white fragility" and do not explicitly talk about whiteness and its categorical privilege double back into a diluted multicultural discourse that sustains a neoliberal orthodoxy that fails to address the workings of race as a system of stratification and its conjugal forms of privilege and oppression. Roderick Ferguson warns us that the neoliberal order has a tendency of "transforming whiteness into a modern formation that seemingly embraces matters of diversity but eschews visions for social change."[6] Attentive to such warnings, *Topographies of Whiteness* compels us to consider whiteness as a necessary lens through which to expand our visions for social change. Through counternarratives of resistance, transformation, and alternative possibilities, the writings in this volume attempt to engage in a project of decentering whiteness through its very centering. While this may seem contradictory at first, such work is a

---

5. Karl Marx, "Letter from Marx to Arnold Ruge," 1843, https://www.marxists.org/archive/marx/works/1843/letters/43_09-alt.htm. Thank you to Greg Leazer for pointing out the need for this "ruthless theorization" in LIS during one of our conversations about race and diversity in the field.

6. Roderick A. Ferguson, "The Distributions of Whiteness," *American Quarterly* 66, no. 4 (2014): 1101-6, doi: 10.1353/aq.2014.0064.

necessary step in order to account for the way that whiteness structures the "field of racial positions" that we all (differentially) occupy.[7]

I hope that future generations of LIS scholars and practitioners take the opportunity to approach this volume with an open mind, and from it, reflect, discuss, debate, and chart new trajectories forward. I use the term *trajectories* in the plural, because there is much work to be done and many different journeys to embark upon, and I look forward to seeing how this volume opens up these new trajectories of exploration and practice. I also have a personal hope that the gap that this volume fills emphasizes that those of us working on these topics are not struggling in isolation, but instead—as this collection makes clear—form part of a larger collective that holds our field accountable for the changes that we often simply talk about. The (ruthless!) critical self-reflection about LIS and our role in it is crucial to make our field more just, equitable, and accessible for all, rather than for the privileged few. And as this volume helps us realize, first we have to be willing to critique the present in order to get there.

Todd Honma
Pitzer College
Claremont, California
January 19, 2017

---

7. Claire Jean Kim, "The Racial Triangulation of Asian Americans," *Politics & Society* 27, no. 1 (1999): 105-38.

Bibliography

Chu, Clara M., Linda Ueki Absher, Renate L. Chancellor, Karen E. Downing, Shari Lee, and Touger Vang. "Race as Multidimensional: The Personal Shaping the Professional in the Library and Information Field." In *Celebrating the James Partridge Award: Essays Toward the Development of a More Diverse, Inclusive, and Equitable Field of Library and Information Science*, Advances in Librarianship 42, edited by Diane L. Barlow and Paul T. Jaeger, 155-70. Bingley, UK: Emerald Group Publishing, 2016.

Ferguson, Roderick A. "The Distributions of Whiteness." *American Quarterly* 66, no. 4 (2014): 1101-6. doi: 10.1353/aq.2014.0064.

Hall, Stuart. "Race, Articulation and Societies Structured in Dominance." In *Sociological Theories: Race and Colonialism*, 305-45. Paris: UNESCO, 1980.

Henk, Mandy. "Mandy Henk's Hikuwai Event: What Is Critical Librarianship?" *Library Juice* (blog), April 21, 2016. http://libraryjuicepress.com/blog/?p=5252.

Kim, Claire Jean. "The Racial Triangulation of Asian Americans." *Politics & Society* 27, no. 1 (1999): 105-38.

Marx, Karl. Letter from Marx to Arnold Ruge. 1843. https://www.marxists.org/archive/marx/works/1843/letters/43_09-alt.htm.

Omi, Michael, and Howard Winant. *Racial Formation in the United States: From the 1960s to the 1990s*. New York: Routledge, 1994.

Acknowledgements

This collection would not be possible without the guidance of Rory Litwin and Alison Lewis, as well as all the work Sujei Lugo put in to get the project going. Many thanks to Shana Higgins and Lua Gregory who, over coffee and margaritas, shared their experiences with editing their own collection. To all of you: your advice has been excellent, and your patience extraordinary.

I thank Todd Honma, whose "Trippin' Over the Color Line: The Invisibility of Race in Library and Information Studies" has inspired so many of us, for providing a foreword for this volume. I also thank Dave Ellenwood and David James Hudson for their willingness to review the introduction—earlier drafts were greatly improved due to your insight and wisdom, and I extend my appreciation to the organizers of the 2015 Canadian Association of Professional Academic Librarians Conference where I first presented many of these ideas. Deepest gratitude to Amber Billey, Annie Pho, and Kyle Shockey for their work as peer reviewers, and I thank Cesar Caballero and my colleagues at California State University, San Bernardino for their support of this project. Finally, I recognize the incredible amount of time and effort the contributors to this anthology have put towards their chapters—it has been an absolute honor to work with each and every one of you. You make our profession better.

A million hugs and kisses to Miguel A. Tarango.

— Gina Schlesselman-Tarango

Introduction

Gina Schlesselman-Tarango

> Just as none of us is outside or beyond geography, none of us is completely free from the struggle over geography. That struggle is complex and interesting because it is not only about soldiers and cannons but also about ideas, about forms, about images and imaginings.
> – Edward Said, *Culture and Imperialism*

In *Culture and Imperialism*, Edward Said reveals the ways in which cartography is intimately linked to power. He writes: "Imperialism after all is an act of geographical violence through which virtually every space of the world is explored, charted, and finally brought under control."[1] It might seem odd, then—or even inappropriate—that a collection which seeks to locate and problematize how whiteness operates in library and information sciences and studies (LIS) would take up mapping as its project. Yet, in the epigraph that opens this introduction, Said also makes the important point that we are all bound up in the struggle over geography, and we know that struggle can be productive. In taking an account of

---

1. Edward W. Said, *Culture and Imperialism* (New York: Alfred A. Knopf, 1993), 225.

that which is often denied, in tracing that which seeks imperceptibility, in insisting that whiteness exists and that it is oppressive, we can also understand mapping as an act of resistance.

This collection does not attempt to provide a complete accounting of whiteness (not least because of spatial constraints), but rather extends to readers a topography, a mere outline or survey of the ways whiteness works on, in, and through our field. As Todd Honma notes in the foreword, whiteness is multidimensional. There are undoubtedly subfields and contexts, theoretical orientations, and pressing problems—buttes and mesas, gulches and valleys, regions and even entire continents—that one will not find covered in this anthology. In providing a lay of the land, it is my hope that readers will leave with a few tools with which to traverse yet unexplored terrains of whiteness that mark LIS.

The struggle over geography that Said describes as complex and interesting is also generative in that it creates space for what he calls imaginings. Contributors to this collection present us with their own imaginings of what it means and looks like to trouble whiteness in LIS, and they also guide us in teasing apart the way we talk about and understand it. These namings of whiteness unearth more fundamental questions about how we define whiteness to begin with. Such questions are not unique to LIS. Even a cursory review of the literature reveals a dozen or more definitions: an identity or self-understanding, an ideology or set of group beliefs, a concept, a form of property, an experience, a number of social practices, a system of power, that which terrorizes—to name but a few. It appears that whiteness, in its ubiquity and with its claims to normalcy, resists definition, consequently rendering it a particularly tricky thing to theorize. The tensions created by problems of definition, too, are beginning to mark discussions within LIS, and this book seeks to insert itself into these conversations. It aims to surface rather than resolve such tensions, ultimately giving us additional tools to identify and fissure whiteness, however defined. Further, readers will find that a number of contributors speak to the relationships between whiteness and gender, neoliberalism, and more, in addition to the relationship of whiteness to broader goals of diversity and social justice.

Yet the value of this collection lies in its explicit address of whiteness and its avoidance of some of the ways in which common understandings and utilizations of diversity and social justice can divest of race.

This collection is interdisciplinary, with many contributors drawing on a variety of sources outside LIS in their navigation of questions of whiteness. This outward orientation is largely born out of necessity, for those in other fields and disciplines have wrestled with such questions for longer and in more sustained ways. However, while this is the first book-length treatment of whiteness in LIS, a number of scholars have—over approximately the last fifteen years—paved the way for interrogations of whiteness in our field, and we too have seen a recent increase in scholarship from an emerging set of thinkers who have sought to continue this work.[2] I can speak with confidence for the

---

2 Earlier writings include, for example: Deborah A. Curry, "Your Worries Ain't Like Mine: African American Librarians and the Pervasiveness of Racism, Prejudice and Discrimination in Academe," *Reference Librarian* 21, no. 45-46 (1994): 299-311, doi: 10.1300/J120v21n45_26; Isabel Espinal, "A New Vocabulary for Inclusive Librarianship: Applying Whiteness Theory to our Profession," in *The Power of Language/El Poder de la Palabra: Selected Papers from the Second REFORMA National Conference*, ed. Lillian Castillo-Speed (Englewood, CO: Libraries Unlimited, 2001), 131-49; Jody Nyasha Warner, "Moving Beyond Whiteness in North American Academic Libraries," *Libri* 51, no. 3 (2001): 167-72, doi: 10.1515/LIBR.2001.167; John D. Berry, "White Privilege in Library Land," *Library Journal*, June 15, 2004, http://lj.libraryjournal.com/2004/06/ljarchives/backtalk-white-privilege-in-library-land/#_; Todd Honma, "Trippin' Over the Color Line: The Invisibility of Race in Library and Information Studies," *InterActions: UCLA Journal of Education and Information Studies* 1, no. 2 (2005): 1-26, http://escholarship.org/uc/item/4nj0w1mp; and Christine Pawley, "Unequal Legacies: Race and Multiculturalism in the LIS Curriculum," *Library Quarterly* 76, no. 2 (2006): 149-68, doi: 10.1086/506955.

For more recent scholarship, see, for example: Lisa Hussey, "The Diversity Discussion: What are We Saying?" *Progressive Librarian*, no. 34-35 (Fall-Winter 2010): 3-10, http://www.progressivelibrariansguild.org/PL_Jnl/pdf/PL34_35_fallwinter2010.pdf; Shane Hand, "Transmitting Whiteness: Librarians, Children, and Race, 1900-1930s," *Progressive Librarian*, no. 38-39 (Spring 2012):34-63, http://progressivelibrariansguild.org/PL_Jnl/pdf/PL38_39.pdf; nina de jesus, "Locating the Library in Institutional Oppression," *In the Library with the Lead Pipe* (September 2014), http://www.inthelibrarywiththeleadpipe.org/2014/locating-the-library-in-institutional-oppression/; Angela Galvan, "Soliciting Performance, Hiding Bias: Whiteness in Librarianship," *In the Library with the Lead Pipe* (June 2015), http://www.inthelibrarywiththeleadpipe.org/2015/soliciting-performance-hiding-bias-whiteness-and-librarianship/; April Hathcock, "White Librarianship in

contributors to this anthology when I state that we are eternally grateful for the work these scholars have done, for their own mappings and for the paths they have cleared for us. A number have contributed in one way or another to this collection, and I am honored to include them alongside the work of emerging scholars, practitioners, and activists.

This collection is organized into three parts. Part one, "Early Formations: Tracing the Historical Operations of Whiteness," consists of contributions that do just that. Shaundra Walker dissects white philanthropic motivation and asks readers to consider the ways in which Historically Black Colleges and Universities (HBCUs) navigated racist incentives to ensure they were able to provide libraries for their students. Nicole M. Joseph, Katherine M. Crowe, and Janiece Mackey interrogate how privilege and exclusion have worked upon the historical record at both HBCUs and Predominantly White Institutions (PWIs) and offer recommendations for building anti-racist and inclusive archives. Ian Beilin explores architecture and space, using Columbia University's Butler Library as a case study to prompt us to consider how whiteness has quite literally shaped the academic research library.

In part two, "Present Topographies: Surveying Whiteness in Contemporary LIS," Sarah Hannah Gómez calls upon windows and mirrors to reflect upon a lifetime of library use, as well as her current work as

---

Blackface: Diversity Initiatives in LIS," *In the Library with the Lead Pipe* (October 2015), http://www.inthelibrarywiththeleadpipe.org/2015/lis-diversity/; Mario H. Ramirez, "Being Assumed Not to Be: A Critique of Whiteness as an Archival Imperative," *American Archivist* 78, no. 2 (2015): 339-56, doi: 10.17723/0360-9081.78.2.339; Freeda Brook, Dave Ellenwood, and Althea Eannace Lazzaro, "In Pursuit of Antiracist Social Justice: Denaturalizing Whiteness in the Academic Library," *Library Trends* 64, no. 2 (2015): 246-84, doi: 10.1353/lib.2015.0048; Gina Schlesselman-Tarango, "The Legacy of Lady Bountiful: White Women in the Library," *Library Trends* 64, no. 4 (2016): 667-86, doi: 10.1353/lib.2016.0015; David James Hudson, "On 'Diversity' as Anti-Racism in Library and Information Studies: A Critique," *Journal of Critical Library and Information Studies* 1, no. 1 (2017): 1-36. This is not a complete list and, by the time this anthology will have been published, there will likely be more. Additionally, there are a number of blogs and other Web resources that also address whiteness in LIS (for example, *Reading While White: Allies for Racial Diversity and Inclusion in Books for Children and Teens*, last accessed January 5, 2017, http://readingwhilewhite.blogspot.com).

a black woman in a white-dominated profession. Jessica Macias details the lived experiences of library professionals as they navigate white beauty and grooming standards, calling attention to the ways in which the bodies of people of color are policed in library spaces. Vani Natarajan explores designer Orla Kiely's fashion show, *Library for Fall 2015*, to interrogate the ways in which sartorial representations of the library and library workers reflect fantasies and imperatives rooted in white femininity, and Megan Watson outlines how white feminism regulates power, influence, and decision making in academic libraries. Rafia Mirza and Maura Seale also look at intersections of gender and whiteness, and using the Center for the Future of Libraries' Trend Library as a case study, trouble the ways in which white masculinity infuses and is centered in discourse surrounding library futurity. David James Hudson rounds out this section with a critique of the discourse of practicality that dominates LIS, exposing the work a practice-oriented imperative does to preclude theoretical engagement with the complexities of white supremacy.

Part three, "Fissures: Imagining New Cartographies," begins with an account of how whiteness can be addressed in the LIS classroom; Katrina Spencer, Jennifer Margolis Jacobs, Cass Mabbott, Chloe Collins, and Rebekah M. Loyd reflect on their learning experiences with educator Nicole A. Cooke. April M. Hathcock and Stephanie Sendaula examine whiteness at the reference desk and propose ways that both librarians of color and white librarians can combat its harmful effects through bystander intervention, micro-affirmations, and a renewed focus on the recruitment and retention of librarians of color. Jorge R. López-McKnight shares his experiences as a librarian of color at two PWIs, demonstrating how counterstories can be tools to deconstruct and disrupt whiteness. Natalie Baur, Margarita Vargas-Betancourt, and George Apodaca also provide an example of how whiteness can be challenged in LIS, as they tell us about the *Desmantelando Fronteras/Breaking Down Borders* collaborative webinar series that carves out a space to counter the histories of uneven relations between US and Latin American library and archival organizations. Finally, Melissa Kalpin Prescott, Kristyn

Caragher, and Katie Dover-Taylor reflect on ways white librarians can engage in anti-racist praxis at different levels and in various communities.

Readers will notice that authors' decisions regarding the capitalization of white(ness), black(ness), and the like have been respected. While such a move does not lend itself to consistency from chapter to chapter, it is important that contributors' choices—no doubt made with great thought and attention to the ways in which writing conventions can reinforce or challenge whiteness—be honored. Many thanks to those involved with Litwin Books and Library Juice Press's Series on Critical Race Studies and Multiculturalism in LIS for their willingness to support this nontraditional editorial approach.

Critical Whiteness Studies: A Very Brief Introduction

There are a number of misgivings I had going into editing this collection, and this is due in no small part to the fact that the ways in which I move about the world are at times at odds with or even contradictory to the anti-racist ideals I profess. For example, after leaving a position as an English teacher in Ukraine with the Peace Corps, I worked for two years as one of many young teachers who comprised an almost exclusively white teaching staff at a charter school in a low-income urban neighborhood (read: a community of color). In both capacities, I could be understood to be functioning under the logic of white feminine benevolence I later critique,[3] and one might bring a similar reading to my work today as a white librarian and educator at a Hispanic-Serving Institution.[4] How does one make sense of or account for their complicity in structures of imperialism, capitalism, and white supremacy, for example, while at the same time engage in the political act of critiquing

---

3. Schlesselman-Tarango, "The Legacy of Lady Bountiful."

4. Hispanic Association of Colleges and Universities (HACU), "Hispanic-Serving Institution Definitions," last accessed January 6, 2017, http://www.hacu.net/hacu/HSI_Definition1.asp. According to HACU, "Hispanic-Serving Institutions (HSIs) are defined in Title V of the Higher Education Act as not-for-profit institutions of higher learning with a full-time equivalent (FTE) undergraduate student enrollment that is at least 25 percent Hispanic."

them? As Honma compels us to ask, "how do we challenge the weight of history that continues to haunt our everyday practices?"[5]

The above questions gesture to the messiness that accompanies any sort of critique. In the following sections, I expand upon and elucidate this messiness as it pertains specifically to whiteness critique by detailing some (though certainly not all) of the debates surrounding critical whiteness studies. Doing so allows me to preface one's reading of this collection with a bit of context, for problematizing whiteness is one thing, but the *act* of studying whiteness is a political project that poses a different, yet related, set of complications and challenges. If our field continues to interrogate whiteness, an understanding of the problems inherent to and the implications of this act, as well as strategies for negotiating the limitations of this broader theoretical project, are required. While not all scholarship that has engaged with whiteness has done so explicitly through the lens of critical whiteness studies (nor, you will find, do most contributors to this collection), this paradigm is a useful site of analysis because it is an established area of inquiry whose concerns align with those more recently taken up in LIS (white privilege, white supremacy, white spaces, etc.). Secondly, criticisms of critical whiteness studies are heavily documented, and it would behoove us to call upon such critiques to inform our own research agenda.

The emergence of what is known today as critical whiteness studies (sometimes referred to simply as *whiteness studies*) is often traced back to Peggy McIntosh's 1988 paper on white privilege.[6] Toni Morrison's 1992 text, *Playing in the Dark: Whiteness and the Literary Imagination*, is equally important to the birth of the framework.[7] This text explores whiteness as determined by blackness in American literature, bringing attention to the fact that while blackness is assigned meaning, "whiteness, alone,

---

5. Foreword, this volume.

6. Peggy McIntosh, "White Privilege: Unpacking the Invisible Knapsack," *Independent School* 49, no. 2 (Winter 1990): 31-35, http://www.wvu.edu/~lawfac/jscully/Race/documents/whiteprivilege.pdf.

7. Toni Morrison, *Playing in the Dark: Whiteness and the Literary Imagination* (Cambridge, MA: Harvard University Press, 1992).

is mute, meaningless, unfathomable, pointless, frozen, veiled, curtained, dreaded, senseless, implacable."[8] This insight—that whiteness is somehow veiled—is considered a key contribution to race studies, and there is general consensus that whiteness seeks invisibility (even while it is not always successful and can also be understood as hypervisible to those who do not benefit from it). A central aim of the study of whiteness, then, is to lay it bare and interrogate the "unexamined norm, implicitly standing for all that is presumed to be right and normal."[9]

Critical whiteness studies shares similarities to studies of masculinity, as both seek to name, problematize, and make (more) visible the center, or that which is dominant.[10] Many have pointed to the necessity and importance of such work, from Hazel Carby's call to "think about the invention of the category of whiteness"[11] to Alfred J. López's suggestion that "for perhaps the first time since its invention some few hundred years ago, whiteness finds itself to some extent caught in the others' gaze; it has come to be aware of itself as a race-object among other race-objects, or at least as an entity that can be and is apprehended that way by the others' gaze."[12] The tensions and contradictions that characterize critical whiteness studies are nevertheless well worth examining.

.

---

8. Ibid., 59.

9. Margaret L. Andersen, "Whitewashing Race: Critical Perspectives on Whiteness," in *White Out: The Continuing Significance of Racism*, ed. Ashley W. Doane and Eduardo Bonilla-Silva (New York: Routledge, 2003), 24.

10. Heloise Brown, "Introduction: White? Women: Beginnings and Endings?" in *White? Women: Critical Perspectives on Gender and Race*, ed. Heloise Brown, Madi Gilkes, and Ann Kaloski-Naylor (York, UK: Raw Nerve Books, 1999), 6.

11. Hazel Carby, "The Multicultural Wars" in *Black Popular Culture*, ed. Gina Dent and Michelle Wallace (Seattle: Bay Press, 1992), 193.

12. Alfred J. López, ed., "Introduction: Whiteness After Empire," in *Postcolonial Whiteness: A Critical Reader on Race and Empire* (Ithaca, NY: State University of New York Press, 2005), 15.

Centering White Scholarship, Centering White Subjects

It is not necessary to look too far before one encounters the contention that critical whiteness studies started to be taken seriously only when white scholars took it up. Indeed, people of color have been thinking and talking about, theorizing, and resisting whiteness long before critical whiteness studies—or what could be understood as the "theoretical apparatus" sanctioned by the white academy[13]—had been taken seriously as a discipline. Thinkers like James Baldwin, Zora Neale Hurston, Langston Hughes, Harriet Jacobs, and countless others had been discussing whiteness in America well before critical whiteness studies was legitimized by the academy.[14] Indeed, in *Black Reconstruction in America, 1860-1880*, published in 1935, W. E. B. Du Bois theorized about what we often refer to today as privilege (what he described as a sort of "public and psychological wage" granted to white laborers that, despite their meager remuneration, "had great effect upon their personal treatment and the deference shown them").[15] Yet, this idea is more often than not attributed to McIntosh, who is white and whose essay was published more than fifty years later. Dismissal of both early writings and contemporary work on whiteness by scholars of color is one of the major critiques leveled against the field.[16] What, then, is unique or new about critical whiteness studies? One is left to assume

---

13. Espinal, "A New Vocabulary for Inclusive Librarianship," 137.

14. See David Roediger, ed., *Black on White: Black Writers on What it Means to Be White* (New York: Schocken Books, 1998) for an excellent compilation of black writers on whiteness.

15. W. E. B. Du Bois, B*lack Reconstruction in America, 1860-1880* (1935; repr., New York: Touchstone, 1995), 700-01; Zach Schwartz-Weinstein, "'White Privilege' Defanged: From Class War Analysis to Electoral Cynicism," *Abolition* (blog), October 27, 2016, https://abolitionjournal.org/white-privilege-defanged/.

16. Zeus Leonardo, Race F*rameworks: A Multidimensional Theory of Racism and Education* (New York: Teachers College Press, 2013), 98-101; Roediger, introduction to *Black on White*, 3-26.

that its novelty simply resides in its "explicit focus upon whiteness as a subject of study and the deliberate use of labels such as 'whiteness studies' to describe the field."[17]

It should come as no surprise, then, that critics of whiteness studies implore white scholars and activists to "consider the intimacy between privilege and the work we do, even in the work we do on privilege."[18] Zeus Leonardo further recommends that "a brutal self-reflection becomes necessary for Whites if Whiteness Studies is expected to avoid reproducing racial privilege at the level of intellectual production, despite the best intentions."[19] Yet, this position might appear to be at odds with others' insistence that white people do their own work,[20] that whites perform the labor of thinking through, working out, or solving problems presented by whiteness, a call that has also been made within LIS.[21] It is important, then, to avoid creating a line of inquiry that centers white scholarship, while at the same time acknowledging the necessity for white people to assume a certain amount of responsibility for the whiteness question.

Additional criticism points to whiteness studies' insular focus on white subjects, which risks affirming or reifying the whiteness that it attempts to problematize in the first place. This fixation is evidenced by proposed solutions in the outstanding debate about what well-meaning white people are to *do* with their whiteness. One camp, a group often referred to as the "abolitionists," aims to simply get rid of whiteness

---

17. Woody Doane, "Rethinking Whiteness Studies," in *White Out: The Continuing Significance of Racism*, ed. Ashley W. Doane and Eduardo Bonilla-Silva (New York: Routledge, 2003), 5.

18. Sara Ahmed, "Declarations of Whiteness: The Non-Performativity of Anti-Racism," *Borderlands* 3, no. 2 (2004): para. 55, http://www.borderlands. net.au/vol3no2_2004/ahmed_declarations.htm.

19. Leonardo, *Race Frameworks*, 98.

20. Cynthia Levine-Rasky, ed., Introduction to *Working Through Whiteness: International Perspectives* (Albany: State University of New York Press, 2002), 1.

21. Chris Bourg, "Whiteness, Social Justice, and the Future of Libraries," *Feral Librarian* (blog), January 9, 2016, https://chrisbourg.wordpress. com/2016/01/09/whiteness-social-justice-and-the-future-of-libraries/.

altogether.[22] How exactly this abolition would be realized is unclear, though the general idea is that if a handful of white abolitionists—also referred to as "race traitors"—flagrantly rejects their allegiance to whiteness, the special privileges granted to those with white skin will be eliminated, and whiteness as a system will destabilize and collapse.

This position has been critiqued for its assumption that white people can simply shed their whiteness; indeed, if whiteness is a social construction—something that is not fixed but is continuously being renegotiated and remade in relation to gender, class, nation, and more—then we ought to remain skeptical of claims that it is possible to will oneself to be once and for all nonwhite. To simply declare oneself not white through individual acts of racial disavowal does not mean that others will stop regarding one as white, that one's whiteness will not continually be revived, rearticulated, and reinforced, or that one will automatically stop being afforded benefits under structures of privilege. Abolitionism naively suggests that personal choice can undo racial identities rooted in social processes and structures extending far beyond the control of the individual.[23] Such a solution places the responsibility of "solving" whiteness—and thus racism—in the hands of individual white subjects, effectively leaving no political space for the work of people of color.[24] Abolitionism has also been critiqued for (re)centering white male figures, such as abolitionist John Brown, as its ideal anti-racist heroes.[25]

In contrast to the abolitionist, the reconstructionist aims to rearticulate whiteness into something worthwhile and non-oppressive.

---

22. John Garvey and Noel Ignatiev, "Toward a New Abolitionism: A *Race Traitor* Manifesto," in *Whiteness: A Critical Reader*, ed. Mike Hill (New York: New York University Press, 1997), 346-49; Noel Ignatiev, "The Point is Not to Interpret Whiteness But to Abolish It" (presentation, The Making and Unmaking of Whiteness, Berkeley, California, April 11-13, 1997), http://racetraitor.org/abolishthepoint.pdf.

23. Andersen, "Whitewashing Race," 31.

24. Leonardo, *Race Frameworks*, 97-112.

25. bell hooks, *Yearning: Race, Gender, and Cultural Politics* (Boston, MA: South End Press, 1990), 167; López, "Introduction," 13; Robyn Wiegman, "Whiteness Studies and the Paradox of Particularity," *boundary* 2 26, no. 3 (1999): 140-41.

Anti-essentialist thinkers insist that because it is a social construct, whiteness ought not to be conflated with white racism, that it need not always be oppressive, and that it can, in a sense, be reinvented.[26] For example, Henry Giroux asserts the need for "an attempt to rearticulate Whiteness as part of a broader project of cultural, social, and political citizenship,"[27] and we can identify similar sentiments from those who seek to "de-colonize" white subjects or forge white, anti-racist political spaces. Yet, Leonardo challenges this strategy, suggesting that "arguing for a proud Whiteness conjures images of 'White pride,' whose history with White supremacy is intimate and familiar."[28] Margaret L. Andersen also questions the invitation to white people to call upon their particular histories, experiences, and cultures as sites of defiance, noting that here, it is again white subjects that do the resisting, reflecting, and empowering—from positions of whiteness.[29]

The turn to the particularities of whiteness is illustrated by the "white trash" school.[30] The analyses that emerge examine how whiteness intersects with, and is fashioned by, other facets of identity such as class. While it would be difficult to argue against the value of intersectional analysis and the work it does to demonstrate how race and other

---

26. See Henry Giroux, "Racial Politics and the Pedagogy of Whiteness," in *Whiteness: A Critical Reader*, ed. Mike Hill (New York: New York University Press, 1997), 294-313; Henry Giroux, "Rewriting the Discourse of Racial Identity: Towards a Pedagogy and Politics of Whiteness," *Harvard Educational Review* 67, no. 2 (1997): 285-321, doi: 10.17763/haer.67.2.r4523gh4176677u8; Henry Giroux, "White Squall: Resistance and the Pedagogy of Whiteness," *Cultural Studies* 11, no. 3 (1997): 376-89, doi: 10.1080/095023897335664; Diana Jeater, "Roast Beef and Reggae Music: The Passing of Whiteness," *New Formations* 118 (Winter 1992): 114-17; Shannon Sullivan, *Good White People: The Problem with Middle-Class White Anti-Racism* (Albany: State University of New York Press, 2014), 117-63; George Yudice, "Neither Impugning nor Disavowing Whiteness Does a Viable Politics Make: The Limits of Identity Politics," in *After Political Correctness: The Humanities and Society in the 1990s*, ed. Christopher Newfield and Ronald Strickland (Boulder, CO: Westview Press, 1995), 255-83.

27. Giroux, "Rewriting the Discourse of Racial Identity," 297.

28. Leonardo, *Race Frameworks*, 88.

29. Andersen, "Whitewashing Race," 31.

30. Wiegman, "Whiteness Studies and the Paradox of Particularity," 122.

identities are co-constitutive, some warn against lingering in specificity and instead point to the need to explore the ways in which whiteness is produced and operates across age, gender, sex, class, and the like. It is worth quoting Richard Dyer at length: "Yet the strength of white representation, as I've suggested, is the apparent absence altogether of the typical, the sense that being white is coterminous with the endless plenitude of human diversity. If we are to see the historical, cultural, and political limitations (to put it mildly) of white world domination, it is important to see similarities, typicalities, within the seemingly infinite variety of white representation."[31]

Further, in calling attention to particularized whiteness and in positioning white subjects as disadvantaged, minoritized, injured, racialized, or as "prewhite" ethnics,[32] we risk creating space for such subjects to "avoid critical confrontations with contemporary U.S. race relations in order to exempt themselves personally from complicity or responsibility."[33] This position further suggests that "only in becoming 'nonwhite,' only in retrieving a prewhite ethnicity, can the anti-racist subject be invented."[34] This is reminiscent of the race traitor position, as it champions a white subject who authenticates their own anti-racism through self-authorized white distancing or disaffiliation.

In attempting to locate and problematize whiteness, anti-racist solutions posed by abolitionists, reconstructionists, and those of the white trash school risk more firmly lodging it in the center. The preceding critique should not be confused with a simple dismissal of the important anti-racist work done under the banner of any of these camps, nor should it be read as an assertion that all whiteness scholarship fits neatly into one or any of these three categories. However, outlining these

---

31. Richard Dyer, "White," in *The Matter of Images: Essays on Representation* (New York: Routledge, 2002), 145.

32. Wiegman, "Whiteness Studies and the Paradox of Particularity," 139.

33. Mimi Thi Nguyen, Introduction to *Evolution of a Race Riot* 1 (1998): 4, https://issuu.com/poczineproject/docs/evolution-of-a-race-riot-issue-1.

34. Wiegman, "Whiteness Studies and the Paradox of Particularity," 139.

positions and the criticisms they invite allows us to see how whiteness can sully even the strategies meant to challenge it.

White Privilege Pedagogy, White Privilege Politics

John D. Berry's 2004 short piece entitled "White Privilege in Library Land" implores white LIS practitioners to become aware of their white privilege.[35] He connects white privilege to diversity (though what he means by diversity is unclear), contending that "accepting this awareness" of privilege "is critical if you have a commitment to the goals and values of diversity and equity."[36] Introducing a list of white privileges he identifies in LIS, Berry further stipulates that such a list "will get at the heart of why diversity matters."[37] He encourages readers to attend diversity events, suggesting that attendance can prompt personal change in white perception and understanding of privilege. Berry's call thus gives rise to a number of questions: Does ignorance of white privilege produce or perpetuate inequity, or that which diversity purportedly is not?[38] How does one go about acknowledging white privilege? Is such acknowledgement a means to an end or an end in itself? What sort of change does individual awareness of privilege enable?

While it is perhaps the first explicit call for white subjects in LIS to consider their privilege, Berry's piece is one of many that followed McIntosh's 1988 essay. Since its publication, many have framed the recognition of privilege as a necessary prerequisite to anti-racism or even as an anti-racist act itself. McIntosh herself insists that "describing white privilege makes one newly accountable,"[39] and accounting

---

35. Berry, "White Privilege in Library Land."

36. Ibid.

37. Ibid.

38. See Hudson, "On 'Diversity' as Anti-Racism" for a critique of diversity discourse, and Hathcock, "White Librarianship in Blackface" for a critique of diversity initiatives. Both suggest that "diversity" as it is currently conceived of and practiced in LIS is not antithetical to whiteness.

39. McIntosh, "White Privilege."

for white privilege has accordingly become something of a trope in critical whiteness studies and among white self-identified anti-racists. The fascination with teaching about privilege—of calling upon white privilege as a way to introduce problems posed by white supremacy and to assert anti-racist solutions—can be understood as what Barbara Applebaum calls "white privilege pedagogy."[40]

The aspiration to learn about and thus recognize white privilege raises questions of agency. If part of the definition of white privilege is that it is something about which white subjects are "meant to remain oblivious,"[41] and if white privilege, like whiteness itself, is invested in its invisibility, then can one ever become fully aware of its various manifestations? If privilege—again, like whiteness—is an elusive yet permeative norm, can we ever see it for what it is? Indeed, Sara Ahmed suggests that one "cannot simply unlearn privilege when the cultures in which learning take place are shaped by privilege."[42] This raises a second question of whether the project of becoming aware of one's privilege is one that "could never attain completion."[43] As many have argued, the "self-work" called for in relation to white privilege—often an exercise in expunging guilt—can easily turn into an endless and all-encompassing project of self-improvement. This leaves one wondering, as Fredrik deBoer asks, "whether our goal is to *be* good or to *do* good."[44]

Even if someone were to become fully aware of their privilege—if they were, in a sense, to attain completion—how do they use such knowledge to counter, resist, or reject privileges that are conferred rather

---

40. Barbara Applebaum, *Being White, Being Good: White Complicity, White Moral Responsibility, and Social Justice Pedagogy* (Lanham, MD: Lexington Books, 2010), 4, 29-34.

41. McIntosh, "White Privilege."

42. Ahmed, "Declarations of Whiteness," para. 40.

43. Sonia Kruks, "Simone De Beauvoir and the Politics of Privilege," *Hypatia* 20, no.1 (2005): 184, doi: 10.1111/j.1527-2001.2005.tb00378.x.

44. Fredrik deBoer, "Admitting that White Privilege Helps You is Really Just Congratulating Yourself," *Washington Post*, January 28, 2016, https://www.washingtonpost.com/posteverything/wp/2016/01/28/when-white-people-admit-white-privilege-theyre-really-just-congratulating-themselves/.

than chosen? Can one un-choose privilege? As Sonia Kruks notes, "the structural asymmetries of privilege, and so also our degrees of implications in it, may sometimes be mitigated but cannot be expunged through our own individual volition."[45] Yet, if we entertain the possibility that one were able to successfully (and fully) first unlearn, then unchoose or resist their privilege—or even, like the abolitionist, reject their whiteness—we must then ask what change this can effect. In other words, what political possibilities can a project of individual reform like white privilege pedagogy facilitate?

The link between (un)learning privilege and social change is perhaps not as clear as we are often led to believe. In a critique directed at critical whiteness studies, Ahmed poses salient challenges to those who consider learning about white privilege to be effective, particularly due to the implication that "the absence of such learning is the 'reason' for inequality and injustice."[46] Indeed, such an idea rests on the common yet unfounded assumption that ignorance breeds racism, an assumption that frames racism solely as an attitudinal or psychological rather than a structural problem.[47] Thus, we must be careful to not frame lack of awareness of white privilege as the *cause* of oppression in and of itself. While I am not suggesting that learning about white privilege is an endeavor without any value, the key distinction—that while racial awareness is necessary to fight injustice, its absence is not the cause of injustice—is often overlooked in white privilege pedagogy and can lead to the erroneous conclusion that the world is unjust because individuals are uneducated or unaware, rather than because there are any number of systems and structures (including those that rely on educational

---

45. Kruks, "Simone De Beauvoir and the Politics of Privilege," 184.

46. Ahmed, "Declarations of Whiteness," para. 37.

47. Ian Haney López, *Dog Whistle Politics: How Racial Coded Appeals Have Reinvented Racism and Wrecked the Middle Class* (New York: Oxford University Press, 2015), 49; David Theo Goldberg, "Racisms and Rationalities," in *Racist Culture: Philosophy and the Politics of Meaning,* (Oxford: Blackwell, 1993), 117-47; Alastair Bonnett, *Anti-Racism* (London: Routledge, 2005).

institutions for their operation) invested in white supremacy and that profit from racial oppression.[48]

As a field, we ought to remain critical of the narratives surrounding learning and liberation, or what Michael J. Monahan calls a "racial morality play" leading to "white . . . redemption,"[49] taking into account what we obscure or even perpetuate when our energies are focused on educating individual subjects.[50] Surely, while white privilege pedagogy carries heuristic benefits as far as race conscientization, when we ask students, practitioners, and the like to consider whiteness only through the framework of privilege, we risk drawing attention away from, and thus perhaps unwittingly contribute to, the maintenance of white supremacy and the structural arrangements that produce such privilege.[51]

In following the trajectory of white privilege pedagogy, it is often the case that once the white subject is adequately "enlightened," the next step is to disclose or even broadcast one's privilege. While we do not see this in Berry's short piece, deBoer contends that this is a ritualistic part of the white privilege "cottage industry," perhaps best exemplified by hip hop duo Macklemore and Ryan Lewis' 2016 song, "White Privilege II."[52] This act is concerning, however, and in utilizing personal testimony as a strategy to explore and examine privilege, a

---

48. The prison industrial complex, for example. For more, see Michelle Alexander, *The New Jim Crow: Mass Incarceration in the Age of Colorblindness* (New York: New Press, 2010) and George Lipsitz, "The Possessive Investment in Whiteness," in *White Privilege: Essential Readings on the Other Side of Racism*, ed. Paula S. Rothenberg (New York: Worth Publishers, 2002), 67-90.

49. Michael J. Monahan, "The Concept of Privilege: A Critical Appraisal," *South African Journal of Philosophy* 33, no. 1 (2014): 81, doi: 10.1080/02580136.2014.892681.

50. See Hudson, "On 'Diversity' as Anti-Racism" and David James Hudson and Gina Schlesselman-Tarango, "On Structures and Self-Work: Locating Anti-Racist Politics in LIS" (presentation, LACUNY Institute, Race Matters: Libraries, Racism, and Antiracism, Brooklyn, New York, May 20, 2016), https://youtu.be/LsmIoDJ4Fz0.

51. Ibid; Applebaum, *Being White, Being Good*, 30.

52. deBoer, "Admitting that White Privilege Helps;" Macklemore and Ryan Lewis (musical group), "White Privilege II," performed by Macklemore and Ryan Lewis, featuring Jamila Woods. Macklemore LLC, 2016.

number of scholars and activists have pointed out that such narratives often devolve into grandiose displays that promote a suffering and pity-inducing white subject.[53] The white individual, riddled by guilt and the burden of penance, thus becomes the subject of investigation and functions as the site of emotional connection for the audience. López writes: "White liberal guilt at its most performative has the . . . effect of diverting attention from the facts of white racism and oppression to how badly the Enlightened White Liberal feels about it."[54]

We can further make sense of the disclosure of white privilege when we understand it as an "unhappy performative."[55] The admission of privilege appears to condemn the white subject, to implicate them in their whiteness. What it asserts, however, is that the subject's understanding of their privilege represents a transcendence of their whiteness and the full realization of a self-critical, anti-racist subjectivity. For Ahmed, then, this admission is empty, meaning that "the conditions are not in place that would allow such 'saying' to 'do' what it 'says'."[56] Unfortunately, disclosure instead operates as a self-congratulatory act in which individuals "pay a kind of grudging penance for their own white privilege and move on, inevitably and fairly quickly, to the white privilege of others."[57]

Leonardo suggests that such displays prevent movement towards constructive investigations of how whiteness affects people of color. While they might be cathartic for white individuals, he contends that public disclosures of privilege are in result "assaulting" for people of color who are reminded "about their lack of privilege" and further "reinforce those [white] privileges when it stays at the level of

---

53. For a LIS-specific critique, see Robin Kurz, "No More Privilege Porn," *Transforming American Libraries* (blog), February 13, 2016, http://www.transformingamericanlibraries.com/2016/02/no-more-privilege-porn.html.

54. López, "Introduction," 23.

55. Ahmed, "Declarations of Whiteness," para. 54.

56. Ibid.

57. deBoer, "Admitting that White Privilege Helps." See also Applebaum, *Being White, Being Good*, 31-32, and Sara Ahmed, "Progressive Racism," *feministkilljoys* (blog), May 30, 2016, https://feministkilljoys.com/2016/05/30/progressive-racism/.

confessionals."[58] He concludes that "White discovery of racial advantage is new mainly *to* Whites,"[59] again pointing to the fact that the "discoveries" of white people regarding whiteness are in fact not discoveries at all. Kara Brown leaves us with what is perhaps a more scathing indictment: "And they simply confirm what we already know: white privilege is fucking amazing."[60]

Finally, in scholarly and activist circles alike, one often encounters the suggestion that once white privilege is (publicly) acknowledged, the white subject should "use" this privilege for "good." Often, this means that white people engage in anti-racist work as what are commonly referred to as "allies" to people of color or members of other oppressed groups. This move demands not only that white individuals take up a particular subject position, but also call upon their privilege as a resource. White privilege pedagogy thus sends its pupils mixed messages, for while we are told that white privilege is something to be resisted or countered, we are also encouraged to leverage it for involvement in anti-racist work. Ewuare X. Osayande illustrates the confusion this call creates, suggesting that white privilege is nothing more than the stuff of white supremacy. He implores us to "imagine a white anti-racist saying, 'I'm going to use my white supremacy to help people of color.'"[61] Like the reconstructionist, the ally who invokes their whiteness as a point of departure into anti-racist work "locate[s] agency in this place. It is also to re-position the white subject as somewhere other than implicated in the critique."[62] Certainly this is not to say that advocating with or sup-

---

58. Leonardo, *Race Frameworks*, 100. As one reviewer noted, Leonardo's claims perhaps generalize the ways in which people of color experience white privilege confessionals.

59. Ibid.

60. Kara Brown, "The Problem with #CrimingWhileWhite," *Jezebel* (blog), December 4, 2014 (3:30 p.m.), http://jezebel.com/the-problem-with-crimingwhilewhite-1666785471.

61 Ewuare X. Osayande, "Word to the Wise: Unpacking the White Privilege of Tim Wise," *Ewuare X. Osayande*, August 26, 2013, http://osayande.org/2013/08/word-to-the-wise-unpacking-the-white-privilege-of-tim-wise/.

62. Sara Ahmed, "A Phenomenology of Whiteness," *Feminist Theory* 8, no. 2 (2007): 164-65, doi: 10.1177/1464700107078139.

porting marginalized groups is a bad thing, but rather that accounting for the dynamics by which allyship can reproduce or reinforce existing power relations is a necessary prerequisite to action.

Navigating Whiteness Critique

As demonstrated, the study of whiteness presents a number of challenges. It is critical, therefore, that as scholars we not only expose whiteness in the field, but also attend to the *act* of studying it. For those of us who identify as white, doing so demands rigorous reflexivity—not to be confused with a self-absorbed fixation on personal improvement— and perhaps without the expectation of any sort of ethical resolution. In considering the implications of studying race, white scholars claiming anti-racism ought to keep in mind the tensions created by doing such work in LIS,[63] a field that has a troubled history of elevating white voices and dismissing scholars of color.[64]

Scholars, and again, particularly those who are white, would do well to embrace ambivalence regarding their involvement both with critical whiteness studies specifically and race studies more generally, situating their work within what Sveta Stoytcheva describes as an "ethics of contingency."[65] In describing such an ethics for librarianship, she suggests that "foregrounding contingency as a lens to think through complex situations . . . can help us formulate an ethical stance through a better understanding of how our work intersects with power."[66] Recognition of context requires that we take seriously the dynamics in which we

---

63. Though it contains potentially problematic personal testimony, George Yancy, ed., *White Self-Criticality Beyond Anti-Racism: How Does It Feel to Be a White Problem?* (Lanham, MD: Lexington Books, 2015) addresses many of the limitations of white anti-racism.

64. Honma, "Trippin' Over the Color Line," 14-18.

65. Sveta Stoytcheva, "Steven Salaita, the Critical Importance of Context, and Our Professional Ethics," *Canadian Journal of Academic Librarianship* 1, no. 1 (2016): 92, http://www.cjal.ca/index.php/capal/article/viewFile/24309/19471.

66. Ibid., 93.

study, theorize, and problematize race. This means that we not only entertain the possibility that our dedication to, or aspiration towards, anti-racism and anti-white supremacy positions us as part of the solution, but also that, in other contexts, it might mean that we are always already part of the problem. Certainly, one's embeddedness within structures of power ought to lead us to treat as suspect any claim to have "arrived" at anti-racism, or any claim to be operating from within a purely anti-racist space.[67]

If our profession is to benefit from its intellectual foray into whiteness critique, none of us should refrain from asking the difficult questions of whether our work contributes to epistemic violence through the intellectual reproduction of whiteness; to the valorization of the white, anti-racist subject; or to the preoccupation with and subsequent privileging of white experience, identity, and self-improvement. In spite of the enormity of the tensions outlined above, I maintain that working within these challenges, however frustrating, can be productive. Such a commitment likely involves lingering in sites of anxiety, but it also creates room for us to remain invested in a "critical engagement with whiteness that does not muffle its own internal conflicts."[68] Remaining committed to criticality allows us to acknowledge these tensions and exploit them for their generative properties. Indeed, in keeping the limitations of whiteness studies in sight, I suggest we not abandon this project altogether. As many of the contributors to this collection do, we might instead draw from other thinkers, theories, and frameworks to tease apart the contradictions of whiteness scholarship, forging a more sophisticated, nuanced, and ultimately transformative critique.

---

67. Aspirations of purity can be problematic. See Kruks, "Simone De Beauvoir and the Politics of Privilege," 185, for an excellent critique of purism as it pertains to white feminism. See also Kristyn Caragher, this volume, for a related critique of perfectionism in anti-racist work.

68. Levine-Rasky, Introduction, 12.

Bibliography

Ahmed, Sara. "Declarations of Whiteness: The Non-Performativity of Anti-Racism." *Borderlands* 3, no. 2 (2004). http://www.borderlands.net.au/vol3no2_2004/ahmed_declarations.htm.

———. "A Phenomenology of Whiteness." *Feminist Theory* 8, no. 2 (2007): 149-68. doi: 10.1177/1464700107078139.

———. "Progressive Racism." *feministkilljoys* (blog), May 30, 2016. https://feministkilljoys.com/2016/05/30/progressive-racism/.

Alexander, Michelle. *The New Jim Crow: Mass Incarceration in the Age of Colorblindness.* New York: New Press, 2010.

Andersen, Margaret L. "Whitewashing Race: Critical Perspectives on Whiteness." In *White Out: The Continuing Significance of Racism,* edited by Ashley W. Doane and Eduardo Bonilla-Silva, 21-34. New York: Routledge, 2003.

Applebaum, Barbara. *Being White, Being Good: White Complicity, White Moral Responsibility, and Social Justice Pedagogy.* Lanham, MD: Lexington Books, 2010.

Berry, John D. "White Privilege in Library Land." *Library Journal* (June 2004). http://lj.libraryjournal.com/2004/06/ljarchives/backtalk-white-privilege-in-library-land/#_.

deBoer, Fredrik. "Admitting that White Privilege Helps You is Really Just Congratulating Yourself." *Washington Post,* January 28, 2016. https://www.washingtonpost.com/posteverything/wp/2016/01/28/when-white-people-admit-white-privilege-theyre-really-just-congratulating-themselves/.

Bonnett, Alastair. *Anti-Racism.* London: Routledge, 2005.

Bourg, Chris. "Whiteness, Social Justice, and the Future of Libraries." *Feral Librarian* (blog), January 9, 2016. https://chrisbourg.wordpress.com/2016/01/09/whiteness-social-justice-and-the-future-of-libraries/.

Brook, Freeda, Dave Ellenwood, and Althea Eannace Lazzaro. "In Pursuit of Antiracist Social Justice: Denaturalizing Whiteness in the Academic Library." *Library Trends* 64, no. 2 (2015): 246-84. doi: 10.1353/lib.2015.0048.

Brown, Heloise. "Introduction: White? Women: Beginnings and Endings?" In *White? Women: Critical Perspectives on Gender and Race*, edited by Heloise Brown, Madi Gilkes, and Ann Kaloski-Naylor, 1-12. York: Raw Nerve Books, 1999.

Brown, Kara. "The Problem with #CrimingWhileWhite." *Jezebel* (blog), December 4, 2014 (3:30 p.m.). http://jezebel.com/the-problem-with-crimingwhilewhite-1666785471.

Carby, Hazel. "The Multicultural Wars." In *Black Popular Culture*, edited by Gina Dent and Michelle Wallace, 187-99. Seattle: Bay Press, 1992.

Curry, Deborah A. "Your Worries Ain't Like Mine: African American Librarians and the Pervasiveness of Racism, Prejudice and Discrimination in Academe." *Reference Librarian* 21, no. 45-46 (1994): 299-311. doi: 10.1300/J120v21n45_26.

Doane, Woody. "Rethinking Whiteness Studies." In *White Out: The Continuing Significance of Racism*, edited by Ashley W. Doane and Eduardo Bonilla-Silva, 3-20. New York: Routledge, 2003.

Du Bois, W. E. B. *Black Reconstruction in America, 1860-1880*, 700-01. 1935. Reprint, New York: Touchstone, 1995.

Dyer, Richard. "White." In *The Matter of Images: Essays on Representations*, 141-63. New York: Routledge, 2002.

Espinal, Isabel. "A New Vocabulary for Inclusive Librarianship: Applying Whiteness Theory to our Profession." In *The Power of Language/El Poder De La Palabra*, edited by Lillian Castillo-Speed, 131-49. Englewood, CO: Libraries Unlimited, 2001.

Galvan, Angela. "Soliciting Performance, Hiding Bias: Whiteness and Librarianship." *In the Library with the Lead Pipe* (June 2015). http://www.inthelibrarywiththeleadpipe.org/2015/soliciting-performance-hiding-bias-whiteness-and-librarianship/.

Garvey, John and Noel Ignatiev. "Toward a New Abolitionism: A
    Race Traitor Manifesto." In *Whiteness: A Critical Reader*, edited
    by Mike Hill, 346-49. New York: New York University Press,
    1997.

Giroux, Henry. "Racial Politics and the Pedagogy of Whiteness." In
    Whiteness: A Critical Reader, edited by Mike Hill, 294-313. New
    York: New York University Press, 1997.

———. "Rewriting the Discourse of Racial Identity: Towards
    a Pedagogy and Politics of Whiteness." *Harvard Edu-
    cational Review* 67, no. 2 (1997): 285-321. doi: 10.17763/
    haer.67.2.r4523gh4176677u8.

———. "White Squall: Resistance and the Pedagogy of White-
    ness." *Cultural Studies* 11, no. 3 (1997): 376-89. doi:
    10.1080/095023897335664.

Goldberg, David Theo. "Racisms and Rationalities." In *Racist Culture:
    Philosophy and the Politics of Meaning*, 117-47. Oxford: Black-
    well, 1993.

Hand, Shane. "Transmitting Whiteness: Librarians, Children, and
    Race, 1900-1930s." *Progressive Librarian*, no. 38-39 (Spring
    2012): 34-63. http://progressivelibrariansguild.org/PL_Jnl/
    pdf/PL38_39.pdf.

Hathcock, April. "White Librarianship in Blackface: Diversity Initia-
    tives in LIS." *In the Library with the Lead Pipe* (October 2015).
    http://www.inthelibrarywiththeleadpipe.org/2015/lis-diver-
    sity/.

Hispanic Association of Colleges and Universities. "Hispanic-Serving
    Institution Definitions," accessed January 6, 2017. http://
    www.hacu.net/hacu/HSI_Definition1.asp.

Honma, Todd. "Trippin' Over the Color Line: The Invisibility of
    Race in Library and Information Studies." *InterActions:
    UCLA Journal of Education and Information Studies* 1, no. 2
    (2005): 1-26. http://escholarship.org/uc/item/4nj0w1mp.

hooks, bell. *Yearning: Race, Gender, and Cultural Politics*. Boston, MA: South End Press, 1990.

Hudson, David James. "On 'Diversity' as Anti-Racism in Library and Information Studies: A Critique." *Journal of Critical Library and Information Studies* 1, no. 1 (2017): 1-36, http://libraryjuicepress.com/journals/index.php/jclis/article/view/6.

Hudson, David James and Gina Schlesselman-Tarango. "On Structures and Self-Work: Locating Anti-Racist Politics in LIS." Presentation at LACUNY Institute, Race Matters: Libraries, Racism, and Antiracism, Brooklyn, New York, May 20, 2016. https://youtu.be/LsmIoDJ4Fz0.

Hussey, Lisa. "The Diversity Discussion: What are We Saying?" *Progressive Librarian*, no. 34-35 (Fall-Winter 2010): 3-10. http://www.progressivelibrariansguild.org/PL_Jnl/pdf/PL34_35_fallwinter2010.pdf.

Ignatiev, Noel. "The Point is Not to Interpret Whiteness But to Abolish It." Presentation, The Making and Unmaking of Whiteness, Berkeley, California, April 11-13, 1997. http://racetraitor.org/abolishthepoint.pdf.

Jeater, Diana. "Roast Beef and Reggae Music: The Passing of Whiteness." *New Formations* 118, (Winter 1992): 107-21.

de jesus, nina. "Locating the Library in Institutional Oppression." *In the Library with the Lead Pipe* (September 2014). http://www.inthelibrarywiththeleadpipe.org/2014/locating-the-library-in-institutional-oppression/.

Kruks, Sonia. "Simone De Beauvoir and the Politics of Privilege." *Hypatia* 20, no. 1 (2005): 178-205. doi: 10.1111/j.1527-2001.2005.tb00378.x.

Kurz, Robin. "No More Privilege Porn." *Transforming American Libraries* (blog), February 13, 2016. http://www.transformingamericanlibraries.com/2016/02/no-more-privilege-porn.html.

Leonardo, Zeus. *Race Frameworks: A Multidimensional Theory of Racism and Education*. New York: Teachers College Press, 2013.

Levine-Rasky, Cynthia, ed. Introduction to *Working Through Whiteness: International Perspectives*, 1-22. Albany: State University of New York Press, 2002.

Lipsitz, George. "The Possessive Investment in Whiteness." In *White Privilege: Essential Readings on the Other Side of Racism*, edited by Paula S. Rothenberg, 67-90. New York: Worth Publishers, 2002.

López, Alfred J., ed. "Introduction: Whiteness After Empire." In *Postcolonial Whiteness: A Critical Reader on Race and Empire*, 1-30. Ithaca, NY: State University of New York Press, 2005.

López, Ian Haney. *Dog Whistle Politics: How Coded Racial Appeals Have Reinvented Racism and Wrecked the Middle Class*. New York: Oxford University Press, 2013.

Macklemore and Ryan Lewis (Musical Group). "White Privilege II." Performed by Macklemore and Ryan Lewis, featuring Jamila Woods. Macklemore LLC, 2016.

McIntosh, Peggy. "White Privilege: Unpacking the Invisible Knapsack." *Independent School* 49, no. 2 (Winter 1990): 31-35. http://www.wvu.edu/~lawfac/jscully/Race/documents/whiteprivilege.pdf.

Monahan, Michael J. "The Concept of Privilege: A Critical Appraisal." *South African Journal of Philosophy* 33, no. 1 (2014): 73-83. doi: 10.1080/02580136.2014.892681.

Morrison, Toni. *Playing in the Dark: Whiteness and the Literary Imagination*. Cambridge, MA: Harvard University Press, 1992.

Nguyen, Mimi Thi. Introduction to *Evolution of a Race Riot* 1 (1998): 4-6. https://issuu.com/poczineproject/docs/evolution-of-a-race-riot-issue-1.

Osayande, Ewuare X. "Word to the Wise: Unpacking the White Privilege of Tim Wise." *Ewuare X. Osayande*, August 26, 2013. http://osayande.org/2013/08/word-to-the-wise-unpacking-the-white-privilege-of-tim-wise/.

Pawley, Christine. "Unequal Legacies: Race and Multiculturalism in the LIS Curriculum." *The Library Quarterly* 76, no. 2 (2006): 149-68. doi: 10.1086/506955.

Ramirez, Mario H. "Being Assumed Not to Be: A Critique of Whiteness as an Archival Imperative." *The American Archivist* 78, no. 2 (2015): 339-56. doi: 10.17723/0360-9081.78.2.339.

Reading While White: Allies for Racial Diversity and Inclusion in Books for Children and Teens. Accessed January 6, 2017. http://readingwhilewhite.blogspot.com.

Roediger, David R., ed. *Black on White: Black Writers on What it Means to be White.* New York: Schocken Books, 1998.

Said, Edward. *Culture and Imperialism.* New York: Knopf, 1993.

Schlesselman-Tarango, Gina. "The Legacy of Lady Bountiful: White Women in the Library." *Library Trends* 64, no. 4 (2016): 667-86. doi: 10.1353/lib.2016.0015.

Schwartz-Weinstein, Zach. "'White Privilege' Defanged: From Class War Analysis to Electoral Cynicism." *Abolition* (blog), October 27, 2016. https://abolitionjournal.org/white-privilege-defanged/.

Stoytcheva, Sveta. "Steven Salaita, the Critical Importance of Context, and Our Professional Ethics." *Canadian Journal of Academic Librarianship* 1, no.1 (2016): 92-103. http://www.cjal.ca/index.php/capal/article/viewFile/24309/19471.

Sullivan, Shannon. *Good White People: The Problem with Middle-Class White Anti-Racism.* Albany: State University of New York Press, 2014.

Warner, Jody Nyasha. "Moving Beyond Whiteness in North American Academic Libraries." *Libri* 51, no. 3 (2001): 167-72. doi: 10.1515/LIBR.2001.167.

Wiegman, Robyn. "Whiteness Studies and the Paradox of Particularity." *boundary 2* 26, no. 3 (1999): 115-50.

Yancy, George, ed. *White Self-Criticality Beyond Anti-Racism: How Does It Feel to Be a White Problem?* Lanham, MD: Lexington Books, 2015.

Yudice, George. "Neither Impugning Nor Disavowing Whiteness Does a Viable Politics Make: The Limits of Identity Politics." In *After Political Correctness: The Humanities and Society in the 1990s*, edited by Christopher Newfield and Ronald Strickland, 255-83. Boulder, CO: Westview Press, 1995.

PART ONE:

EARLY FORMATIONS:

TRACING THE HISTORICAL

OPERATIONS OF WHITENESS

Chapter 1

A REVISIONIST HISTORY OF ANDREW CARNEGIE'S LIBRARY GRANTS TO BLACK COLLEGES

Shaundra Walker

Introduction

For American libraries and their constituents, philanthropy has been a significant influence. This has been especially true for African Americans in their pursuit of access to the library and the benefits associated with such access. While philanthropy has the potential to do enormous good, because such donations often reflect the values and interests of the benefactor, it also has the potential to do harm. Using critical race theory (CRT) as an analytical framework, this essay explores the role of philanthropy on the provision of academic library buildings for Black colleges. Specifically, it reviews several of the fourteen academic library buildings provided by Andrew Carnegie (and later the Carnegie Foundation) on Black college campuses.

Within the literature of library science, rarely has the embedded normal nature of racism been challenged. Our discipline is replete with "stock stories," or narratives that explain the lack of racial progress in libraries in ways that affirm the prevailing culture. For example, most treatments of philanthropists' contributions to libraries have failed to critique their positions on matters of race and social class and the degree to which their donations reflected and strengthened existing class structures. This should not be surprising because, according to Richard Delgado, one of the primary architects of CRT, "racism is an ingrained feature of our landscape, it looks ordinary and natural to persons in the culture."[1] This essay seeks to present a revisionist view of Carnegie's library building grants to Black colleges, offering a counterstory to the prevailing narrative. Using a range of primary resources, it will argue that a critical view of industrial philanthropists' influence on African American library access provides a prime example of the workings of Whiteness, "an ideology based on beliefs, values, behaviors, habits and attitudes, which result in the unequal distribution of power and privilege based on skin colour."[2]

Theoretical Framework

CRT is an appropriate analytical framework to explore and critique the allocation of resources, such as those provided by access to the library. Emerging in the mid-1970s out of critical legal studies (CLS), a movement that rejected the belief that the law was neutral, CRT uses race and racism as central points of analysis. Defining racism as "a structure in society that systematically advantages Whites and disadvantages people of color,"[3] CRT uses several key tenets or characteristics: the embedded normal nature of racism, the permanence of racism, a critique of liberalism, interest convergence, Whiteness as property, storytelling, and the goal of dismantling racism.[4] This essay will utilize Whiteness as property and interest convergence to bound an analytical framework

---

1. Richard Delgado, *Critical Race Theory: The Cutting Edge* (Philadelphia, PA: Temple University Press, 1995), xiv.

2. "Understanding Whiteness," University of Calgary, last accessed November 9, 2016, http://www.ucalgary.ca/cared/whiteness.

3. Sherry Marx, "Critical Race Theory," in *The SAGE Encyclopedia of Qualitative Research Methods*, ed. Lisa M. Given (Thousand Oaks, CA: SAGE Publications, 2008), 163.

4. Ibid.

for reconsidering the role of philanthropy as it has historically shaped African Americans' relationship with and access to libraries.

CRT posits that the dominant group, in this case Whites, only permits racial progress when such progress also results in benefits for Whites. This tenet, interest convergence, is most notably associated with the *Brown v. Board of Education* case. Legal scholar Derrick Bell, in introducing CRT, opines as follows: "Civil rights advances for blacks always seemed to coincide with changing economic conditions and the self-interest of elite whites. Sympathy, mercy, and evolving standards of social decency and conscience amounted to little, if anything."[5] Another tenet that proves useful for this essay is the concept of Whiteness as property. Legal scholar Cheryl I. Harris explains the tenet this way:

> As whiteness is simultaneously an aspect of identity and a property interest, it is something that can both be experienced and deployed as a resource. Whiteness can move from being a passive characteristic as an aspect of identity to an active entity that—like other types of property—is used to fulfill the will and to exercise power. The state's official recognition of a racial identity that subordinated Blacks and of privileged rights in property based on race elevated whiteness from a passive attribute to an object of law and a resource deployable at the social, political, and institutional level to maintain control.[6]

Library philanthropist Carnegie was familiar with the value of the property interest inherent within Whiteness. In speaking about the history and appropriateness of manual labor for African Americans, he opined that "there is no objection to negroes being craftsmen thruout the South because under slavery the clever slaves did the larger part of such work, white craftsmen being few. Manual labor was only for slaves. Poor whites were above that degradation. They were poor, but gentlemen – at least they were white."[7]

---

5. Delgado and Stefancic, *Critical Race Theory*, 46.

6. Cheryl I. Harris, "Whiteness as Property," *Harvard Law Review* 106, no. 8 (1993): 1734, doi:10.2307/1341787.

7. Andrew Carnegie, *The Negro in America: An Address Delivered Before the Philosophical Institution of Edinburgh, 16th October 1907* (Cheyney, PA: Committee of Twelve for the Advancement of the Interests of the Negro Race, 1908), 27.

The Whiteness as property tenet is based on the belief that being White affords one with inalienable and unearned rights, one of which is the right to exclude, as illustrated by Carnegie's quote above. The degree to which the exclusionary rights inherent within Whiteness operated within the Carnegie academic library grants to Black colleges has yet to be explored.

Background and Context

A fuller understanding of the problem necessitates placing this topic within the context of educational history, specifically the history of Black higher education. As noted by Freeda Brook, Dave Ellenwood, and Althea Eannace Lazzaro, "academic libraries, as products and representations of their parent institutions, are situated within the well-documented systemic and institutional racism of higher education in the United States."[8]

Gaining a more useful understanding of the impact of philanthropists' contributions to the library field requires acknowledging the fact that their curiosity in Black academic libraries was secondary to their primary interest, which was to influence—and according to some, control—African American education and labor. Therefore, exploring this problem requires a detour into the history of education for African Americans, particularly higher education as represented in the historically Black college/university (HBCU).

Historically Black Colleges and Universities

According to the Higher Education Act of 1965, HBCUs are accredited higher education institutions founded prior to the Civil Rights Act of 1964 with the expressed purpose of educating African Americans.[9]

---

8. Freeda Brook, Dave Ellenwood, and Althea Eannace Lazzaro, "In Pursuit of Antiracist Social Justice: Denaturalizing Whiteness in the Academic Library," *Library Trends* 64 no. 2 (2015): 246, doi:10.1353/lib.2015.0048.

9. Higher Education Act of 1965, Pub. L. No 89-329, 79 Stat. 1219 (1965).

Today, there are 103 HBCUs; only two, Wilberforce University and Lincoln University, were founded prior to emancipation.

Historians generally divide Black higher education history into distinct time periods, each of which has been shaped by the hand of philanthropy. The first period, usually spanning from emancipation to Reconstruction, is marked by the interest and involvement of White Christian missionary philanthropists and African American church denominations.[10] Although these groups were not universally in agreement on all matters, they were united in their belief in the intellectual ability of African Americans and the appropriateness of a classical education, modeled after the liberal arts schools of the day, to uplift their race. They envisioned the development of a "talented tenth" of leaders who would guide others within their race.[11] While these schools offered some industrial course work and many started off only offering a grade school education, such offerings were not at the expense of a classical education. In the estimation of Christian missionary philanthropists and African American denominations, a curriculum including languages, mathematics, science, history, and philosophy was necessary to develop the mind of this new Black leadership.[12]

Following Reconstruction, Black higher education experienced its next phase, which lasted through the end of the World War I. Although the second phase was similar to the first in that it was also marked by philanthropy, it was distinct in that the philanthropy was driven by a different set of benefactors with different values, beliefs, and interests. The Christian missionary philanthropists and African American denominations were overshadowed by a powerful and resourceful group of White industrial philanthropists. Historian J. M. Stephen Peeps maintains that

---

10. James D. Anderson, *The Education of Blacks in the South, 1860-1935* (Chapel Hill: University of North Carolina Press, 1988), 240.

11. J. M. Stephen Peeps, "Northern Philanthropy and Black Higher Education – Do Gooders, Compromisers, or Co-Conspirators?" *Journal of Negro Education* 50, no. 3 (1981): 255-56, doi:10.2307/2295156.

12. Ibid, 244.

this second period of philanthropy was distinguished from the first by "its tendency to accommodate the wishes of white supremacy."[13]

The Industrial Philanthropists

The turn of the century saw the birth of the first major industrial philanthropy, the General Education Board (GEB), which was established in 1902 through a $1 million donation from John D. Rockefeller, Jr. The board, which consisted of "all white businessmen, educators, and clergymen,"[14] is said to have had more influence over African American education than any of its contemporaries; of the $325 million it contributed to education before it ceased to operate in 1960, $63 million went toward improving education for African Americans.[15] The GEB is said to have held "virtual monopolistic control of educational philanthropy for the South and for the Negro."[16]

The sentiment of some key representatives of the GEB provides insight into their beliefs, values, behaviors, habits, and attitudes regarding African Americans. GEB member and president William H. Baldwin, Jr. had this to say about African Americans in 1899: "The Negro should not be educated out of his environment. Industrial work is his salvation; he must work . . . at trades and on the land . . . Except in the rarest of instances, I am bitterly opposed to the so-called higher education for Negroes."[17] J. M. L. Curry, a GEB board member from the South who was previously involved with the Peabody Education Fund, shared a similar perspective: "The White people are to be the leaders, to have the initiative, to have the directive control in all matters pertaining to

---

13. Ibid, 256.

14. Waldemar A. Nielsen, *The Big Foundations* (New York: Columbia University Press, 1972), 334.

15. *Encyclopedia of African-American Education*, s.v., "General Education Board."

16. Louis Harlan, *Separate and Unequal: Public School Campaigns and Racism in the Southern Seaboard States, 1901-1915* (New York: Athenum, 1968), 86.

17. Nielsen, *The Big Foundations*, 355.

civilization and the highest interests of our beloved land. History demonstrates that the Caucasian will rule. He ought to rule. This white supremacy does not mean hostility to the Negro, but friendship to him."[18]

Dr. Wallace Buttrick, who served as the first executive leader of the GEB was in agreement: "The Negro is an inferior race . . . The Anglo-Saxon is superior. There cannot be any question about that."[19]

Although he did not use such strong language, Carnegie expressed a similar opinion. Speaking in 1903, he said:

> We cannot produce cotton enough for the entire world. We should be in the position in which South Africa is today but for the faithful, placable, peaceful, industrious, lovable colored man; for industrious and peaceful he is compared with any other body of colored men on the earth—not up to the standards of the colder North in continuous effort, but far in advance of any corresponding class anywhere. South Africa has just had to admit contracted Chinese workers, although there are between five and six million or colored people who will not work. We should be in the same position but for our colored people, who constitute one of the most valuable assets of the Republic, viewed from an economic standpoint. It is certain we must grow more cotton to meet the demands of the world, or endanger our practical monopoly of that indispensable article. Either the efforts of Europe will be successful to grow in other parts, even at a greater cost for a time, or the world will learn to substitute something else for it. We cannot afford to lose the Negro. We have urgent need of all and of more. Let us therefore turn our efforts to making the best of him.[20]

In a classic manifestation of Whiteness, the industrial philanthropists' collective behavior resulted in the very "unequal distribution of power and privilege based on skin colour" that is inherent in the ideology.[21] Beginning in the 1880s and continuing until after World War I, they practiced an informal policy of "fiscal disinterest" in Black colleges that

---

18. Ibid, 355.

19. Ibid.

20. Anderson, *The Education of Blacks*, 92-93.

21. "Understanding Whiteness," University of Calgary.

did not embrace an industrial educational curriculum.[22] This powerful group, which included Carnegie and the Carnegie Foundation, was unified in their beliefs about Black education and worked collectively to promote an industrial-vocational model for African Americans.[23] The evidence to support such a claim is difficult to refute. In 1915, the two Black colleges that most strongly identified with the industrial education model, Hampton Institute and Tuskegee Institute, possessed endowments of $2.7 and $1.9 million respectively. Collectively, their endowments totaled more than half of the endowments of all the Black private colleges combined. Ten years later, Hampton Institute, the prototype for industrial Black higher education and a favorite of the industrial philanthropists, boasted an endowment of $8.5 million, making it first among Black colleges and seventeenth among the 176 colleges in the United States holding an endowment of more than $7 million.[24]

Although it was strongly supported by industrial philanthropists, the industrial-vocational educational model did not go unchallenged. A network of private Black liberal arts colleges was chiefly responsible for Black higher education between Reconstruction and the Great Depression. Despite the fact that sixteen Black land-grant colleges and seven Black public colleges were established between 1870 and 1915, the schools existed as colleges in name only. As late as 1917, only one of the Southern Black land grants offered college-level classes.[25] Supporters of a classically-oriented model of education were outspoken in their beliefs about its appropriateness for African Americans. In the May 11, 1901 issue of *Outlook,* James G. Merrill, president of Fisk Institute (later Fisk University), a private Black liberal arts college, described the need for classical education this way: "When the time comes that White students who planned to become teachers, doctors, lawyers, ministers and professors should learn to hoe and plow and lay bricks rather than

---

22. Peeps, "Northern Philanthropy," 261.

23. Anderson, *The Education of Blacks,* 247.

24. Peeps, "Northern Philanthropy," 262.

25. Anderson, *The Education of Blacks,* 238.

go to literary and classical schools, it will be the right policy to shut off all of our literary and classical schools for Negroes in the South."[26]

It must be acknowledged that, although the industrial philanthropists preferred industrial-vocational education for the masses of the African American race, they conceded that a limited number of leaders, such as teachers, doctors, and ministers, were both necessary and allowable. While speaking on the status of the "Negro" in Edinburgh, Scotland, Carnegie described the proper balance between Black manual laborers and Black professionals as follows:

> All the signs are encouraging, never so much so as to-day. One is quite justified in being sanguine that the result is to be a respectable, educated, intelligent race of colored citizens, increasing in numbers, possest of all civil rights, and who in return will by honest labor remain notably the chief factor in giving the world among other things its indispensable supply of cotton and, to no inconsiderable extent, of the products of cotton, while individual members gifted beyond the mass will worthily fill places in all of the professions. Nor will the race fail to be distinguished? from time to time in the future as in the past by the advent of great men, fit successors of Frederick Douglas and Booker Washington.[27]

A few schools that could develop teachers, ministers, and doctors were therefore necessary, but industrial-vocational education was the preferred path for the masses of African Americans.

The philosophical struggle regarding African American education has been personified by the beliefs of two African American leaders, Booker T. Washington and W. E. B. Du Bois. A formerly enslaved man born in 1850 in Virginia, Washington was educated at Hampton Institute, the model industrial-vocational school for Blacks. His autobiography, *Up from Slavery*, details his experience pulling himself up by his bootstraps. In 1881, Samuel Chapman Armstrong recommended Washington to serve as the first leader of Tuskegee Institute, an industrial-vocational school

---

26. James G. Merrill, "Literary Education for the Negro," *Outlook*, May 11, 1904.

27. Carnegie, *The Negro in America*, 30-31.

modeled after Hampton. Based largely on his experience at Hampton, Washington argued that an industrial-vocational education was best suited for the masses of the descendants of a formerly enslaved people. In his infamous 1895 "Atlanta Exposition Speech," which took place at the Cotton States and International Exposition in Atlanta, Washington explained the fate of African Americans this way:

> Our greatest danger is, that in the great leap from slavery to freedom, we may overlook the fact that the masses of us are to live by the productions of our hands and fail to keep in mind that we shall prosper in proportion as we learn to dignify and glorify common labor and put brains and skill into the common occupations of life . . . no race can prosper till it learns that there is as much dignity in tilling a field as in writing a poem.[28]

While Washington's achievements are significant in their own right, a key factor in his rise to fame was the support of industrial philanthropists, including Carnegie and his ilk. The industrial philanthropists virtually developed Tuskegee Institute and played the central role in propelling Washington onto the national scene as the new leader of the Black race.[29] In 1903, the president of the GEB, James Baldwin, was a central figure in helping Washington secure a $600,000 endowment from Carnegie. Carnegie was impressed with Washington's story and the work he performed to develop Tuskegee into a model industrial-vocational school. He described Washington as "the modern Moses, who leads his race and lifts it through Education, to even better and higher things than a land overflowing with milk and honey. History is to tell of two Washingtons, one white, the other black, both Fathers of their people. I am satisfied that the serious problem of the South is to be solved wisely only through Mr. Washington's policy of Education."[30]

---

28. Booker T. Washington, "Atlanta Exposition Speech" (speech, Cotton States and International Exposition, Atlanta, GA, September 18, 1895).

29. Anderson, *The Education of Blacks*, 103.

30. Andrew Carnegie to William Henry Baldwin, Jr., April 17, 1903, in *The Booker T. Washington Papers*, ed. Louis R. Harlan (Urbana: University of Illinois Press, 1972-1989), 121.

Famed historian and sociologist W. E. B. Du Bois emerged as the Black antithesis to Washington's beliefs regarding industrial-vocational education for Blacks. Born in Great Barrington, Massachusetts in 1868 and a graduate of Fisk, Du Bois was the first African American to earn a doctorate from Harvard. He maintained that a classical, liberal arts education, one that would prepare a "talented-tenth" for leadership roles within their communities, was necessary for African Americans to improve their place in society. In contrast to Washington's argument in the "Atlanta Compromise," Du Bois advocated for equal rights for African Americans.

In addition to their contrasting views on education for African Americans, Du Bois and Washington had conflicting beliefs about the role of philanthropy in Black education. Suspicious of their motives, Du Bois was an outspoken critic of the industrial philanthropists throughout his career, reflecting late in his life that "education is not and should not be a private philanthropy; it is a public service and whenever it becomes a gift of the rich it is in danger."[31]

These divergent philosophies would not only influence the trajectory of African American higher education, but would also significantly shape the industrial foundations' interest in and influence on academic libraries for African Americans. The degree to which these philosophies influenced African American library access has not fully been explored.

Andrew Carnegie and the Black College Libraries

Carnegie, the Scottish-born steel magnate, is perhaps the best-known library philanthropist. Initially on his own, and later through the charitable arm of his corporation, Carnegie is credited with establishing a large number of libraries throughout the United States. He is most often acclaimed for donating public library buildings, while his contributions to build academic libraries are lesser known. Even more obscure are his

31. W. E. B. Du Bois, June 10, 1946, "The Future and Function of the Private Negro College," W.E.B. Du Bois Papers. Special Collections and University Archives, University of Massachusetts Amherst Libraries.

donations of library buildings on the campuses of HBCUs. David Kaser provides the most thorough retelling of these donations, detailing Carnegie's library gifts to fourteen Black colleges between 1900 and 1907.[32]

When Carnegie began his academic library grant program in 1900, only sixty-two American colleges and universities possessed freestanding library buildings that were built specifically for that purpose.[33] The situation among Black colleges was even more dire; only four Black colleges, all private, possessed freestanding libraries at the turn of the century.[34] Each of these four libraries was funded through the donation of a wealthy White patron. To be clear, not one of the Black land-grant schools or Black state colleges had a dedicated library building in 1900. This lack of access is particularly significant because African Americans were barred by law from attending Southern White land-grant schools and White state colleges. It is fairly safe to say that at the turn of the century, the rights to grant, access, use, enjoy, and dispose of a freestanding academic library building were enjoyed almost exclusively by Whites. The Carnegie Library Grant program that started in 1900 followed this pattern; only fourteen of the 108 library buildings that were awarded went to Black colleges. More interesting still is the fact that among the fourteen, slightly more than one-third of the Black college library grant recipients leveraged the agency and influence of Washington.

It was under these conditions that Tuskegee's Washington became the first president of a Black college to secure a library building grant from Carnegie and one of the first, period. [35] When Carnegie's 1900 library donation to Tuskegee Institute is placed against the backdrop of Black higher education, his selection of the industrial-vocational

---

32. David Kaser, "Andrew Carnegie and the Black College Libraries," in *For the Good of the Order: Essays in Honor of Edward G. Holley*, ed. Edward G. Holley and Delmus Eugene Williams (Greenwich, CT: JAI Press, 1994), 131.

33. Ibid., 119

34. Ibid. The HBCUs with freestanding libraries in 1900 were Lincoln University (PA), St. Augustine's College, Claflin College, and Hampton Institute. Notable among these is the Collis P. Huntington Library at Hampton, a $100,000 gift of the railroad tycoon's widow following his death in 1900.

35. Ibid, 121.

institution as the first of the Black colleges to receive a freestanding library building takes on a deeper meaning. In his request to Carnegie for the Tuskegee library grant, Washington played on the millionaire's beliefs about the value of Black labor by stating: "All the work for the building, such as brickmaking, brickmasonry, carpentry, blacksmithing, etc., would be done by the students. The money which you would give would not only supply the building, but the erection of the building would give a large number of students an opportunity to learn the building trades, and the students would use the money paid to them to keep themselves in school."[36]

Washington was not content to gain a library for Tuskegee alone. In a letter encouraging another Black college president, Henry W. Groler of Livingstone College, to apply, he described his interest in Carnegie's library grant program as follows: "I am very anxious that while Mr. Carnegie is giving away his money that our race be benefited as much as possible."[37] Washington remained true to his word, assisting Atlanta, Benedict, Fisk, Livingstone, Wilberforce, and Wiley in their successful applications for Carnegie library building grants. He understood well the power of Whiteness, was able to tap into it due to his affiliation with the industrial philanthropists, and used it to his and his allies' benefit when he could. In general, Black colleges were able to tap into the resources of industrial philanthropists when they could affirm that their interests converged with those of the industrial philanthropists. As illustrated above, when it came to academic library buildings, assurance of philosophical alignment would often come through the endorsement of Washington, the leading Black advocate for industrial-vocational education.

---

36. Booker T. Washington to Andrew Carnegie, December 15, 1900, Carnegie Corporation of New York Records. Rare Book and Manuscript Library. Columbia University Libraries, Series II.A.1.b Reel 39.

37. Booker T. Washington to William Harvey Goler, July 4, 1904, in The Booker T. Washington Papers, ed. Louis R. Harlan (Urbana: University of Illinois Press, 1972-1989), 3.

Another example of the of the exclusionary power of Whiteness as it operated within the Carnegie library building grant program is the difficulty that several of the Black colleges faced in meeting the matching requirement of the grants. In addition to leveraging their relationship with Washington to obtain library grants, several schools also received his help in having Carnegie's matching requirement waived. For example, at Fisk, which received a building grant in 1905, the Carnegie library building initiative languished for two years because the school could not make the match. Washington, whose wife Margaret James Murray Washington was a Fiskite, convinced Carnegie's secretary, James Bertram, to waive the matching requirement. Likewise, when private Wiley College struggled to come up with the necessary endowment to match Carnegie's gift, Washington interceded, mentioning that his own secretary, Emmett J. Scott, was an alumnus of the school and that Wiley was worthy of investment. Although the schools did not receive intervention from Washington, Carnegie library buildings at Cheyney and Johnson C. Smith also languished as the schools struggled to come up with their portions of the match.

Certainly Washington's ability to persuade Carnegie to forego the matching requirement illustrates both his influence on Carnegie and Carnegie's confidence in his recommendations. Yet the need for such intervention also reveals much about the financial status of the classically-oriented Black colleges that required Washington's assistance, and the endowments of Black colleges in general. It is worth remembering that in 1915, the endowments of Hampton Institute and Tuskegee Institute totaled $2.7 and $1.9 million respectively, which represented more than half of the endowments of all the Black private colleges combined. During the second historical era of Black higher education, private Black colleges such as those mentioned above were ill-prepared to match Carnegie's donations, as many faced an uncertain existence. Because the giving decisions of industrial philanthropists were based largely on the way an institution's curriculum fit into their plans for the Black race, the ability of Black private colleges to access the Carnegie academic library grant program was limited. Black colleges needed help and an association with Washington, however loose, proved to be advantageous in several instances.

In addition to Tuskegee Institute and the six colleges that received Carnegie donations through the assistance of Washington, eight other Black colleges received Carnegie libraries.[38] A cursory review of those colleges would seem to contradict the basic argument of this essay, as many failed to strongly identify with the industrial-vocational model that was promoted by Washington and that was the preference of industrial philanthropists such as Carnegie.

While there is no direct evidence that Carnegie or his corporation explicitly stated a preference for funding Black college libraries at institutions that subscribed to an industrial-vocational curriculum, the degree to which some of the classically-oriented colleges felt the need to "put on industrial blackface" in their applications and communications with Carnegie (and later the Carnegie Corporation) is quite telling. Some of the applications bore an uncanny resemblance to Washington's 1900 appeal to Carnegie on behalf of Tuskegee. For example, at Wiley College, President Matthew Dogan included the following statement with his application: "Our students are noted for their efforts at self-help. A large administration building was built largely by their efforts during the last three years."[39] Likewise, in a letter urging Washington to intercede on Wiley College's behalf, Washington's secretary, Wiley alumnus Emmett J. Scott, wrote: "You will note that they are doing industrial work and I can testify it is all of a high character."[40] When Biddle University (now Johnson C. Smith) applied for a grant, its president tried

---

38. The Black colleges that received Carnegie library grants were: Alabama A&M, Atlanta University, Benedict College, Biddle University (now Johnson C. Smith), Cheyney State University, Fisk University, Florida A&M University, Knoxville College, Howard University, Livingstone College, Talladega College, Tuskegee Institute, Wilberforce University, and Wiley College.

39. Matthew W. Dogan to Andrew Carnegie, January 20, 1905. Carnegie Corporation of New York Records. Rare Book and Manuscript Library. Columbia University Libraries, Series II.A.1.b. Reel 39.

40. Emmett J. Scott to Booker T. Washington, November 29, 1905, Carnegie Corporation of New York Records. Series II.A.1.b. Reel 39.

to assuage Carnegie with this statement: "We are at this time planning for the purchase of a farm in the neighborhood of the university where the students can be trained industrially and given an opportunity for self support. All of this makes it necessary to call upon our friends to increased benevolence."[41] Wilberforce University's president also used this style in the private, church-affiliated school's application, stating: "All the work of the building such as brickmaking, brick masonry, carpentering, blacksmithing, etc., would be done by the students."[42] Likewise, in writing to Carnegie to appeal for additional funding, Talladega College's President B. M. Nyce stressed that "we are putting considerable student labor in the building, much of the furniture will also be made by our students."[43] At Atlanta University, a private classically-oriented school, mention was made of the school's contribution of teachers to work in the "state industrial colleges for Negroes" and of its graduates who had found work at Washington's famed Tuskegee Institute.[44] In reality, Wiley, Talladega, Wilberforce, and Atlanta never acquiesced to the industrial-vocational model. Although these colleges remained true to their classical roots, they felt inclined to suggest that their work was in line with the industrial philanthropists' preferred philosophy in order to participate in the library building grant program.

Relatedly, obtaining a Carnegie academic library building grant sometimes required Black colleges to reference cordial relationships with well-respected White citizens within their local communities. Talladega's president affirmed its favorable position in the community by stating, "you will observe that our application receives the hearty endorsement of the leading white citizens of Talladega, who are well acquainted

---

41. D. J. Sanders to Andrew Carnegie, February 24, 1906, Carnegie Corporation of New York Records. Rare Book and Manuscript Library. Series II.A.1.b Reel 37.

42. Horace Talbert to James Bertram, April 16, 1903, Carnegie Corporation of New York Records. Series II.A.1.b. Reel 39.

43. B. M. Nyce to Andrew Carnegie, August 12, 1904, Carnegie Corporation of New York Records. Series II.A.1.b. Reel 39.

44. Horace Bumstead to Andrew Carnegie, February 5, 1904, Carnegie Corporation of New York Records. Series II.A.1.b. Reel 37.

with the history and work of the College."[45] Washington employed this type of reference himself when he appealed to Carnegie on behalf of Atlanta University, revealing that the school had "the confidence and good will of the leading white people in Atlanta. Several of the leading white people are on its board of trustees."[46]

The situation at Florida A & M highlights the unique struggles experienced by Black state colleges along these lines. Although the school received a $10,000 library building grant in 1905, it lacked the ability to meet the matching endowment requirement. Carnegie agreed to forego the match if the school produced a letter of support from the chairman of its controlling board, which it did.[47] Further evidence from the college's bulletin indicates that outside assistance from another influential White man, the son of Ralph Waldo Emerson, also influenced the decision.[48] Another letter in the school's file came from the State Superintendent of Public Instruction of Florida, who affirmed its adherence to the industrial-vocational model, stating: "There are conducted sixteen industrial departments in this school. It is the most important factor for the development and salvation of the colored race in this State."[49]

Collectively, these experiences illustrate the extension of White men's property rights to Black colleges which they deemed worthy of investment. With the exception of Washington, a powerful black man whose educational philosophy closely aligned with the will of industrial philanthropists, Black college presidents were inclined to leverage their

---

45. G. W. Anderson to Andrew Carnegie, December 17, 1905, Carnegie Corporation of New York Records. Series II.A.1.b. Reel 39.

46. Booker T. Washington to Andrew Carnegie, November 13, 1909. *The Booker T. Washington Papers*, 196.

47. Kaser, "Andrew Carnegie," 127-28.

48. Florida Agricultural and Mechanical College. *Bulletin of the Florida Agricultural and Mechanical College (for Negroes)*. University of Florida Digital Collections. George A. Smathers Libraries. October 1911, last accessed November 9, 2016, http://ufdc.ufl.edu//AM00000096/00001.

49. William N. Sheats to Andrew Carnegie, December 16, 1904. Carnegie Corporation of New York Records. Rare Book and Manuscript Library. Columbia University Libraries, Series II.A.1.b. Reel 37.

associations with and the approval of White "friends" in their attempts to gain library grants. Even though local whites did not grant libraries outright, they were able to influence the colleges' access to libraries. Black colleges existed within a racial caste system that placed powerful men such as Carnegie on top, local White citizens in the middle, and Black colleges squarely on the bottom. Obtaining resources such as those offered by an academic library required successful negotiation of both local as well as national beliefs and attitudes about the type of education that was appropriate for African Americans.

Conclusion

Over a three-year period from 1904-1907, the Carnegie library building grant program invested $240,490 into the physical plants of Black colleges.[50] One way to measure the value of an investment is to consider its appreciation, or increase in value over time. Several studies of the status of Black education that emerged in the years following the end of the library grant program provide glimpses into the state of Black college libraries. When Thomas Jesse Jones surveyed the status of Black high schools and colleges in 1917, he concluded that only Howard and Fisk were proficient enough to offer college-level course work. His overall assessment of Black college and high school libraries was dismal, with most of the schools having no library at all and "only 11 . . . known to have a fair collection of books, arranged and managed so as to contribute to the education of the pupils."[51] Ten years later, conditions had improved little; a 1927 assessment of the situation stated that books in Black colleges were scarcer than in rural communities.[52]

---

50. Kaser, "Andrew Carnegie," 131.

51. Thomas Jesse Jones, the Phelps-Stokes Fund, and the United States Department of the Interior, *Negro Education: A Study of the Private and Higher Schools for Colored People in the United States.* (Washington, DC: Department of the Interior, Bureau of Education, 1917), 173.

52. Edwin R. Embree and Julia Waxman, *Investment in People: The Story of the Julius Rosenwald Fund* (New York: Harper, 1942), 63-64.

Similarly, a 1942 study added the challenge of insufficiently trained staff to the list of problems plaguing Black college libraries.[53] If these findings are accepted as true, they suggest that, while the Carnegie academic library building grants did improve the physical plants of the recipient campuses, their overall impact on the educational output of Black colleges is questionable.

The "stock stories" that dominate discussions of diversity in library science frequently seek to illuminate progressive explanations for the lack of racial progress within the profession, ones that do not indict the dominant culture. Meanwhile, CRT argues that, rather than following a linear progression, racial progress often sputters back and forth. Advances, such as the provision of library buildings through the Carnegie library building grant program, are often followed by digressions into topics such as the lack of quality library collections and insufficiently trained library staff described above. The root cause of many of the challenges faced by Black college libraries was, and is, a lack of resources. Most often this lack of access to resources has been driven by racism, and more specifically Whiteness—a system of resource allocation based on skin color. In keeping with the ultimate goal of CRT, which is to dismantle racism, this essay endeavored to call out one manifestation of Whiteness within the history of the library profession, to highlight the lived experiences of an oppressed group, and perhaps to inspire similar interrogations of library "stock stories."

Bibliography

Anderson, James D. *The Education of Blacks in the South, 1860-1935*. Chapel Hill, NC: University of North Carolina Press, 1988.

Brook, Freeda, Dave Ellenwood, and Althea Eannace Lazzaro. "In Pursuit of Antiracist Social Justice: Denaturalizing Whiteness in the Academic Library." *Library Trends* 64, no. 2 (2015): 246-84. doi:10.1353/lib.2015.0048.

---

53. Ina Corinne Brown et al., *National Survey of the Higher Education of Negroes* (Washington, D.C: United States Government Printing Office, 1942), 102.

Brown, Ina Corinne, Martin David Jenkins Lloyd E. Blauch, Ambrose Caliver, and United States Office of Education. *National Survey of the Higher Education of Negroes.* Washington, DC: U.S. Government Printing Office, 1942.

Carnegie, Andrew. *The Negro in America: An Address Delivered Before the Philosophical Institution of Edinburgh, 16th October 1907.* Cheyney, PA: Committee of Twelve for the Advancement of the Interests of the Negro Race, 1907.

Carnegie Corporation of New York Records. Rare Book and Manuscript Library. Columbia University Libraries, Series II.A.1.b Reels 37-39.

Delgado, Richard. *Critical Race Theory: The Cutting Edge.* Philadelphia: Temple University Press, 1995.

Delgado, Richard, and Jean Stefancic. *Critical Race Theory: An Introduction.* New York: New York University Press, 2012.

Du Bois, W. E. B. June 10, 1946, "The Future and Function of the Private Negro College," W.E.B. Du Bois Papers. Special Collections and University Archives, University of Massachusetts Amherst Libraries.

Embree, Edwin R., and Julia Waxman. *Investment in People; The Story of the Julius Rosenwald Fund.* New York: Harper, 1949.

Florida Agricultural and Mechanical College. *Bulletin of the Florida Agricultural and Mechanical College (for Negroes).* University of Florida Digital Collections. George A. Smathers Libraries. October 1911. Accessed November 9, 2016. http://ufdc.ufl.edu//AM00000096/00001.

Harlan, Louis. *Separate and Unequal: Public School Campaigns and Racism in the Southern Seaboard States, 1901-1915.* New York: Atheneum, 1968.

Harris, Cheryl I. "Whiteness as Property." *Harvard Law Review* 106, no. 8 (1993): 1707-91. doi:10.2307/1341787.

Jones, Thomas Jesse, the Phelps-Stokes Fund, and the United States
Department of the Interior. *Negro Education: A Study of the
Private and Higher Schools for Colored People in the United States.*
Washington, DC: Department of the Interior, Bureau of
Education, 1917. Kaser, David. "Andrew Carnegie and the
Black College Libraries." In *For the Good of the Order: Essays
in Honor of Edward G. Holley,* ed. Delmus Williams, 119-33.
Greenwich, CT: JAI Press, 1994.

Marx, Sherry. "Critical Race Theory." In *The SAGE Encyclopedia of
Qualitative Research Methods,* edited by Lisa M. Given, 163-67.
Thousand Oaks, CA: SAGE Publications, 2008.

Merrill, James. G. "Literary Education for the Negro." *Outlook*, May
11, 1901.

Nielsen, Waldemar. *The Big Foundations.* New York: Columbia University Press, 1972.

Peeps, J. M. Stephen. "Northern Philanthropy and the Emergence of
Black Higher Education - Do Gooders, Compromisers, or
Co-Conspirators?" *Journal of Negro Education* 50, no. 3 (1981):
251-69. doi:10.2307/2295156.

University of Calgary. "Understanding Whiteness." Accessed November 9, 2016. http://www.ucalgary.ca/cared/whiteness.

Washington, Booker T. "The Atlanta Exposition Speech." Speech
presented at the Cotton States and International Exposition,
Atlanta, GA, September 18, 1895.

———. *The Booker T. Washington Papers.* Edited by Louis R. Harlan.
14 vols. Urbana: University of Illinois Press, 1972-1989.

Chapter 2

Interrogating Whiteness in College and University Archival Spaces at Predominantly White Institutions

Nicole M. Joseph, Katherine M. Crowe, and Janiece Mackey

Introduction

College and university archives at Predominantly White Institutions (PWIs) in many ways perpetuate a master narrative of whiteness, in large part due to foundational archival theory and best practices. It is critical that archivists in college and university archives understand how archival theory and practice supports whiteness in the historical record so that they can begin to address, problematize, and ultimately fissure whiteness in their work and their archives.

This chapter will examine the cultural and historical context within which archives at many PWIs and Minority-Serving Institutions (MSIs)—specifically Historically Black Colleges and Universities (HBCUs)—came to be. The following questions will be addressed: How do archives of PWIs both reflect and perpetuate a master narrative around whiteness? How do the archives of HBCUs and similar institutions create necessary counter-narratives that interrogate whiteness and white supremacy in the historical record? How can college and university archives at PWIs actively work to support the development of inclusive and actively anti-racist archives by supporting and promoting awareness and access to the counter-narratives present in the historical records of their own institutions and those of HBCU archives?

The authors will use critical race theory (CRT) and legal scholar Dr. Cheryl Harris's definition of whiteness as "the right to exclude" to examine the cultural context around which archives in the United States, particularly at PWIs and HBCUs, were established and constructed as sites where this exclusion is perpetuated.[1] This chapter will include personal reflections from Ms. Crowe, who identifies as white, about her work as an archivist with a goal of creating a more inclusive, compositionally diverse, and actively anti-racist university archives at the University of Denver. The article will also draw upon Dr. Joseph's extensive experience as a researcher in the archives of multiple HBCUs, as well as her work with Ms. Crowe to document the history of African American alumnae at the University of Denver. Ms. Mackey, a doctoral student at the University of Denver, has worked with Dr. Joseph on research into the preservation of underrepresented narratives and histories, using CRT to amplify the multiple realities of these (sometimes) shared narratives and histories between and among faculty, students, and staff at HBCUs.

Defining and Disrupting Whiteness at Work

The disruption of whiteness at work in archives requires an examination of how the concept of whiteness and white privilege has been defined and discussed across the disciplines. This examination is critical, because scholarship and these definitions are predicated to some degree on the evidence present in (or excluded from) the historical record accessible to scholars. In addition, the concept of "counter-narratives" (i.e. narratives that challenge dominant or otherwise "authoritative" narratives), a major component of CRT, is also dependent to some

---

1. Cheryl I. Harris, "Whiteness as Property." *Harvard Law Review* 106, no. 8 (1993): 1714.

degree on scholars' ability to draw from the historical record and/or primary sources. If archivists at PWIs do not examine, deconstruct, and disrupt archives' histories as sites of privilege and exclusion, the historical record is necessarily less inclusive, and scholars' work in these areas is circumscribed.

Sociologists Eduardo Bonilla-Silva and Ruth Frankenberg's work on structural racism and whiteness as a social construct illustrates how whiteness and white privilege can contribute to dominance and exclusion in society and, by extension, within the historical record. Bonilla-Silva defines "racialization" as "the process of attaching meaning to a people," informing how "racism provides the rules for perceiving and dealing with the 'other' in a racialized society."[2] Race, in Bonilla-Silva's framework, becomes the "'organizational map' that guides the actions of racial actors in society . . . [becoming] as material as the racial relations it organizes."[3] Frankenberg's take is similar; she defines whiteness as "the production and reproduction of dominance rather than subordination, normativity rather than marginality, and privilege rather than disadvantage."[4] Bonilla-Silva also uses his structural framework to illustrate racialization and racism's influence on white/American Indian and white/Black relations in American history, as well as the "whitening" of Irish and Jewish immigrants initially perceived as not-white.[5] In all of Bonilla-Silva's examples, he uses the lens of racism to show how the dominant group has used racialization of the subordinate group to justify further subordination or exclusion of any persons in that group who question the dominant paradigm.[6]

Legal scholar Cheryl Harris's definition of "whiteness" and white identity as a kind of property interest shows how, from a legal perspective,

---

2. Eduardo Bonilla-Silva, "Rethinking Racism: Toward a Structural Interpretation," *American Sociological Review* 62, no. 3 (1997): 472, 474.

3. Ibid.

4. Ruth Frankenberg, *White Women, Race Matters: The Social Construction of Whiteness* (Minneapolis: University of Minnesota Press, 1993): 236.

5. Ibid., 476.

6. Ibid., 473.

whiteness can function as a social (in her case, legal) construct that allows for power, beliefs, acts, and decisions to permeate society in a manner that is unconscious and often unquestioned.[7] Harris argues:

> Whiteness is not simply and solely a legally recognized property interest. It is simultaneously an aspect of self-identity and of personhood, and its relation to the law of property is complex. Whiteness has functioned as self-identity in the domain of the intrinsic, personal and psychological; as reputation in the interstices between internal and external identity; as property in the extrinsic, public, and legal realms.[8]

Harris's definition of whiteness within this legal framework of property rights focuses on whiteness's "right to exclude,"[9] for "whiteness has been characterized, not by an inherent unifying characteristic, but by the exclusion of others deemed to be 'not white.'"[10] In this way, "possessors of whiteness were granted the legal right to exclude others from the privileges inhering in whiteness; whiteness became an exclusive club whose membership was closely and grudgingly guarded. The courts played an active role in enforcing this right to exclude – determining who was or was not white enough to enjoy the privileges accompanying whiteness."[11] The ramifications of this "right to exclude" are clear in the history of HBCUs and PWIs—HBCUs have historically existed in opposition to and apart from PWIs—their existence is predicated upon this exclusion and the corresponding decision by the Black community in *de jure* segregated states to create its own system of education in response.

Scholars in multiple disciplines have also examined race and white privilege as inextricably linked to other aspects of identity such as class and gender. Legal scholar Kimberlé Crenshaw coined the term

---

7. Harris, "Whiteness as Property," 1714.

8. Ibid., 1725.

9. Ibid., 1714.

10. Ibid., 1736.

11. Ibid.

"intersectionality" to illustrate this concept in a 1989 article in which she discussed the impossibility of discussing issues of race separate from gender. Crenshaw's writing on this topic is specific to Black women's experiences in the legal system and public policy. She writes: "Black women are sometimes excluded from feminist theory and antiracist policy discourse because both are predicated on a discrete set of experiences that often does not accurately reflect the interaction of race and gender."[12] Bonilla-Silva has also written about how race interacts as a part of the "systemic matrix of the social system," with "class, gender, and race . . . as elements" of this matrix that ultimately favors "the interest of the dominant race/class/gender."[13] Historian Darlene Clark Hine, when asked why she sometimes refers to herself as a "womanist" and sometimes as a "feminist," said: "feminism . . . can sometimes obscure the racism that some white women direct against black women."[14] The poet Audre Lorde brings sexual orientation and gender identity into the conversation; in her "biomythography," *Zami: A New Spelling of My Name,* she recounts her experiences as a Black lesbian moving through a predominantly white lesbian community. In her remembrances she describes encountering several white lesbians who are quick to proclaim that, because they are all part of a marginalized group, their experiences of oppression are the same as Lorde's—an idea that Lorde flatly rejects.[15]

These scholars' definitions of whiteness are foundational to an understanding of how race, privilege, and power work in the world. By extension, this work is also critical to an understanding of how power,

---

12. Kimberlé Crenshaw, "Demarginalizing the Intersection of Race and Sex: Toward a Black Feminist Critique of Antidiscrimination Doctrine, Feminist Theory, and Antiracist Politics," *University of Chicago Legal Forum* 1, article 8 (1989): 140, http://chicagounbound.uchicago.edu/uclf/vol1989/iss1/8.

13. Eduardo Bonilla-Silva, "Rethinking Racism: Toward a Structural Interpretation," *Center for Research on Social Organization: Working Papers Series* no. 526 (1994): 3, http://hdl.handle.net/2027.42/51290.

14. Roger Adelson, "Interview with Darlene Clark Hine," *Historian* 57, no. 2, (1995): 273.

15. Audre Lorde, *Zami: A New Spelling of My Name* (Trumansburg, NY: Crossing Press, 1982), 225.

privilege, and exclusion manifests in foundational archival theory and best practice, which in turn manifests in the historical record present in college and university archives. Scholars' explorations of whiteness in the historical record are to some degree contingent upon the evidence present in or excluded from that record. Additionally, at times one's ability to locate "counter-narratives"—stories that challenge dominant or otherwise "authoritative" narratives—is also dependent on the ability to draw from the historical record.[16] Therefore, if archivists at PWIs do not examine, deconstruct, and disrupt archives' histories as sites of privilege and exclusion, the historical record is necessarily less inclusive and scholars' work in these areas is circumscribed.

Archives, Archivists, and White Supremacy in the Historical Record

> If you want the history of a white man, you go to the library. If you want the history of black women, you go to the attics, the closets, and the basements. [17]
> -Alta Jett, project coordinator for the community-focused *Black Women in the Middle West* archives project

The above statement encapsulates the issue of archives as sites of power and privilege, exclusion and erasure, specific to gender, class, and particularly race and whiteness. The early foundational texts of modern archival theory (Muller, Feith, and Fruin [1898], Jenkinson [1937], and, to some degree, Schellenberg [1965]) are built around the assumption that archives should consist entirely of official government or other corporate or business organizational records, leaving "private and personal archives to the purview of libraries and librarians."[18] In this way,

16. Delgado and Stefancic, *Critical Race Theory*, 212.

17. Paul E. Bushnell, "*The Black Women in the Middle West Project: A Comprehensive Resource Guide, Illinois and Indiana* by Darlene Clark Hine," *Illinois Historical Journal* 81, no. 2 (1988): 152.

18. Samuel Muller, Arthur H. Leavitt, and R. Fruin, *Manual for the Arrangement and Description of Archives* (New York: The H.W. Wilson Company, 1940);

according to archivist and historian of archival theory and practice Terry
Cook, "those in power decided who was allowed to speak and who was
forced into silence, both in public life and in archival records . . . indeed,
archives had their institutional origins in the ancient world as agents for
legitimizing such power and for marginalizing those without power."[19]

Despite this distinction in the professional literature about what
"archives" should be and what they should not collect, many college
and university archives at both PWIs and HBCUs have chosen to collect
"historical manuscripts" (i.e. personal papers and other materials that
are not official organizational records of the institution) in addition to
the official records of the institution.[20] However, the archival theories
espoused by Jenkinson and Schellenberg continue to inform archivists'
conceptions of their professional roles as "the professional preservers,
the keepers, the handmaidens," rather than "interpreters, mediators, or
co-constructors" of social memory.[21] Beginning in the 1970s, propo-
nents of the "new social history" began to challenge archivists on their
attempts to remain "neutral" and "objective."[22] The most notable early
example of this was the historian Howard Zinn who, in a speech given
to the Society of American Archivists in 1970, noted several examples
of the real impact of "objectivity" on the racial diversity of archival
collections, in particular: "Recently I came across a list of letterpress
publications sponsored, assisted, and endorsed by the National Historical

---

Hilary Jenkinson, *A Manual of Archive Administration* (London: P. Lund,
Humphries & Company, Ltd: 1937); T. R. Schellenberg, *The Management
of Archives*. Columbia University Studies in Library Service 14 (New York:
Columbia University Press, 1965); Terry Cook, "What is Past is Prologue: A
History of Archival Ideas Since 1898, and the Future Paradigm Shift," *Archi-
varia* 43, no. 1 (1997), 27

19. Cook, "Past is Prologue," 18.

20. Nicholas C. Burckel and J. Frank Cook, "A Profile of College and University Archives in the United States," *American Archivist* 45, no. 4, (1982): 411.

21. Terry Cook, "The Archive(s) is a Foreign Country: Historians, Archivists, and the Changing Archival Landscape," *American Archivist* 74, no. 2,
(2011), 615.

22. Dale Mayer, "The New Social History: Implications for Archivists,"
American Archivist 48, no. 4 (1985): 388.

Publications Commission of the General Services Administration. The papers of thirty-three Americans are being published. There is one black person on the list, and that person is Booker T. Washington."[23] Compounding the issue is the relative lack of racial diversity within the archival profession as a whole; of the 5,133 archivists who responded to a 2004 survey of the profession, 87.8 percent identified as "White/ Caucasian," and only 2.8 percent identified as African American.[24]

The relative racial homogeneity of the archival profession has been a subject of some discussion in the professional literature as well. In 2015, Mario Ramirez's article "Being Assumed Not to Be" critiqued the profession's continuing emphasis on a "benign discourse of 'diversity'" over an interrogation of the "predominance of whiteness."[25] The archivist Mark Greene, a primary subject of Ramirez's critique (which was aimed at the profession generally, but singled out a particular article written by Greene), in many ways supported Ramirez's arguments about the profession's "resistance to self-reflexivity" by pivoting the bulk of his response away from both substantive self-critique and critique of the profession's approach to addressing race and inequality, focusing instead on colleagues of "at least three different races and an unknown number of faiths" who had assured him that Ramirez's article "did descend to [ad hominem] personal attacks."[26]

The racial homogeneity of the profession is matched by the relative racial homogeneity of the histories of PWIs as they are represented and presented within the archives of PWIs. Many PWIs have lengthy

---

23. Howard Zinn, "Secrecy, Archives, and the Public Interest," *Midwestern Archivist* 2, no. 2 (1977): 22.

24. Victoria Walch and Elizabeth Yakel, "The Archival Census and Education Needs Survey in the United States (A*CENSUS)," *OCLC Systems and Archives: International Digital Library Perspectives* 22, no. 1, (2006): 22 doi: 10.1108/10650750610640757.

25. Mario H. Ramirez, "Being Assumed Not to Be: A Critique of Whiteness as an Archival Imperative," *American Archivist* 78, no. 2 (2015): 342, doi: 10.17723/0360-9081.78.2.339.

26. Ramirez, "short form of title," 339; Mark A. Greene, "A Brief Preliminary Comment on 'Being Assumed Not to Be' – And a Pledge This Will Not Become Ad Hominem Ad Infinitum," *American Archivist* 78, no. 2 (2015): 601, doi: 10.17723/0360-9081.78.2.599.

histories of matriculating students of color, employing faculty and staff
of color, and operating within cities and towns that have their own complex histories with communities of color, both in the *de jure* segregated
American South and the *de facto* segregated majority of the remainder of
the country. Despite this, projects focused on documenting the history
of people of color that center on more than just "significant individuals"
or "firsts" are relatively recent, and are often the focus of small groups
of passionate and committed but under-resourced faculty, students, and
staff, rather than institutionally supported efforts.[27] Given the recent
call for a critical re-examination of the public histories—specifically,
the problematic and often overtly racist naming of buildings on many
college campuses and the connection of the founders and histories of
several Ivy League colleges to the Transatlantic slave trade and to the
removal and genocide of indigenous peoples[28]—an equally critical re-
examination of the archives that document and often uncritically uphold
these histories is long overdue.

---

27. See "About The Project," *Black at Bryn Mawr: Past as Legacy and Project:
Re-Remembering Black Experiences at Bryn Mawr College*, last accessed August 1,
2016, http://blackatbrynmawr.blogs.brynmawr.edu/about/; David Tenenbaum, "Recovering the History of UW's First African American Students,"
University of Wisconsin-Madison News, July 12, 2016, http://news.wisc.edu/
recovering-the-history-of-uws-first-african-american-students/; Katherine
M. Crowe and Nicole Joseph, "Reconstructing History: African American
Alumnae at the University of Denver," *Reconstruction* 16, no. 1 (2016), http://
reconstruction.eserver.org/Issues/161/Crowe_Joseph.shtml.

28. Zach Schwarz Weinstein, "Broken Window Theory: Corey Menafee
and the History of University Service Labor," *Weapon of Class Destruction* (blog), July 21, 2016, http://weaponofclassinstruction.blogspot.
com/2016/07/broken-window-theory-corey-menafee-and.html; Ellen Brait,
"Princeton Students Demand Removal of Woodrow Wilson's Name From
Buildings," *The Guardian*, November 23, 2015, https://www.theguardian.
com/education/2015/nov/23/princeton-woodrow-wilson-racism-students-
remove-name; Natasha Senjanovic, "MTSU President Calls for Forrest Hall
Name Change, But Calls out 'Unruly' Debate," Nashville Public Radio. April
28, 2016, http://nashvillepublicradio.org/post/mtsu-president-calls-forrest-
hall-name-change-calls-out-unruly-debate#stream/0; Craig Steven Wilder,
Ebony & Ivy: Race, Slavery, and the Troubled History of America's Universities (New York: Bloomsbury Press, 2013): 11; "John Evans Study Committee
Report and Supporting Documents," *University of Denver*, last accessed August
1, 2016, https://portfolio.du.edu/evcomm.

Jett's statement about Black women, archives, and the historical record encapsulates many of the problems detailed above: foundational texts that advise archivists to avoid the collection of manuscripts and personal papers in favor of organizational records; foundational theory based on the assumption that archivists can and should try to operate as objective neutral actors; the overwhelming whiteness of the profession; professional discourse that struggles to interrogate the profession's whiteness; and the limited collection development and documentation strategies of the PWIs within which these archives are situated.

Archives and Archivists at Historically Black Colleges and Universities

Many of the problems related to whiteness and white privilege in archives at PWIs also mark HBCUs, but manifest in specific ways unique to the complex and distinctive history of HBCUs in the United States. Indeed, HBCUs/MSIs still exist within a structurally racist culture (and, in fact, their existence is in many cases due to that very culture of exclusion in the form of *de jure* segregation) and, we would argue, should not be considered without an eye to intersectionality and CRT. However, we argue that HBCUs's archives can offer necessary counter-narratives to the historical record largely present and available through the archives of PWIs. We also argue that HBCU and PWI archives have opportunities to partner on actively anti-racist documentation and collection development strategies that support historical counter-narratives. In particular, PWI archives and HBCU archives have a shared history due to a significant side effect of "separate but equal" in *Plessy v. Ferguson* (1896) that, in many cases, sent Black alumni of HBCUs to schools in the North to pursue post-baccalaureate degrees in law, medicine, and other programs that HBCUs in their states could not or did not provide.[29]

In many cases, much like the successes of the HBCUs themselves, the successes of the archives and archivists at HBCUs and at other archives

---

29. United States Department of Education Office for Civil Rights, *Historically Black Colleges and Universities and Higher Education Desegregation* (Washington, DC, 1991), http://www2.ed.gov/about/offices/list/ocr/docs/hq9511.html.

focused on Black history are often a direct result of either individuals or groups from within the Black community, and with the support of the Black community, working to create their own spaces and their own histories—their own counter-narratives—despite a lack of resources. Archivists, librarians, community members, and scholars interested in the history of the Black community have largely been the forces behind writing grants, collecting materials, volunteering time, and working to make the materials within these institutions, and even those within the community itself, more discoverable. In many cases, despite these efforts, the contributions of Black scholars have been erased from the history of intellectual thought,[30] just as the contributions and presence of Black people have been largely erased or not collected as a part of the archives in PWIs.

In addition, due to the under-resourced nature of HBCU archives and the lack of focus on collecting records that support historical counter-narratives at PWIs, researchers with an interest in the history of education in the Black community often need to draw on their own community connections to find evidence for their scholarship. Indeed, we can see that HBCUs have a long, uneven history of being able to allocate funds to their respective archives and special collections. Based on an examination of a 1966 directory of college and university archives, some private HBCUs, as with private PWIs, were older than state schools, and, in some rare cases, well-resourced enough to have established archives early in the twentieth century (e.g. Fisk University in 1928).[31] In most cases, however, institutions either did not respond (listed as "no report"), reported that they did not have a formal archive (Spelman College and Morehouse College), or, as in the case of Tougaloo

---

30. See Aldon D. Morris, *The Scholar Denied: W. E. B. Du Bois and the Birth of Modern Sociology* (Oakland: University of California Press, 2015) for Du Bois' erasure from the field of sociology and Rabia Gibbs, "The Heart of the Matter: The Developmental History of African American Archives," *American Archivist* 75, no. 1 (2012): 198, for the erasure of African Americans from historiography.

31. Society of American Archivists, *College and University Archives in the United States and Canada.* (Ann Arbor: The Society of American Archivists, 1966): 90.

College, indicated that they did have an archive, but that it was small and not open to scholars.[32] Later, a lengthy survey and inventory project, the Cooperative Historically Black College and University Archives Survey Project (CHASP), was conducted from the late 1980s through the mid-1990s with archivists, librarians, and administrators at more than seventy HBCUs interviewed.[33] Taronda Spencer, one of the archivists involved in the project, reported: "Nearly one-third of the respondents indicated that a formalized archives program had been established with adequate facilities of material. The remaining two-thirds reported situations that ranged from the archives being closed for the lack of funds to material being warehoused with no foreseeable plans for archival preservation."[34] The group tasked with the initial survey sought and received National Endowment for the Humanities (NEH) funding to build on the results of the survey to create better description and more access to the collections at a pilot group of seven institutions, which later expanded (after a move to Spelman College and an additional round of NEH funding) to include many more.

Another common thread that appears in the history of HBCUs is a sense of social and community support within and among HBCUs, as well as archives and organizations focused on Black history. For example, CHASP began as a survey created by the National Alliance of Black School Educators (NABSE).[35] Booker T. Washington spoke of the founding of Tuskegee in terms that implicated the whole of the Black community in the success or failure of the school:

> I knew that, in a large degree, we were trying an experiment – that of testing whether or not it was possible for Negroes to build up and control the affairs of a large education institution. *I knew that if we failed it would*

---

32. Ibid., 51.

33. Taronda Spencer, "The Evolution of the Cooperative Historically Black College and University Archival Survey Project (CHASP)," *Provenance* 17, no. 1 (1999): 70, http://digitalcommons.kennesaw.edu/provenance/vol17/iss1/5.

34. Ibid., 70.

35. Spencer "The Evolution of the Cooperative Historically Black College," 67.

injure the whole race [italics added]. I knew that the presumption was against us. I knew that in the case of white people beginning such an enterprise it would be taken for granted that they were going to succeed, but in our case I felt that people would be surprised if we succeeded. All this made a burden which pressed down on us, sometimes, it seemed, at the rate of a thousand pounds to the square inch.[36]

Washington's words illustrate the challenges faced by the Black community and, by extension, HBCUs, and the corresponding drive (with limited resources and a lack of broad support outside the Black community) to create and support a counter-narrative focused on "racial uplift" and the stakes of this "experiment."[37] Archives—the records of the HBCUs themselves—and manuscripts (papers of alumni, faculty, and administrators) are critical components for the support of this counter-narrative. The Black community's understanding and awareness of the stakes of the "experiment" explains much of the immense amount of (often unpaid) time and energy that they have poured and continue to pour into support for HBCUs, including their archives.

Scholars of Black History: What Archivists Can Learn from Their Research Strategies

Though not specifically focused on collecting and preserving the history of HBCUs, the research experiences of Dr. Nicole Joseph, as well as those documented by Dr. Darlene Clark Hine and Dr. Vanessa Siddle Walker, provide an additional window into the unique challenges of trying to reconstruct some aspects of Black history through primary sources—especially when those records aren't held, in whole or in part, by traditional archives. In all three cases, these scholars had a particular research question related to Black history that required the use of archival materials, and in all three cases, the records required were, in whole or in part, available only through their connections to the Black community,

---

36. Booker T. Washington, *Up From Slavery: An Autobiography* (Auckland, NZ: The Floating Press, 2009): 161.

37. Ibid., 182.

not in traditional research archives. These scholars' research questions and processes can shed light on the types of records that archives at PWIs and HBCUs can and should be working to collect in support of researchers whose questions can only be answered effectively with access to archival records created by and for the Black community.

Dr. Siddle Walker, a researcher on the history of education during *de jure* segregation, focused her project, *Their Highest Potential*, on reconstructing the history of the Caswell County Training School (CCTS), a segregated school that operated in rural North Carolina from 1934 to 1969.[38] Siddle Walker, who had attended the school as a child, noted that her personal relationship to the school, while it benefited her in terms of access to records still held by community members, concerned her in terms of bias and objectivity in relationship to her research data. Her description of the records of CCTS—and their ultimate fate—is instructive as an example of the implications of appraisal and disposition (i.e., review and, in many cases, destruction) of "inactive records" and the absences they create: "In general, because CCTS school files— with the exception of one thin folder—were discarded at the onset of desegregation, primary documents relating to the school were almost uniformly located in the homes of members of the local African American community."[39]

The work of historian Dr. Hine followed a similar trajectory, except that in her case the project (and the community members with the records) sought her out. Hine's project began in the early 1980s when, as a professor at Purdue University, two Black women literally showed up at her house with a car full of personal papers and organizational records and informed her that she was going to write a book on the history of Black women in Indiana, because, as a Black woman in a tenure-track position at a prestigious research university, "she owed them this book."[40]

---

38. Vanessa Siddle Walker, *Their Highest Potential: An African American School Community in the Segregated South* (Chapel Hill: University of North Carolina Press, 1996): 221-22.

39. Ibid.

40. Andrew H. Malcolm, "Black Women Find History in the Attic: A Project

Hine did write the book, which was published as *When the Truth is Told: Black Women's Community and Culture in Indiana: 1875-1950*,[41] but the papers were returned to the families and organizations that had donated them for the duration of the project. Realizing that no other scholars were likely to ever have the opportunity to examine this material unless she acted, she wrote an NEH grant to support the documentation of Black women in the region which became the community-driven *Black Women in the Middle West* project.[42]

Dr. Joseph's work on Black history is similar to that of Dr. Siddle Walker in terms of her interest in the educational framework related to science, technology, and mathematics advanced by teachers at HBCUs during *de jure* segregation in the American South. Joseph visited the archives of multiple HBCUs for her research and in the process noticed many of the issues reported in the CHASP survey: lack of resources, inadequate staffing, or archives which in some cases were closed to the public entirely. Joseph and Ms. Crowe, both of whom work at the University of Denver (DU), a PWI, also encountered the erasure of Black women's history at their place of work when, in 2014, they embarked on a shared documentary project related to the DU's 150th anniversary to highlight the history of Black alumnae.[43] The success of and interest in this project can be attributed in no small part to personal connections that Joseph made with living Black alumnae at events where she presented about the project. Joseph's interest in representation in the archives of PWIs—in particular, DU—is also informed by her work as the faculty advisor to the Sistah Network, an affinity group she formed to support women graduate and doctoral students who identify as Black. As Joseph and Crowe noted in a previous article about their project,

---

Unearths a Lost Chapter of Midwest Society," New York Times, February 2, 1987: C10.

41. Darlene Clark Hine, *When the Truth Is Told: A History of Black Women's Culture and Community in Indiana, 1875-1950* (Indianapolis: National Council of Negro Women, Indianapolis Section, 1981).

42. Malcolm, "Black Women Find History," C10.

43. Crowe and Joseph, "Reconstructing History."

"the documentation of underrepresented communities in cultural heritage institutions, especially those that are part of predominantly white institutions, run by white archivists, is only possible through partnerships with engaged and invested community members who choose to tell their stories and are empowered to do so in a way that is authentic and honest."[44]

For all of these projects, these scholars' abilities to draw upon connections to Black communities were instrumental in gaining access to some or all of the records required to address their research questions in depth—and in each case, the scholars' identities and experiences as Black women and their connections to Black communities, rather than visits to the archives (even archives at HBCUs), also formed key components of their research. Based on the above researchers' experiences, and the context within which PWI and HBCU archives are situated, we recommend that archives and archivists at PWIs pursue one or more of the avenues detailed in the next section in order to actively support anti-racist archiving practices that support the creation of counter-narratives relevant to PWIs within the historical record.

Archives and Archivists at Predominantly White Institutions: Creating Counter-Narratives

The authors recommend a combination of the following practices to support the creation of a framework for working toward inclusive, actively anti-racist archives at PWIs, beginning and ending with self-reflection and consciously inclusive practices. First and foremost, it is critical that white archivists and administrators at PWIs begin by asking (and continuing to ask): "Who is not at the table?"—in Harris's words, who is being excluded? Next, white archivists need to do their own work to begin "dismantling whiteness from within," with the recognition that mistakes will be made and errors in judgment will happen as part of the

---

44. Ibid.

process.[45] As scholarly communications librarian April Hathcock writes in a related post in her blog *At the Intersection*, working to dismantle whiteness within librarianship and archives as a white person means "you're gonna screw up . . . no matter who you are, no matter how good your intentions, no matter how careful you are, you will make a mistake. You will make many mistakes . . . You're going to say the wrong thing and make some or many people of color very angry and disappointed and frustrated with you . . . You will be hurt [but] you will survive."[46] This approach reflects the one taken by Crowe within the DU archives. As a white, cisgender, heterosexual woman responsible for university archives at a PWI, she recognizes how critical the work of understanding and working on a daily basis to purposefully and thoughtfully correct the implicit and explicit biases that come with privileged identities is to support the creation of inclusive and actively anti-racist archives.

We also recommend that archivists take a pluralistic approach to collection development that respects and accounts for multiple ways of knowing, memory-making, and memory-keeping when working with members of the Black community with connections to a given PWI. We also advocate for an acknowledgement and acceptance of combining a post-custodial (i.e., not held directly by or within a traditional archives setting) and community archives-focused approach to collecting and documentation, in addition to traditional archival collection practices. As with Siddle Walker, Hine, and Joseph's research projects, personal papers and manuscripts related to a particular aspect of a PWI's history might live in places (such as the homes of private citizens) that are not traditional archives. Individuals and organizations tied to the Black community that are also important to the history of a given PWI will inevitably generate their own records, which they may not think to

---

45. April Hathcock, "White Librarianship in Blackface: Diversity Initiatives in LIS," *In the Library with the Lead Pipe* (October 2015), http://www.inthelibrarywiththeleadpipe.org/2015/lis-diversity/.

46. April Hathcock, "You're Gonna Screw Up," *At the Intersection* (blog), April 13, 2016, https://aprilhathcock.wordpress.com/2016/04/13/youre-gonna-screw-up/.

donate; even if they wish to preserve the records and their history, they may not trust the PWI sufficiently to deposit their records. In either case, it is incumbent upon archivists to, as digital archivist Jarrett Drake puts it: "[Face] forward to the future of the archive as a space with. . . the consciousness to recognize the inequality, violence, and injustice of modernity and ensure that the communities most directly impacted by them have equal access to archival processes."[47] With this in mind, archivists at PWIs can and should partner with community activists and citizen archivists to support the preservation of content that documents the histories of Black community members that is relevant to the history of the PWI but is external to its official archives. In so doing, white archivists can, when wanted and welcomed, play a role in preserving the history of marginalized and, in some cases, brutalized communities without requiring community members to relinquish autonomy over their history, ways of knowing, and/or their own narrative(s).

Archivists at PWIs can and should also partner, when appropriate, with archivists at MSIs/HBCUs that share history (common alumni or geographic region, etc.) to collaborate on collection development and documentation strategies specific to higher education and Black history. Within some PWIs, that could take the form of a shared approach to documenting post-baccalaureate Black alumni, faculty, and staff from states with *de jure* segregation who matriculated into Northern schools. As Siddle Walker has noted, "the policy of Georgia and other southern states to send their African American graduate degree candidates North, rather than admit them to southern White institutions,"[48] especially in professions requiring specialized professional degrees (such as law and medicine not typically available at HBCUs), means that institutions in the North likely hold (or could begin to collect or better describe) records

---

47. Jarrett M. Drake, "RadTech Meets RadArch: Toward a New Principle for Archives and Archival Description," *Medium* (blog). April 4, 2016, https://medium.com/on-archivy/radtech-meets-radarch-towards-a-new-principle-for-archives-and-archival-description-568f133e4325.

48. Vanessa Siddle Walker, "African American Teaching in the South: 1940-1960," *American Educational Research Journal* 38 no. 4, (2001): 766.

related to African American graduates of both HBCUs and PWIs, creating a richer historical record that documents this shared history.

Archivists at PWIs can also actively seek to document and bring to light the complex racial histories of their universities in partnership with communities of color on campus. University archivists are often perceived as walking repositories of campus history; therefore, archivists at PWIs can be visible and outspoken advocates for open dialogue about their particular campus's complex racial history. Archivists can also use the documentation present in the PWI's archives (or accessible through partnerships with community members) to advocate for public acknowledgement and social justice actions (e.g., building renaming, advocacy for scholarships for descendants of communities negatively impacted by the founding of the PWI in question) related to these campus histories.

We hope that these recommendations can serve as a roadmap for beginning the work of dismantling whiteness in the archives of PWIs. First and foremost, as we note above, this work should begin in self-reflection on the part of the archivist, as well as the acknowledgement that the move from reflection to action will likely be messy, difficult, and require developing a comfort with discomfort and with "messing up." In some cases, partnership with community members on these types of projects may not result in the acquisition of the papers of Black alumni, especially if the individuals or groups choose to maintain their own archival records. Without these efforts, however, the overwhelming, hegemonic effects of whiteness will continue to dominate PWIs and, ultimately, their archives and the larger historical record.

Bibliography

"About the Project." *Black at Bryn Mawr: Past as Legacy and Project: Re-Remembering Black Experiences at Bryn Mawr College.* Accessed August 1, 2016. http://blackatbrynmawr.blogs.brynmawr.edu/about/.

Adelson, Roger. "Interview with Darlene Clark Hine." *Historian* 57, no. 2 (1995): 258-74.

Bonilla-Silva, Eduardo. "Rethinking Racism: Toward a Structural Interpretation." *Center for Research on Social Organization: Working Papers Series* no. 526 (1994): 1-64. http://hdl.handle.net/2027.42/51290.

———. "Rethinking Racism: Toward a Structural Interpretation." *American Sociological Review* 62 no. 3 (1997): 465-80.

Brait, Ellen. "Princeton Students Demand Removal of Woodrow Wilson's Name from Buildings." *The Guardian*, November 23, 2015. https://www.theguardian.com/education/2015/nov/23/princeton-woodrow-wilson-racism-students-remove-name. Retrieved August 1, 2016.

Burckel, Nicholas C. and J. Frank Cook. "A Profile of College and University Archives in the United States." *The American Archivist* 45, no. 4 (1982): 410-28.

Bushnell, Paul E. "*The Black Women in the Middle West Project: A Comprehensive Resource Guide, Illinois and Indiana* by Darlene Clark Hine." *Illinois Historical Journal* 81, no. 2 (1988): 152-53.

Cook, Terry. "What is Past is Prologue: A History of Archival Ideas Since 1898, and the Future Paradigm Shift." *Archivaria* 43, no. 1 (1997): 17-63.

———. "The Archive(s) is a Foreign Country: Historians, Archivists, and the Changing Archival Landscape." *The American Archivist* 74, no. 2 (2011): 600-32.

Crenshaw, Kimberlé. "Demarginalizing the Intersection of Race and Sex: Toward a Black Feminist Critique of Antidiscrimination Doctrine, Feminist Theory, and Antiracist Politics. *University of Chicago Legal Forum* 1, article 8 (1989): 139-67. http://chicagounbound.uchicago.edu/uclf/vol1989/iss1/8.

Crowe, Katherine M., and Nicole Joseph. "Reconstructing History: African American Alumnae at the University of Denver." *Reconstruction* 16, no. 1 (2016). http://reconstruction.eserver.org/Issues/161/Crowe_Joseph.shtml.

Delgado, Richard, and Jean Stefancic. *Critical Race Theory: An Introduction.* New York: NYU Press, 2012.

Drake, Jarrett M. "RadTech Meets RadArch: Toward a New Principle for Archives and Archival Description." *Medium* (blog), April 4, 2016. https://medium.com/on-archivy/radtech-meets-radarch-towards-a-new-principle-for-archives-and-archival-description-568f133e4325.

Frankenberg, Ruth. *White Women, Race Matters: The Social Construction of Whiteness.* Minneapolis: University of Minnesota Press, 1993.

Gibbs, Rabia. "The Heart of the Matter: The Developmental History of African American Archives." *The American Archivist* 75, no. 1 (2012): 195-204.

Greene, Mark A. "A Brief Preliminary Comment on 'Being Assumed Not to Be' – And a Pledge This Will Not Become Ad Hominem Ad Infinitum." *The American Archivist* 78, no. 2 (2015): 599-601. doi: 10.17723/0360-9081.78.2.599.

Harris, Cheryl I. "Whiteness as Property." *Harvard Law Review* 106, no. 8 (1993): 1707-91.

Hathcock, April. "White Librarianship in Blackface: Diversity Initiatives in LIS." *In the Library with the Lead Pipe* (October 2015). http://www.inthelibrarywiththeleadpipe.org/2015/lis-diversity/.

————. "You're Gonna Screw Up." *At the Intersection* (blog), April 13, 2016. https://aprilhathcock.wordpress.com/2016/04/13/youre-gonna-screw-up/.

Hine, Darlene Clark. *When the Truth is Told: A History of Black Women's Culture and Community in Indiana, 1875-1950.* Indianapolis: National Council of Negro Women, Indianapolis Section: 1981.

Jenkinson, Hilary. *A Manual of Archive Administration.* London: P. Lund, Humphries & Company, Ltd: 1937.

"John Evans Study Committee Report and Supporting Documents." *University of Denver.* https://portfolio.du.edu/evcomm.

Lorde, Audre. *Zami: A New Spelling of My Name.* Trumansburg, NY: Crossing Press, 1982.

Malcolm, Andrew H. "Black Women Find History in the Attic: A Project Unearths a Lost Chapter of Midwest Society." *The New York Times,* February 2, 1987: C10.

Mayer, Dale. "The New Social History: Implications for Archivists." *The American Archivist* 48, no. 4 (1985): 388-99.

Morris, Aldon D. *The Scholar Denied: W. E. B. Du Bois and the Birth of Modern Sociology.* Oakland: University of California Press, 2015.

Muller, Samuel, Arthur H. Leavitt, and R. Fruin. *Manual for the Arrangement and Description of Archives.* New York: The H.W. Wilson Company, 1940.

Ramirez, Mario H. "Being Assumed Not to Be: A Critique of Whiteness as an Archival Imperative." *The American Archivist* 78, no. 2 (2015): 339-56. doi: 10.17723/0360-9081.78.2.339.

Schellenberg, T. R. *The Management of Archives.* Columbia University Studies in Library Service 14. New York: Columbia University Press, 1965.

Senjanovic, Natasha. "MTSU President Calls for Forrest Hall Name
     Change, But Calls out 'Unruly' Debate." *Nashville Public Radio*
     (website), April 28, 2016. http://nashvillepublicradio.org/
     post/mtsu-president-calls-forrest-hall-name-change-calls-
     out-unruly-debate#stream/0.

Siddle Walker, Vanessa. *Their Highest Potential: An African American
     School Community in the Segregated South.* Chapel Hill: University
     of North Carolina Press, 1996.

———. "African American Teaching in the South: 1940-1960."
     American Educational Research Journal 38, no. 4 (2001): 751-79.

Society of American Archivists. *College and University Archives in the
     United States and Canada.* Ann Arbor: The Society of Ameri-
     can Archivists, 1966.

Spencer, Taronda. "The Evolution of the Cooperative Histori-
     cally Black College and University Archival Survey Project
     (CHASP)." *Provenance* 17 no. 1 (1999): 67-84. http://digitalc-
     ommons.kennesaw.edu/provenance/vol17/iss1/5.

Tenenbaum, David. "Recovering the History of UW's First African
     American Students." *University of Wisconsin-Madison News,* July
     12, 2016. http://news.wisc.edu/recovering-the-history-of-
     uws-first-african-american-students/.

United States Department of Education Office for Civil Rights.
     *Historically Black Colleges and Universities and Higher Education
     Desegregation.* Washington, DC: United States Department of
     Education, 1991. http://www2.ed.gov/about/offices/list/
     ocr/docs/hq9511.html.

Walch, Victoria and Elizabeth Yakel. "The Archival Cen-
     sus and Education Needs Survey in the United States
     (A*CENSUS)." *OCLC Systems and Archives: International
     Digital Library Perspectives* 22, no. 1 (2006): 15-22. doi:
     10.1108/10650750610640757.

Washington, Booker T. *Up from Slavery: An Autobiography*. Auckland, NZ: The Floating Press, 2009.

Weinstein, Zach Schwarz. "Broken Window Theory: Corey Menafee and the History of University Service Labor." *Weapon of Class Instruction* (blog), July 21, 2016. http://weaponofclassinstruction.blogspot.com/2016/07/broken-window-theory-corey-menafee-and.html.

Wilder, Craig Steven. *Ebony & Ivy: Race, Slavery, and the Troubled History of America's Universities*. New York: Bloomsbury Press, 2013.

Zinn, Howard. "Secrecy, Archives, and the Public Interest." *The Midwestern Archivist* 2, no. 2 (1977): 14-26.

Chapter 3

THE ACADEMIC RESEARCH LIBRARY'S WHITE PAST AND PRESENT

Ian Beilin

Academic Libraries, Diversity, and Whiteness

The term *academic library* refers to a library that serves any type of post-secondary institution.[1] But because a great variety of such institutions exists, there is an equal variety of academic libraries as well. Even within the general subdivisions of community colleges, small liberal arts colleges, research universities, etc., there is a wide range of differences. As

---

1. As a usable definition for academic library, the American Library Association refers to that used by the National Center for Education Statistics, which defines an academic library "as the library associated with a degree-granting institution of higher education. Academic libraries are identified by the post-secondary institution of which they are a part and provide all of the following:

1. An organized collection of printed or other materials or a combination thereof;

2. A staff trained to provide and interpret such materials as required to meet the informational, cultural, recreational, or educational needs of clientele;

3. An established schedule in which services of the staff are available to clientele; and

4. The physical facilities necessary to support such a collection, staff, and schedule."

American Library Association, "Academic Libraries," last accessed February 13, 2016, http://www.ala.org/research/librarystats/academic.

with United States education generally, the differences often have much to do with funding and endowments. They also have to do with history, tradition, status, location, public/private status, and more.

Many library workers move between these different spaces over the course of their careers. This has been true for me, even in my relatively brief time as a librarian, because my former place of work, the Ursula C. Schwerin Library of New York City College of Technology (CUNY), and Columbia University Libraries are different in almost every way. These two libraries and their host institutions present obvious differences in terms of wealth (with correspondingly large differences in tuition and resources), physical size, and reputation or public perception, to name just a few. Another major difference is the composition of the student bodies.[2]

Librarianship has long been one of the whitest professions, and the demographics of librarianship have hardly shifted over the last generation. Recently, more people have questioned publicly why programs intended to increase diversity in the profession have failed to make a significant difference (though their absence would presumably make things much worse).[3] Librarianship has "a whiteness problem," Chris

---

2. For statistics on the demographics of the two institutions, see, for City Tech: Charlie Edwards, Jody Rosen, Maura Smale, and Jenna Spevack, "Building a Place for Community: City Tech's OpenLab," *Journal of Interactive Technology and Pedagogy* no. 5 (May 2014), http://jitp.commons.gc.cuny.edu/building-a-place-for-community/; and for Columbia: "Columbia University Headcount Enrollment by School, Race/Ethnicity, and Citizenship, Fall 2015," last accessed May 15, 2016, http://www.columbia.edu/cu/opir/abstract/opir_enrollment_ethnicity_1.htm.

3. See Annie Pho and Turner Masland, "The Revolution Will Not Be Stereotyped: Changing Perceptions Through Diversity," in *The Librarian Stereotype: Deconstructing Perceptions and Presentations of Information Work*, ed. Nicole Pagowsky and Miriam Rigby (Chicago: Association of College and Research Libraries, 2014), 257-82; Angela Galvan, "Soliciting Performance, Hiding Bias: Whiteness and Librarianship," *In the Library with the Lead Pipe* (June 2015), http://www.inthelibrarywiththeleadpipe.org/2015/soliciting-performance-hiding-bias-whiteness-and-librarianship/; April Hathcock, "White Librarianship in Blackface: Diversity Initiatives in LIS," *In the Library with the Lead Pipe* (October 2015), http://www.inthelibrarywiththeleadpipe.org/2015/lis-diversity/; Jennifer Vinopal, "The Quest for Diversity in Library Staffing: From Awareness to Action," *In the Library with the Lead Pipe* (January 2016),

Bourg has bluntly reminded us.[4] But this problem is not limited to professional staff demographics. Areas such as collections, cataloging and description, and public programming and exhibitions have shown a similar stubborn resistance to change, even though they have been addressed in many ways, for a long time.[5]

This chapter will consider a less-often mentioned aspect of whiteness in libraries and librarianship. It will examine the ways in which the physical space of the library may inscribe, overdetermine, and perpetuate the library as a white space. The specific prompt for this exploration was the library building in which I work every day. Its marked contrast with my previous library in terms of age, aesthetics, size, and complexity has encouraged me to consider the connections between physical space and the whiteness of the library experience and librarianship. I look at the library not only as a place where people (students, faculty, and staff) work, study, and gather, but as a distinct(ive) part of the university, one which preserves, reproduces, and transmits certain values and regimes of knowledge. I also try to foreground the ways in which a library may be designed to foreclose certain uses, or certain groups, from asserting their agency, or even being. Reflecting on this dimension of the library will show that even if we were to remedy our longstanding diversity and whiteness problems in terms of personnel or staff, we would still find

http://www.inthelibrarywiththeleadpipe.org/2016/quest-for-diversity/.

4. Chris Bourg, "Whiteness, Social Justice, and the Future of Libraries," *Feral Librarian* (blog), January 9, 2016, https://chrisbourg.wordpress.com/2016/01/09/whiteness-social-justice-and-the-future-of-libraries/.

5. See for example Hope Olson, *The Power to Name: Locating the Limits of Subject Representation in Libraries* (Boston: Kluwer Academic Publishers, 2002); K. R. Roberto, ed., *Radical Cataloging: Essays at the Front* (Jefferson, NC: McFarland, 2008); Christine Pawley, "Hegemony's Handmaid? The Library and Information Studies Curriculum from a Class Perspective," *Library Quarterly* 68, no. 2 (1998): 123-44, doi: 10.1086/602955; Wayne Wiegand, "Tunnel Vision and Blind Spots: What the Past Tells Us about the Present; Reflection on the Twentieth-Century History of American Librarianship," *Library Quarterly* 69, no. 1 (Jan. 1999), 1-32, doi: 10.1086/603022; and Emily Drabinski, "Queering Library Space: Notes Toward a New Geography of the Library," in *Thinking Critically: Alternative Perspectives and Methods in Information Studies, 2008 Conference Proceedings*, ed. E. Buchanan and C. Hansen (Milwaukee: University of Wisconsin-Milwaukee, 2008), 30-37.

ourselves in spaces of whiteness and spaces that reproduce whiteness. In concluding, I will suggest some pedagogical implications of these observations about space, because I believe that library classrooms, along with reference and consultation spaces, are the most important sites of resistance to entrenched structures of oppression in the library.

The Library as a White Space

In recent years, several librarians and library and information science (LIS) scholars have sought to better understand why it is that most librarians are white, and especially why higher administration in libraries is even whiter (and more male).[6] Less often referenced in these writings (which often focus on hiring, retention, and other personnel issues) is how our libraries physically organize, represent, and construct knowledge in ways that reproduce whiteness and white supremacy. We have sophisticated critiques that show how cataloging practices, collection development policies, and the allocation of resources work to reproduce structural oppression and inequalities.[7] Gina Schlesselman-Tarango has reminded us that we have to take an intersectional approach to understanding whiteness in librarianship since it has historically (at least since the early 20th century) been the white female librarian who has been the representative and bearer of white supremacy in the library.[8] Likewise, Fobazi Ettarh urges us to move beyond the simplistic binary of white vs. nonwhite and learn to practice an intersectional librarianship

---

6. Bourg, "Whiteness, Social Justice, and the Future of Libraries"; Hathcock, "White Librarianship in Blackface"; Galvan, "Soliciting Performance, Hiding Bias."

7. See for example Christine Pawley, "Unequal Legacies: Race and Multiculturalism in the LIS Curriculum," *Library Quarterly* 76, no. 2 (2006), 149-68, doi: 10.1086/506955.

8. Gina Schlesselman-Tarango, "The Legacy of Lady Bountiful: White Women in the Library" (presentation, Gender and Sexuality in Information Studies Colloquium, University of Toronto, Canada, October 18, 2014), http://scholarworks.lib.csusb.edu/cgi/viewcontent.cgi?article=1033&context=library-publications.

instead.[9] Others have talked about how a library can be perceived as a white space for those acculturating into a white or white-dominated society. Fiona Blackburn has addressed this with respect to the question of "competence" in Australian libraries.[10] Freeda Brook, Dave Ellenwood, and Althea Eannace Lazzaro address various aspects of whiteness in the library beyond personnel, and consider especially "the physical spaces of service delivery, public services staff, and service delivery methods and values."[11] They also address the whiteness of architecture and spatial organization. This chapter is mainly concerned with that specific aspect, as well as how the library itself, physically—and maybe even metaphysically—is a *white place*. Is the library, by definition, a white place? Or can only some be identified as such, and what is it specifically that makes them white spaces?

I use the term whiteness as it was developed by critical race theory and critical whiteness studies. Stated very succinctly, I understand whiteness to be a socially constructed classification or status conferred upon certain people (whose identity has been in flux throughout history) enjoying a wide range of privileges, advantages, and comforts that any group or individual deemed nonwhite is not automatically granted. Most crucially for my considerations here, whiteness is a status that sets the standard for normality and reality itself (at least in much of North America and Europe). Deviations from whiteness are usually perceived as disruptions, disturbances, subversions, or offenses. Hence a telltale sign of whiteness is the policing of its borders, both literal and figurative. Because the vast majority of white people in Europe and North America live within the sphere of whiteness (again, literally and figuratively, physically

9. Fobazi Ettarh, "Making a New Table: Intersectional Librarianship," *In the Library with the Lead Pipe* (July 2014), http://www.inthelibrarywiththeleadpipe.org/2014/making-a-new-table-intersectional-librarianship-3/.

10. Fiona Blackburn, "The Intersection Between Cultural Competence and Libraries," *In the Library with the Lead Pipe* (December 2015), http://www.inthelibrarywiththeleadpipe.org/2015/culturalcompetence/.

11. Freeda Brook, Dave Ellenwood, and Althea Eannace Lazzaro, "In Pursuit of Antiracist Social Justice: Denaturalizing Whiteness in the Academic Library," *Library Trends* 64, no. 2 (2015): 246-84, doi: 10.1353/lib.2015.0048.

and psychologically), they are usually unaware, or unable to recognize, the very category of their privileged status. This includes a long list of unearned privileges famously outlined by Peggy McIntosh.[12]

Architectural theorist Craig Wilkins, who writes about whiteness and space, has elaborated on this: "For white people, race functions as a large ensemble of practices and rules that provide all sorts of small and large advantages in life. As such, whiteness is the source of many privileges and, to mask its benefits, whiteness is often discursively hidden within concepts like neutrality or universality."[13] In Wilkins's description, "whiteness studies reveals and illuminates the construction of a social framework in which assumptions, judgments, and decisions are made that generally support the image of all things white as the normative and anything non-white as the anomaly. The unquestioned assumption of neutrality in what is in truth a carefully constructed social view inevitably renders people of color not necessarily criminal, but suspect, for no other reason than being different, than for not being white."[14] The close association of whiteness and neutrality should be a red flag for anyone who works in critical librarianship and critical library pedagogy, as neutrality endures as one of the values of librarianship that we challenge and question in our work, and which continues to be defended vigorously by many of our colleagues.[15]

A few scholars working in LIS have used the framework provided by critical whiteness studies to analyze the ways that librarianship has

12. Peggy McIntosh, "White Privilege: Unpacking the Invisible Knapsack," *Independent School* 49, no. 2 (Winter 1990): 31-35, http://www.wvu.edu/~lawfac/jscully/Race/documents/whiteprivilege.pdf.

13. Craig Wilkins, *The Aesthetics of Equity: Notes on Race, Space, Architecture, and Music* (Minneapolis: University of Minnesota Press, 2007), 10.

14. Ibid., 11.

15. See the introduction (1-7) and contributions to Alison Lewis, ed., *Questioning Library Neutrality: Essays from Progressive Librarian* (Duluth, MN: Library Juice Press, 2008); see also Candise Branum, "The Myth of Library Neutrality," (2008), https://candisebranum.wordpress.com/2014/05/15/the-myth-of-library-neutrality/; Madison Sullivan, "Librarianship Doesn't Need Professionals," *ACRLog* (blog), January 19, 2016, http://acrlog.org/2016/01/19/professionalism/.

helped perpetuate white supremacy. This work, in addition to the present volume, shows that there is a growing interest in pursuing whiteness studies in LIS. However, given the relatively large volume of work in critical librarianship and information literacy over the past decade or more, it is surprising that there hasn't been more. Todd Honma makes this point in an important and frequently-cited article.[16] He observes that much of LIS continues to operate as though the scholarship on race and race studies doesn't exist.[17] He writes that libraries have always been designed and operated with a "distinctively racial motive" that has been left unanalyzed.[18] In general, he says, "libraries have historically served the interests of a white racial project by aiding in the construction and maintenance of a white American citizenry as well as the perpetuation of white privilege in the structures of the field itself."[19] In a footnote he makes the crucial point that "whiteness in its various forms needs to be recognized, deconstructed, and reinterpreted in order for the field to advance and for scholars and practitioners to recognize the problematic nature of race and librarianship in the United States."[20] Five years before Honma, Isabel Espinal called upon her colleagues in LIS to take up the study of whiteness. She noted that "unless we address whiteness, unless we identify and name it, many of the problems that plague us collectively and as individual librarians of color will continue."[21] Her words have proven to be true: fifteen years later the problems are indeed still present. Espinal suggests that "the traditional North American library

---

16. Todd Honma, "Trippin' Over the Color Line: The Invisibility of Race in Library and Information Studies," *InterActions: UCLA Journal of Education and Information Studies* 1, no. 2 (2005): 1-26, http://escholarship.org/uc/item/4nj0w1mp.

17. Ibid., 1.

18. Ibid., 4.

19. Ibid.

20. Ibid., 21, note 3.

21. Isabel Espinal, "A New Vocabulary for Inclusive Librarianship: Applying Whiteness Theory to Our Profession," in *The Power of Language/El Poder de la Palabra: Selected Papers from the Second REFORMA National Conference*, ed. Lillian Castillo-Speed (Englewood, CO: Libraries Unlimited, 2001): 133.

institution is an example of a white institution and white public space."[22] It is this point that I will now take up.

Columbia's Butler Library as a White Space

Wilkins argues that whiteness "becomes embedded in the foundation of, and is critical to, the determination of desirable space, place, and property."[23] This observation should make us think carefully about the space, place, and property of the library. In the United States (and elsewhere), when we talk about library space, it is important to recognize the very close relationship between place, space, and race throughout history. This relationship is one of the most important aspects of the history of Columbia University. Geographically, the key sociological and historical feature of Columbia's main campus (since the late 1890s) is its proximity to Harlem. As a predominantly white institution for much of its history, its enmeshment with inarguably one of the most important African American places from the 1920s onward helps spotlight the problematic relationship of race and space for the university.

Columbia's fraught relationship with Harlem played out most dramatically in April 1968. As on many campuses across the country, the assassination of Martin Luther King Jr. helped spark student protests against university policies and practices. Specifically, students demanded a halt to the university's plans to build a gymnasium in Morningside Park, whose very name in some ways reflected the uneasy relationship between town and gown. The neighborhood surrounding the university acquired the name Morningside Heights only in the early- to mid-twentieth century. It was never given this name officially.[24] The usage became more standardized as Harlem became a more identifiably black neighborhood.

---

22. Ibid., 137.

23. Wilkins, *The Aesthetics of Equity*, 17.

24. Andrew Dolkart, *Morningside Heights: A History of its Architecture and Development* (New York: Columbia University Press, 1998).

Since Morningside Park, which separates the campus from Harlem proper, shares the same name as the neighborhood, the university may have assumed that the park belonged to it, rather than to the residents of Harlem. As Stefan Bradley writes, "the university assumed that the neighboring communities, mostly black and Puerto Rican, did not have the power to stop Columbia. This . . . belief was based on several premises, including paternalism, white privilege, and class privilege."[25]

The events of 1968 had deep roots. Columbia's history as an elite institution going back to colonial America meant that it was intimately connected to slavery, as Craig Wilder has chronicled.[26] Until the 1960s, Columbia had enrolled almost no African American students. These factors, and the characteristics of its geography and space (which obviously includes the university libraries), speak to a long history of demarcation and exclusion. To put it succinctly, the university has its own specific history of colonization, and even today under the guise of expansion and gentrification, that colonization—at least to many in the community—continues. For much of its existence, including the period when its library buildings and library collections were built, the institution was very much perceived as exclusively white by those in the surrounding community, and especially by the very small number of students of color who attended.[27] What may be missed or ignored is the fact that the university's great libraries are a part of that history in more ways than we might realize.

---

25. Stefan M. Bradley, *Harlem vs. Columbia University: Black Student Power in the Late 1960s* (Urbana: University of Illinois Press, 2009), 1. Bradley recounts the history of Columbia's plans to build a gymnasium in Morningside Park, as well as the university's long history of strained relations with surrounding communities of color. He explains that one of the main reasons for the success of the protest was because of the leadership of the Students' Afro-American Society, which grew out of the significant, though still very small, black presence on campus.

26. Craig S. Wilder, *Ebony and Ivy: Race, Slavery, and the Troubled History of America's Universities* (New York: Bloomsbury Press, 2013).

27. See Bradley, *Harlem vs. Columbia University*, 10-11.

The Library Building: Inside and Out

The first physical fact of any library to be noted is most likely its architecture. While we may be accustomed to bland and utilitarian public architecture, many people, perhaps especially librarians, want library architecture to project something essential to a library's purpose. But if we consider library architecture and aesthetics from the perspective of race, our perception can change. Brook, Ellenwood and Lazzaro explicitly note that many library patrons perceive a link between classical or medieval-style architecture and the imposition of whiteness and white hegemony.[28] Although many people might associate the library, especially the academic library, with these styles, much of contemporary library architecture since the mid-twentieth century is built in a modernist or postmodernist design. But the association of European classical and medieval architecture with libraries and higher learning in general persists, partly as a romanticized vision of academia, but also because of an association with elitism, exclusivity, and class distinction.[29] Scholars such as nina de jesus rightly link the mission of the modern library (especially the academic library) with the European Enlightenment and its racist and colonialist legacies. When a library (or a university) is built in styles deliberately evoking European precedents, it places the space within a certain tradition. It also links the building with other structures that share a similar style: courts, government buildings of various kinds, etc. These structures are meant to invoke and/or promote power, often the power of the state, as Brook, Ellenwood, and Lazzaro observe, but in this case it is the power of (elite) knowledge and perhaps of the

---

28. Brook, Ellenwood, and Lazzaro, "In Pursuit of Antiracist Social Justice," 14-17.

29. See for example nina de jesus's illustration in her article on oppressive library structures, of the very classical Queens Hall, State Library of Victoria, which she captions simply, 'oppressive institution.' nina de jesus, "Locating the Library in Institutional Oppression," *In the Library with the Lead Pipe* (September 2014), http://www.inthelibrarywiththeleadpipe.org/2014/locating-the-library-in-institutional-oppression/.

institution as well. We should remind ourselves that this is another way that libraries are never neutral.[30]

Butler Library has earned more than its share of notoriety for particular architectural features that seem to promote (or imply) patriarchy, elitism, classism, and racism.[31] While it is fairly common for a research university library to occupy a central position on campus, at Columbia this is very prominently the case. At first glance, there appear to be two massive libraries facing each other in the center of campus. The original library, built in 1897 and still called Low Memorial Library, simply has: "The Library of Columbia University" chiseled into its frieze. Its 1934 replacement, Butler Library, sits directly across from it. This placement sends a message, perhaps not so loud and clear as it once was, that the library is the main repository and source of knowledge and enlightenment, the core of the university's identity, and an equal counterweight, or complement perhaps, to the university administration which has been housed in Low ever since the library left. Columbia's leaders (specifically its long-serving president Nicolas Murray Butler, after whom the library was renamed and a large painting of whom adorns the main staircase of the building) wanted to make this abundantly clear, so instead of simply proclaiming the building as the library of the university, they had the names of famous white male writers, ancient and modern, chiseled

---

30. Brook, Ellenwood, and Lazzaro, "In Pursuit of Antiracist Social Justice," 254-56. Of course, adopting a bland and utilitarian style of contemporary architecture does not magically produce a neutral and equitable space. Such buildings are just as capable of being ableist, racist, sexist, and colonialist, arguably even more so because modernism often projects a universality or neutrality even more aggressive than classical or medieval architecture. On racism, sexism, ableism, and architecture, see Wilkins, *The Aesthetics of Equity*; see also Leslie Weisman, *Discrimination by Design: A Feminist Critique of the Man-made Environment* (Urbana: University of Illinois Press, 1992); Daphne Spain, *Gendered Spaces* (Chapel Hill: University of North Carolina Press, 1992); Paulette Rothbauer, "Locating the Library as Place among Lesbian, Gay, Bisexual, and Queer Patrons," in *The Library as Place: History, Community, and Culture*, ed. John E. Buschman and Gloria Leckie (Westport,, CT: Libraries Unlimited, 2007), 101-16.

31. Jeffrey Bellin, "It's Time to Renovate Butler," *Columbia Daily Spectator*, March 25, 1994, http://spectatorarchive.library.columbia.edu/cgi-bin/columbia?a=d&d=cs19940325-01.2.11&e=-------en-20--1--txt-txIN------.

along the upper and lower friezes of the façade.[32] The most prominent names along the upper frieze all belong to men from the Greco-Roman West European tradition. The lower frieze of names spells out the names of exclusively US American white male writers. The practice of permanently putting the names of canonical Western writers on the facades of libraries was not Columbia's invention, nor is it unique to Columbia. It reflects a moment in early- to mid-twentieth century American history when the concept of "Western civilization" was codified through a canon of literary and artistic works. This reflects the values of the ruling elite of Protestant white men in the United States, and reveals both their sense of historical destiny and racial superiority. Not coincidentally, the period also witnessed the rise of white supremacist ideologies, scientific racism, official anti-Semitism, and anti-immigrant legislation that closed the country to most nonwhite peoples.

To enter the library requires that one process all of this information, though one can choose to ignore it if one tries.[33] Once inside, however, visitors finds themselves in a much more intimate space. Apart from the large main reading room, the spaces of the library vary in size. Most are small, and some of them are perhaps even claustrophobic. In many ways, the library functions extremely well as the multi-purpose, flexible institution that many college libraries strive to be today. It is not the uni-functional or rigid space that Brook, Ellenwood, and Lazzaro critique as oppressively white. Yet, the modest grandeur of its entrance and main staircase do project, in a quiet way perhaps, a message about

32. Butler, for much of his lifetime a well-known and ubiquitous figure in the United States and abroad, is not much recognized or remembered today. But from the perspective of Columbia's history he made a profound and lasting impact, not least on the university's libraries. See Michael Rosenthal, *Nicholas Miraculous: The Amazing Career of the Redoubtable Dr. Nicholas Murray Butler* (New York: Columbia University Press, 2015).

33. Students may try, but once they have gazed at the names, it can be hard for them to shake the impression made by those names. See for example one student's reactions: Kara Schechtman, "A Man is but What He Knoweth: Coming to Terms with Butler," *Columbia Daily Spectator* (April 26, 2016), http://columbiaspectator.com/eye/2016/04/26/man-what-he-knoweth-coming-terms-butler.

learning, knowledge, and research. The main staircase reminds the visitor of the university's past: a portrait of Dwight D. Eisenhower when he was president of the university; a huge painting of a ceremony in Low Library honoring a visit of King George VI (the last Emperor of India) and Queen Elizabeth in 1939; a portrait of Butler; and a huge portrait by Joshua Reynolds of George Grenville, a British Prime Minister during the reign of George III.[34] Visitors might simply describe the effect of these paintings as stuffy, or they might find them aesthetically appealing or providing a sense of history to the place. But such images can also be interpreted and absorbed, both consciously and unconsciously, as emblems of the library's whiteness (and maleness). By the time one has reached the third floor, where the main entrance to the stacks is located (and where reference and research services and instruction are found), a message has been delivered. It is a message that is not unique to this library, or to libraries specifically, but it is one that a library truly committed to inclusivity should try to modify.

These observations about the whiteness of my library are prompts to consider ways in which the library might become something other than (primarily) white. In what sense can it become a place not of oppression or the (re)imposition of one group's hegemony, but one that actively works towards becoming a place of freedom, liberation, and justice? Bourg writes that "libraries ought to be the places on campus where community members, students especially, feel the most free to talk about difficult topics, to express and explore the full range of opinions and ideas on the highly charged topics that are part of their social world."[35] I think that most of my colleagues share a commitment to this goal for our libraries, including and perhaps especially Butler. This is a part of the transformation I envision, but it would be more than this.

---

34. When the painting was donated by an alumnus in 1962, a university administrator commented that the work "fits superbly into the setting and tradition of Columbia University." See "Reynolds Portrait Given to Columbia," *Columbia Daily Spectator* 107, no. 44 (December 10, 1962), http://spectatorarchive.library.columbia.edu/cgi-bin/columbia?a=d&d=cs19621210-01.2.16&e=-------en-20--198--txt-txIN-gopstein-----.

35. Bourg, "Whiteness, Social Justice, and the Future of Libraries."

Bourg also recommends that we "educate and motivate those [of] us in leadership positions to start to work on the structural and systemic issues."[36] I also advocate for this, but I would add that librarians such as myself, who are not in leadership positions but who are nonetheless privileged in many ways within the library, the institution, and society at large, can do many things to work on the structural and systemic issues in the things we do every day: collecting, consulting, liaising, and teaching. It is through these activities, in part, that we can call attention to the ways in which we work under specific structural constraints that prevent us from becoming that place of freedom, liberation, and justice we pretend or seek to be.

Pedagogical Implications

Even though an academic research library has abundant resources, and students may come prepared to do research there, the legacies and continued distortions of the information and research landscape that our libraries produce, in addition to the problematic spaces in which research takes place, actually demand *more* attention, not less. Library instruction is an opportunity to expose and to challenge the whiteness of the library, in both its external (architectural and design) and internal (collections and services) manifestations. A critical library pedagogy that acknowledges students as producers of knowledge may be the best challenge to inherited oppressive structures that literally surround students when they walk into the library. George Yancy, following bell hooks, embraces such "a liberatory education . . . that encourages excitement and transgression."[37] Yancy has taken hooks' wisdom and applied it to the teaching of philosophy, which he calls "one of the most elitist and

---

36. Ibid.

37. George Yancy, "Engaging Whiteness and the Practice of Freedom: The Creation of Subversive Academic Spaces," in *Critical Perspectives on bell hooks*, ed. Maria del Guadalupe Davidson and George Yancy (Florence: Routledge, 2009), 40.

whitest of subjects."[38] Yancy writes that "the ethos of the banking system of education in the United States . . . is complicit with the prolongation of uncritical practices of liberation that sustain the hegemony of whiteness."[39] He reminds us that most white students who enter the classroom "have come to identify whiteness with what it means to be human or what it means to be American or simply a person."[40] Indeed, the names on the frieze of Butler Library reinforce this belief. Admittedly, as in so many other areas, the library classroom is a very limited venue for pursuing social justice, if for no other reason than our limited time. Yancy notes that "white students have learned to cut whiteness off from its historical formation, its colonial history, its history of terror, and its current hegemonic practices. Hence, whiteness, in their eyes, is incidental to their identity."[41] So it might be challenging, to the say the least, to open their eyes to the whiteness of the library that surrounds them. This can be done by engaging white students and students of color alike in a conversation about library space. All students should share their reactions and impressions of the library's spaces and how they perceive their places in them. This might bring to the surface some of the differences in their relationships to library space that are either assumed or unspoken. In this way, the library classroom could potentially provide the opportunity to focus on all of the dimensions of the whiteness problem in the library context: our lack of diversity among librarians, our racist and colonialist cataloging practices, our biased and limited collections, our flawed pedagogies, and our white spaces. Here is where we can all really get to work.

---

38. Ibid., 49.
39. Ibid., 43.
40. Ibid., 44.
41. Ibid., 47.

Bibliography

American Library Association. "Academic Libraries." Accessed February 13, 2016. http://www.ala.org/research/librarystats/academic.

Bellin, Jeffrey. "It's Time to Renovate Butler." *Columbia Daily Spectator*, March 25, 1994. http://spectatorarchive.library.columbia.edu/cgi-bin/columbia?a=d&d=cs19940325-01.2.11&e=------en-20--1--txt-txIN------.

Blackburn, Fiona. "The Intersection Between Cultural Competence and Libraries." *In the Library with the Lead Pipe* (December 2015). http://www.inthelibrarywiththeleadpipe.org/2015/culturalcompetence/.

Bourg, Chris. "Whiteness, Social Justice, and the Future of Libraries." *Feral Librarian* (blog), January 9, 2016. https://chrisbourg.wordpress.com/2016/01/09/whiteness-social-justice-and-the-future-of-libraries/.

Bradley, Stefan. *Harlem vs. Columbia University: Black Student Power in the Late 1960s*. Urbana: University of Illinois Press, 2009.

Branum, Candise. "The Myth of Library Neutrality." *candisebranum.wordpress.com* (2008). https://candisebranum.wordpress.com/2014/05/15/the-myth-of-library-neutrality/.

Brook, Freeda, Dave Ellenwood, and Althea Eannace Lazzaro. "In Pursuit of Antiracist Social Justice: Denaturalizing Whiteness in the Academic Library." *Library Trends* 64, no. 2 (2015): 246-84. doi: 10.1353/lib.2015.0048.

"Columbia University Headcount Enrollment by School, Race/Ethnicity, and Citizenship, Fall 2015." *www.columbia.edu*. Accessed May 15, 2016. http://www.columbia.edu/cu/opir/abstract/opir_enrollment_ethnicity_1.htm.

Dolkart, Andrew. *Morningside Heights: A History of its Architecture and Development*. New York: Columbia University Press, 1998.

Drabinski, Emily. "Queering Library Space: Notes Toward a New Geography of the Library." In *Thinking Critically: Alternative Perspectives and Methods in Information Studies, 2008, Conference Proceedings*, edited by E. Buchanan and C. Hansen, 30-37. Milwaukee: University of Wisconsin-Milwaukee, 2008.

Edwards, Charlie, Jody Rosen, Maura Smale, and Jenna Spevack. "Building a Place for Community: City Tech's OpenLab." *Journal of Interactive Technology and Pedagogy*, no. 5 (2014). http://jitp.commons.gc.cuny.edu/building-a-place-for-community/.

Espinal, Isabel. "A New Vocabulary for Inclusive Librarianship: Applying Whiteness Theory to Our Profession." In *The Power of Language/El Poder de la Palabra*, edited by Lillian Castillo-Speed, 131-49. Englewood, CO: Libraries Unlimited, 2001.

Ettarh, Fobazi. "Making a New Table: Intersectional Librarianship." *In the Library with the Lead Pipe* (July 2014). http://www.inthelibrarywiththeleadpipe.org/2014/making-a-new-table-intersectional-librarianship-3/.

Galvan, Angela. "Soliciting Performance, Hiding Bias: Whiteness and Librarianship," *In the Library with the Lead Pipe* (June 2015). http://www.inthelibrarywiththeleadpipe.org/2015/soliciting-performance-hiding-bias-whiteness-and-librarianship/.

Hathcock, April. "White Librarianship in Blackface: Diversity Initiatives in LIS," *In the Library with the Lead Pipe* (October 2015). http://www.inthelibrarywiththeleadpipe.org/2015/lis-diversity/.

Honma, Todd. "Trippin' Over the Color Line: The Invisibility of Race in Library and Information Studies." *InterActions: UCLA Journal of Education and Information Studies* 1, no. 2 (2005): 1-26. http://escholarship.org/uc/item/4nj0w1mp.

de jesus, nina. "Locating the Library in Institutional Oppression." *In the Library with the Lead Pipe* (September 2014). http://www.inthelibrarywiththeleadpipe.org/2014/locating-the-library-in-institutional-oppression/.

Josey, E. J. "Libraries, Reading, and the Liberation of Black People." *The Library Scene* 1, no. 1 (1972): 4-7. http://eric.ed.gov/?id=EJ080423.

Lewis, Alison, ed. *Questioning Library Neutrality: Essays from Progressive Librarian*. Duluth, MN: Library Juice Press, 2008.

McIntosh, Peggy. "White Privilege: Unpacking the Invisible Knapsack." *Independent School* 49, no. 2 (Winter 1990): 31-35. http://www.wvu.edu/~lawfac/jscully/Race/documents/whiteprivilege.pdf.

Olson, Hope. *The Power to Name: Locating the Limits of Subject Representation in Libraries*. Boston: Kluwer Academic Publishers, 2002.

Pawley, Christine. "Hegemony's Handmaid? The Library and Information Studies Curriculum from a Class Perspective." *Library Quarterly* 68, no. 2 (April 1998): 123-44. doi: 10.1086/602955.

———. "Unequal Legacies: Race and Multiculturalism in the LIS Curriculum." *The Library Quarterly 76*, no. 2 (2006): 149-68. doi: 10.1086/506955.

Pho, Annie, and Turner Masland. "The Revolution Will Not Be Stereotyped: Changing Perceptions Through Diversity." In *The Librarian Stereotype: Deconstructing Perceptions and Presentations of Information Work*, edited by Nicole Pagowsky and Miriam Rigby, 257-82. Chicago: Association of College and Research Libraries, 2014.

"Reynolds Portrait Given to Columbia." *Columbia Daily Spectator*, December 10, 1962. http://spectatorarchive.library.columbia.edu/cgi-bin/columbia?a=d&d=cs19621210-01.2.16&e=------en-20--198--txt-txIN-gopstein-----.

Roberto, K. R., ed. *Radical Cataloging: Essays at the Front*. Jefferson, NC: McFarland, 2008.

Rosenthal, Michael. *Nicholas Miraculous: The Amazing Career of the Redoubtable Dr. Nicholas Murray Butler*. New York: Columbia University Press, 2015.

Rothbauer, Paulette. "Locating the Library as Place among Lesbian, Gay, Bisexual, and Queer Patrons." In *The Library as Place: History, Community, and Culture*, edited by John E. Buschman and Gloria Leckie, 101-16. Westport: Libraries Unlimited, 2007.

Schechtman, Kara. "A Man is but What He Knoweth: Coming to Terms with Butler." *Columbia Daily Spectator*, April 26, 2016. http://columbiaspectator.com/eye/2016/04/26/man-what-he-knoweth-coming-terms-butler.

Schlesselman-Tarango, Gina. "The Legacy of Lady Bountiful: White Women in the Library." Presentation at Gender and Sexuality in Information Studies Colloquium, University of Toronto, Canada, October 18, 2014. http://scholarworks.lib.csusb.edu/cgi/viewcontent.cgi?article=1033&context=library-publications.

Spain, Daphne. *Gendered Spaces*. Chapel Hill: University of North Carolina Press, 1992.

Sullivan, Madison. "Librarianship Doesn't Need Professionals." *ACRLog* (blog), January 19, 2016. http://acrlog.org/2016/01/19/professionalism/.

Vinopal, Jennifer. "The Quest for Diversity in Library Staffing: From Awareness to Action." *In the Library with the Lead Pipe* (January 2016). http://www.inthelibrarywiththeleadpipe.org/2016/quest-for-diversity/.

Weisman, Leslie. *Discrimination by Design: A Feminist Critique of the Man-made Environment*. Urbana: University of Illinois Press, 1992.

Wiegand, Wayne. "Tunnel Vision and Blind Spots: What the Past Tells Us About the Present; Reflection on the Twentieth-Century History of American Librarianship." *Library Quarterly* 69, no. 1 (Jan. 1999): 1-32. doi: 10.1086/603022.

Wilder, Craig S. *Ebony and Ivy: Race, Slavery, and the Troubled History of America's Universities*. New York: Bloomsbury Press, 2013.

Wilkins, Craig L. *The Aesthetics of Equity: Notes on Race, Space, Architecture, and Music.* Minneapolis: University of Minnesota Press, 2007.

Yancy, George. "Engaging Whiteness and the Practice of Freedom: The Creation of Subversive Academic Spaces." In *Critical Perspectives on bell hooks*, edited by Maria del Guadalupe Davidson and George Yancy, 34-54. Florence: Routledge, 2009.

PART TWO:

PRESENT TOPOGRAPHIES:

SURVEYING WHITENESS IN

CONTEMPORARY LIS

Chapter 4

THE WEIGHT OF BEING A MIRROR: A LIBRARIAN'S SHORT AUTOBIOGRAPHY

Sarah Hannah Gómez

Snapshots of a Lifetime of Library Use

There is a section of the library where, according to a sign, I belong. That's good. I don't want to invade the space of others. I want a space that's for me. This space has three spinners with worn out paperbacks. The spines don't match with the alphabetical signage on the racks, so even though I looked up what I want in the catalog, I can't find it. Every time I move the rack, it squeaks. It makes me jump, and I know everyone around me is as annoyed by the noise as I am. Everyone is looking at me. I am thirteen.

There is a section at the front of the library advertising new books and express checkouts. Everything is for adults. I go back to the teen section. It's the same shabby collection of paperbacks, but that issue of *YM* might be new. It's hard to tell, because they all have the same generic white celebrity on the covers. I am sixteen.

There is an advertisement for a "teen advisory board" meeting, and even though it is at a branch I have never been to and will never visit again, my mom drives me eighteen miles. A librarian asks us if we prefer cheese or pepperoni, what grade we're in, and whether we like to read. At the meeting, I sit at a conference table and notice that I am the only nonwhite face there. My mom and I drive the forty minutes back. I am fourteen.

I exhaust my school library's supply of fantasy books that take place in our world. My librarian, as she often does, chides and praises me for having read them a million times each. I ask, for the bazillionth time, if she has any more books like them, but maybe with kids who look like me or who live in the Southwest. She has no suggestions. I am ten.

I am browsing the library at my new school, looking for something to read. Everything in the fiction section is for adults or for children. I realize I cannot find a single book about a black person that is not historical fiction. I am fourteen.

I am in the library at the private school where I work, and the mother of one of the students comes in. She hugs me and asks how I am doing. We have met one time before this. She tells me I am always welcome at her house for Thanksgiving. I hug her back. She is Nigerian, I am American. Her daughter is one of a small handful of black students at this school. I hug her harder. I am twenty-five.

I am eating lunch with the only one of my coworkers who is a black woman. "I swear," I tell her. "some days, I feel like the only service I am providing the students is just being there and proving that black people can be successful." My coworker, who has an MBA and a JD, says, "I have felt that way many times." She tells me I shouldn't stay at my job for long and that maybe I should think about law school. I am twenty-six.

I am in the children's area of the public library, sitting on the floor and pulling out picture books, looking for any covers that have something other than animals or white children on them. A little black girl, maybe six, needs to get past me, and I scoot closer to the shelf to give her room. She doesn't move right away. She looks me in the eye and gives me the biggest smile, as if we've known each other for years. I feel we have. We are both black girls surrounded by the things we love best, but we don't have any in our hands because we haven't found *our* books yet. In that mutual stare, I think we're saying to each other, "I see you. I'm a reader, too. I'm here. I see you." I am twenty-seven.

An Unlikely Librarian

I have always been a library user, but I never particularly liked being in the library. As soon as I was too old for storytime and old enough to understand how the reserves system worked, my library usage was restricted to a regular cycle of returning books, picking up holds, checking them out, and leaving. There were no programs to participate in when I was a teen, no author visits, no parties. I did not "study" in the school library during high school unless dragged there by my friends, and then I only studied because the library did not have a particularly teen-friendly collection. During my undergraduate years, I am certain I entered the library no more than ten times, and some of these visits might only have been to use the bathroom.

I saw the value in libraries, and not just in the services I used. I understood that a library was a safe place away from the 100+-degree Tucson heat with free water fountains, an invaluable gift to the homeless. I knew storytimes did great things for child development. I knew that "free" was, for some people, the only price they could afford. But I didn't *like* the library. From the time I was old enough to spend time in the library alone, I felt like I didn't belong. I felt *watched* constantly, but I never felt *seen*. I may never have been chased out of a library with pitchforks, but I feel that my persistent use of libraries over the course of my life has largely been out of a stubborn desire to spite the library for what it didn't give me, not because of what it did. But then, I can be dramatic.

That dramatic attitude is what led me to library school. I wanted to get a master's degree in children's literature, and the school I wanted to attend offered a dual degree in library science. Having recently read a book in which I learned that not all librarians were as boring as common conception would have you believe, I thought this would be a nice way of getting the degree I really wanted while still guaranteeing a job after graduation—a job that I would likely be good at and probably enjoy, more or less. Magnanimously, I thought maybe I could be the librarian I didn't have as a teenager, and then kids like me wouldn't hate the library the way I had.

Everything went according to plan, and two months before I graduated, I had a job offer as a librarian on a team of three at an independent middle and high school for girls, where about fifty percent of students were white.

Mirrors and Windows

Since Rudine Sims Bishop brought the phrase into popularity in 1990, the expression "mirrors and windows" has become shorthand for the two functions that literature (especially for young people) must perform. It must mirror the reader's world back to them, or it must provide the reader with a window through which to see a life that is not their own. Bishop notes, "reading, then, becomes a means of self-affirmation."[1] A liberal understanding of this phrase would lead you to apply the terms together to any book, since no character will, in its entirety, exactly mirror the experience of any single reader and thus can simultaneously be both a mirror and a window. But to misuse the term in that way obscures its real point: to recognize that books more often portray dominant social groups than marginalized ones, and thus that members of dominant social groups suffer from a lack of window books, while members of marginalized groups experience a dearth of mirror texts.

As a woman of color, I have experienced and continue to experience this lack of books that speak to my identity and background, so as a

---

1. Rudine Sims Bishop, "Mirrors, Windows, and Sliding Glass Doors," *Perspectives* 6, no. 3 (1990): 9-11.

librarian, I immediately set to work making sure that in my library, the balance of mirror and window books was going to flip—or at least it was going to look like it had, thanks to creative displays, shelving, and booktalking. With a mix of activist and self-serving energy, I made every effort I could to buy, booktalk, or promote stories about marginalized characters. In other words, I tried to make all of my active and passive book-related services about "diverse books"[2] to the exclusion of stories of comparable quality that starred characters from dominant social groups, which I felt sold themselves. I did not have the foresight to monitor quantitative circulation data at the beginning and end of my tenure at the school, nor was I the only librarian with a role in purchasing, weeding, and promotion, but a (white) colleague and regular library user said that she noticed a significant increase in the diversity of offerings in the library collection during the time I was there.

Books matter. To Bishop, denying a child a mirror book teaches them "a powerful lesson about how they are devalued in the society of which they are a part."[3] In adolescence, teens have a "newfound capacity to reflect on themselves and their futures," and so they "pay careful attention to the world around them for information about who they might become."[4] I felt an immense responsibility not just to perform my job well, but to go the extra mile for the students of color (who essentially start one rung lower on the ladder, regardless of their socioeconomic status) by prioritizing what I imagined to be their needs and desires when it came to reading material. By having diverse options in both active (booktalks, reader's advisory) and passive (displays, Pinterest content) spaces, I could show my minority students that I *saw* them, even if they

---

2. Another shorthand term for a book that features characters with "diverse experiences, including (but not limited to) LGBTQIA, people of color, gender diversity, people with disabilities*, and ethnic, cultural, and religious minorities." We Need Diverse Books, "FAQ," last accessed November 1, 2016, weneeddiversebooks.org/faq.

3. Bishop, "Mirrors, Windows," n.p.

4. Sabrina Zirkel, "Is There a Place for Me? Role Models and Academic Identity among White Students and Students of Color," *Teachers College Record*. 104, no. 2 (2002): 357-76.

didn't want to interact with me. This also meant that even white students were picking up diverse books, because they weren't being presented to them as anything but books—potentially a mirror *or* a window, and I wasn't going to guide them one way or the other. Neither a mirror nor a window text should be given to someone because it's medicine or a learning experience. It may well turn out to be, but the best reason for picking up a book is the desire to read it.

But the students weren't all readers, and they didn't only come to the library for books. Whenever they did walk into the library, however, I wasn't just one of the three librarians they were going to come across. I was the librarian who was black. I was the librarian who was *at most* fifteen years older than the youngest student on campus. I was one of at most ten people of color employed in a student-facing job. I could not afford to forget any of those things. Zirkel suggests that gender- and race-matching role models' greatest contributions to adolescents are not their specific skillsets or occupations, but the fact that they are successful at what they are doing while being the specific type of person they are, because they "focus a young person's attention on the future and suggest opportunities available to him or her independent of the nature of the activities in which the role model engages."[5] Any time a student of color, especially a black one, walked into the library for any reason, I wanted them to see someone who was welcoming (but not a robot), educated (but not uppity), fun (but not with a fake "blaccent"), and respected by her peers.

To my patrons, I may just have been the librarian, but in my own head, I was a young person, fresh out of graduate school and in a new career, trying to make sense of things. I felt exhausted and alone, and like I was always performing. We all put on performances at work, toning down some elements of our personalities, watching our language, dressing in something other than sweatpants. For me, though, there were the added stressors of being a black woman—one who had been raised by

---

5. Zirkel, "Is There a Place," 359.

nonblack parents and who had to navigate blackness without a model, to boot—figuring out who I wanted to be professionally, marrying it with who I am personally, and making sure it fit within the parameters of my workplace. If I used sarcasm, was I sure that it would come across with the humor I intended, or would I seem like an "Angry Black Woman"? Was it worth pointing out a double standard in dress code when my hips and behind looked different in a dress identical to that woman's over there? I found myself changing language registers and code-switching more than I had even in graduate school, all so that I could be approachable but authoritative to students, professional and slightly obsequious to the higher-ups, ever cheerful to my colleague and my boss—then doing it all over again based on whether I was talking to a white person or another person of color, where at least there was some relief and we could both take a break from acting. And even then, if a pin dropped and the spell broke, both of us would look around, feeling guilty for having been ourselves.

As I continued on in my job, I grew professionally dissatisfied and felt stunted. I found myself on edge all the time, wondering what people were thinking of me, how they viewed my job performance, and what their assessment of my character was. I didn't see my needs being met or my concerns heard, and I didn't know if that was because I didn't deserve them or because I didn't explain them well enough. In social science, the feeling I experienced is called "attributional ambiguity," which is a state of being chronically stressed by microaggressions or other workplace occurrences brought about by uncertainty about the motivation behind anyone's actions or inaction. Jessica D. Remedios and Samantha H. Snyder describe the situation this way:

> The uncertainty of not knowing whether others are acting in prejudiced or genuine ways is distressing . . . All people strive to feel certain about their environments because certainty helps people to predict and to control their circumstances . . . The possibility of encountering prejudice, thus, limits the ability of stigmatized people to have the sense of control that all people value . . . Because feedback may be inaccurate and based

on prejudice, and because targets may not trust genuine feedback, attributional ambiguity also diminishes stigmatized targets' abilities to assess personal strengths and weakness and to set realistic goals for themselves.[6]

The stress of this ambiguity made it difficult to get through the workday, though ironically it strengthened my resolve to serve, especially those students who might grow up to be in my shoes someday. I didn't want my students to feel so trapped.

Ultimately, exhaustion won out over the joy of spending time with students I loved. This is not surprising since, according to Remedios and Snyder, women of color have the added task of determining whether they are the recipients of racism, sexism, or both (notwithstanding other marginalized identities that might intersect with those), and even if we possess the intellectual capacity to grapple with it or speak out against it, the effort spent coming to that conclusion and dealing with any emotional by-products may leave us "cognitively depleted."[7] I imagine these are what keep in place a cycle of disenfranchisement and under-service to marginalized groups. Those of us best equipped to help the next generation are bogged down by experiencing what we are trying to keep others from experiencing.

After two years of working in a school library, I left my job and moved back to my home state, intending to go into another field of work altogether. I ended up finding ways to use my library training in other forms, from collaborating on literacy and book projects with We Need Diverse Books, to administering a local free books program and planning events for the kids who are subscribers to that program. I joined Emporia State University's School of Library and Information Management as a (remote) adjunct professor in the summer of 2016. Teaching online courses is not only more suited to my personality, but it also makes me feel like I can contribute without being cognitively depleted. I have the opportunity to shape the next generation of librarians now.

---

6. Jessica D. Remedios and Samantha H. Snyder, "How Women of Color Detect and Respond to Multiple Forms of Prejudice," *Sex Roles* 73, no. 9 (2015): 371-83, doi: 10.1007/s11199-015-0453-5.

7. Ibid., 376.

While they may not yet be the most diverse group of individuals, I am now in a position where I get to influence the books and articles they read and the way we talk about various topics related to library and information science. I make a point of having an overwhelmingly non-majority reading list on my syllabus, and I assign articles outside of library journals so that more perspectives are represented and so that the concepts inextricably linked to my life as a woman of color—like privilege, equity, and microaggressions—are familiar to my students. Since I cannot see them in person and only know them as well as they choose to let me, I cannot say for sure that I know their backgrounds, but the landscape of library science in general and my limited interactions with them tells me that they are primarily white. I feel that if I can help them see early on how environments can be hostile, exhausting, or just unwelcoming, they will be the librarians who are able not just to support their colleagues and patrons of color, but to truly understand what these colleagues and patrons face. And just maybe the environment the next librarian of color faces will be that much less stressful.

Bibliography

Bishop, Rudine Sims. "Mirrors, Windows, and Sliding Glass Doors." *Perspectives* 6, no. 3 (1990): 9-11.

Remedios, Jessica D., and Samantha H. Snyder. "How Women of Color Detect and Respond to Multiple Forms of Prejudice." *Sex Roles* 73, no. 9 (2015): 371-83. doi: 10.1007/s11199-015-0453-5.

We Need Diverse Books. "FAQ." Accessed November 1, 2016. weneeddiversebooks.org/faq.

Zirkel, Sabrina. "Is There a Place for Me? Role Models and Academic Identity among White Students and Students of Color." *Teachers College Record* 104, no. 2 (2002): 357-76.

Chapter 5

LOOKING THE PART

Jessica Macias

As library information science (LIS) professionals—and women of color—the standard grooming and dress code policies in libraries across America often create a box that we simply do not fit into. The quandary that these policies create for people of color act as a basis for upholding White beauty and grooming standards. As of 2014, the American Library Association (ALA) reported that 87.1 percent of its members were White, and this statistic is reflected within the library profession as a whole.[1] Minority library faculty and staff often find themselves alone— different and alienated—among the predominately White landscape of libraries. Increased retention efforts have made for higher numbers of minorities entering LIS schools, but the field remains unbalanced with regard to racial and ethnic diversity.[2] Demographics aside, it is the policies and standards on appearances that serve as guidelines that prompt library professionals to maintain the legacies of Whiteness that persist in librarianship. In conjunction with upholding White standards of appearance, the profession suffers from a system of exclusion for people

1. American Library Association Office for Research and Statistics, *ALA Demographics Studies* (Chicago: American Library Association, September 2014), http://www.ala.org/research/sites/ala.org.research/files/content/initiatives/membershipsurveys/September2014ALADemographics.pdf.

2. April Hathcock, "White Librarianship in Blackface: Diversity Initiatives in LIS," *In the Library with the Lead Pipe* (October 2015), http://www.inthelibrary-withtheleadpipe.org/2015/lis-diversity/.

of color through the normativity of Whiteness.[3] The challenges faced by minority LIS professionals are further complicated by implicit barriers that are created by White standards of appearance. These barriers come in the form of dress codes that ban features such as "unnatural or distracting hairstyles" and "unkempt hair or clothing."[4] The undertones of such guidelines can prove to be unfairly restrictive for people of color. Thus, the profession is shaped by excluding characteristics of appearance that are traditionally associated with minorities, creating a climate that discourages diversity.

What we look like matters. It matters to our employers, the people that we work with, and the communities that we serve. It is not a secret that I am choosing to unveil. Rather, what is often breezed over in discussions about why people of color rarely enter and seldom stay in the profession, is all of the backlash, the belittling, and the diminishing language used to further alienate and discredit people of color based on their appearance.[5] Those who enter the profession, whether by personal choice or through the persuasion of other library professionals, are poised to be the Other right from the start. From the moment we present ourselves in interviews, actions are taken to water down the presentation of our cultures and ethnicities. We must stand out, but also be palatable enough to get a second interview.[6] Later, if we get the job, we will go through this process again for orientation and as we ready ourselves for the probation period of our positions. For library professionals confident or brave enough to display traditional ethnic styles, it is not long before the policing of our bodies begins.

---

3. Ibid.

4. Gina Hernandez (librarian) in discussion with the author, May 2016.

5. Robert K. Robinson, Geralyn McClure Franklin, Karen Epermanis, and Nicole Forbes Stowell, "Employee Appearance Policies and Title VII: New Challenges for Sex Differentiated Standards," *Journal of Individual Employment Rights* 12, no. 4 (2007), 287-302, doi: 10.2190/IE.12.4.b.

6. Barbara Burgess-Wilkerson, "Lessons from Ugly Betty: Business Attire as a Conformity Strategy," *Business Communication Quarterly* 72, no. 3, (2009): 365-68, doi: 10.1177/1080569909340684.

To better understand how the outward appearances of racial and ethnic minorities are regulated, the discourse of diversity itself needs to be engaged from a viewpoint in which inclusion alone is not enough. People of color can enter the field, but it is what happens after they enter that truly impacts the landscape of librarianship. The enduring barriers to professional growth that minority LIS professionals face are sustained on a direct and intimate level that diminishes their educational and technical skills.[7] As we move the discussion beyond access and recruitment, it is important to examine the written and implied practices and policies that affect minority LIS professionals. These guidelines for appearances—often never formally articulated, but real nonetheless—are duly upheld by institutions and LIS professionals. Considerations and conversations focus on hair and clothing rather than quantifiable aspects of one's job performance.[8] In instances where the biases regarding dress standards are not explicitly stated, minority LIS professionals are forced to navigate obstacles they can't wholly see or address. These experiences can come in the form of casual comments about the professionalism of particular hygiene product scents, hair styles, or fashion choices. In 2009, during my very first job performance evaluation at a college library, the director spent the first half of the meeting discussing whether my semi-visible tattoos of flowers and poetry could be considered evidence of gang affiliation to patrons. The implicit take-away message was that a Latina with tattoos should not be seen at the library circulation desk. The sentiments of such an introduction to the profession are echoed in story after story from minority LIS professionals.[9] Biased rules and regulations go unwritten so that organizations can claim to be safe and welcoming spaces for diversity, even as their minority employees are

7. Ione T. Damasco and Dracine Hodges, "Tenure and Promotion Experiences of Academic Librarians of Color," *College and Research Libraries* 73, no.3, (May 2012): 279-301, doi: 10.5860/crl-244.

8. Angela Galvan, "Soliciting Performance, Hiding Bias: Whiteness and Librarianship. *In the Library with the Lead Pipe* (June 2015),http://www.inthelibrarywiththeleadpipe.org/2015/soliciting-performance-hiding-bias-whiteness-and-librarianship/.

9. Gina Hernandez (librarian) in discussion with the author, May 2016.

forced to play a balancing act to keep their "distracting" hair and bodies out of sight. Whiteness is the standard, and deviations from that standard are deemed off-putting at best and criminal at worst.

As the field pushes for professionalism and diversity as core values, minority staff and faculty can feel neglected or made invisible through their lived experiences within libraries.[10] As with most other library professionals, I have sat through numerous diversity initiative meetings, training sessions, and workshops meant to increase diversity and help the staff better reflect the communities that we serve. All the while, the same institutions that rallied behind these initiatives for years created and maintained policies that reminded me and others to never wear our hair in an "unprofessional" or "unkempt" fashion. The underlying message was clear—do not wear your hair "unruly" or natural as it may be viewed as messy and distracting to others. In 2015, a young Black staff member began wearing her hair in long, box braids. As her supervisor, I was asked to remind her to wear her hair back so that it would not fall forward in her face, on the desk, or on the materials that library patrons were borrowing. Suddenly, the library had turned into a restaurant, and our books were likened to food that her hair could contaminate. There were multiple long-haired White women on my staff, none of whom had ever been asked to wear their hair back, so I was discouraged to see my co-workers rally in unison around the assertion that my Black colleague's hair made her unfit for her position. This moment taught me that I had to be careful. This is not the 1950s, and many people of color work in higher education. Yet, in 2015, this staff member with the long, box braids marked the second Black woman to work at the library in forty years. My relationship with this young lady quickly became a threat to the norm. I received my first complaints regarding noise levels at the front desk when she and I would talk. These complaints never came from patrons but rather from my co-workers. On various occasions, the library staff and faculty would search for mistakes in her work and

---

10. American Library Association, "Diversity in the Workplace," last accessed March 1, 2016, http://www.ala.org/advocacy/diversity/workplace.

in the work I completed with her. I was told things like "give her extra training, she's never seen a copy machine this complicated in that part of Los Angeles." When they could no longer find things wrong with our work or her appearance, the library staff and faculty began to find things wrong with my appearance. I was told that my lipstick was for evening wear, my hair (partially shaved but similar to that of a White librarian co-worker) should be grown out, and my fingernails were too long—"we are not filming a rap video here." The policing of beauty and dress standards makes minorities feel excluded and exists only to set the norm back to White beauty standards.[11] Within six months of taking my job at the university, I felt alone and longed for the opportunity to work in a different field.

The appropriate length of hair or nails is not explicitly stated in the employee handbook, but these rules were easily enforced by people who knew that we would comply. Just enough persuasion, bullying, and questioning of my skills and experience caused me to conform. I had only been in the profession for a handful of years at the time and was still a year away from completing my MLIS, so I knew what was at stake: valuable library experience in a state where positions are difficult to come by. Monitoring and policing often came from other minorities. They had conformed and internalized the need to uphold the White standards of beauty and appearance. In Angela Galvan's essay, she reminds us that "framing diversity as the problem implicitly suggests a final outcome, locating responsibility and discomfort away from White librarians while marginalizing colleagues who do not perform whiteness to the satisfaction of gatekeepers."[12] When diverse people are hired, they are alienated and forced to conform and diminish their own unique qualities, skills, and abilities to perform well. It is only through courage and confidence that people of color are able to move forward as library professionals.

Mentorships and diversity initiatives help, but they are not enough to leave people of color unscathed by the intolerance of others. Galvan

---

11. Hathcock, "White Librarianship in Blackface."
12. Galvan, "Soliciting Performance."

discusses the "White savior" and those who rush in to recruit people of color into librarianship.[13] This occurs more often now and with good intentions, but until institutions allow people of color to exist as freely as their White counterparts, people of color will continue to exit the profession as quickly as they entered. The way that each library defines professional attire and grooming is usually fairly benign until a Mexican woman with long nails and a quick tongue or a Black woman with locs and a hearty laugh enter the sphere. Policing people of color based on their appearance diminishes their spirit as well as their qualifications. We buy clothes to help us fit in, pay for hair straightening treatments and weaves, and learn to lose our identities. It must not be ignored or breezed over when we see the rules suddenly changing because White people are not comfortable. The goal should always be acceptance and support in a community that upholds the spread of information to all who seek it. As the profession attempts to stay relevant and modern, discussions of diversity must include the climate of exclusion that minorities face due to White Standards of appearance.

Bibliography

American Library Association, "Diversity in the Workplace." Accessed March 1, 2016, http://www.ala.org/advocacy/diversity/workplace.

American Library Association Office for Research and Statistics. *ALA Demographics Studies.* Chicago: American Library Association, 2014. http://www.ala.org/research/sites/ala.org.research/files/content/initiatives/membershipsurveys/September2014ALADemographics.pdf.

Burgess-Wilkerson, Barbara. "Lessons from Ugly Betty: Business Attire as a Conformity Strategy." *Business Communication Quarterly* 72, no. 3, (2009): 365-68. doi: 10.1177/1080569909340684.

---

13. Ibid.

Comstock, Sharon L., Jerica Copeny, and Cynthia Landrum. "Code as Code: Speculations on Diversity, Inequity, and Digital Women." *The Code4Lib Journal* 28 (2015). http://journal.code4lib.org/articles/10470.

Damasco, Ione T., and Dracine Hodges. "Tenure and Promotion Experiences of Academic Librarians of Color." *College and Research Libraries* 73, no. 3 (2012): 279-301. doi: 10.5860/crl-244.

Elzweig, Brian, and Donna K. Peeples. "Tattoos and Piercings: Issues of Body Modification and the Workplace." *SAM Advanced Management Journal* (Winter 2011): 13-23.

Galvan, Angela. "Soliciting Performance, Hiding Bias: Whiteness and Librarianship." *In the Library with the Lead Pipe* (June 2015). http://www.inthelibrarywiththeleadpipe.org/2015/soliciting-performance-hiding-bias-whiteness-and-librarianship/.

Hathcock, April. "White Librarianship in Blackface: Diversity Initiatives in LIS.." *In the Library with the Lead Pipe* (October 2015). http://www.inthelibrarywiththeleadpipe.org/2015/lis-diversity/.

Jaeger, Paul T., L. C. Sarin, and K. J. Peterson. "Diversity, Inclusion, and Library and Information Science: An Ongoing Imperative (Or Why We Still Desperately Need to Have Discussions About Diversity and Inclusion)." *Library Quarterly* 85 no. 2 (2015): 127-32.

Kim, K., and Sin, S. J. "Increasing Ethnic Diversity in LIS: Strategies Suggested by Librarians of Color." *Library Quarterly* 78, no. 2 (April 2008): 153-77.

Robinson, Robert K., Geralyn Franklin McClure, Karen Epermanis, and Nicole Forbes Stowell. "Employee Appearance Policies and Title VII: New Challenges for Sex Differentiated Standards." *Journal of Individual Employment Rights* 12, no. 4 (2007): 287-302. doi: 10.2190/IE.12.4.b.

Wenger, Etienne. *Communities of Practice: Learning, Meaning, and Identity.* Cambridge, UK: Cambridge University Press, 2011.

Williamson, Kristy. "Research in Constructivist Frameworks Using Ethnographic Techniques." *Library Trends* 55, no. 1 (2006): 83-101.

Chapter 6

Nostalgia, Cuteness, and Geek Chic: Whiteness in Orla Kiely's *Library*

Vani Natarajan

The imperative to "look professional" impacts workers in many fields, including librarianship. "What will I wear today?" might be the first reference question I hear on a typical work day, as it's a question I pose to myself. Sometimes it's simply directional ("Where did I leave that sweater?"). More often than not, it prompts me to revisit history, memory, identity, and the host of social codes that weigh on my decisions as a South Asian American woman navigating, with my own cisgender, upper-middle-class privilege, an overwhelmingly white profession. Librarianship carries legacies of colonialism, racism, classism, and patriarchy, among other intersecting vectors of oppression. These ongoing legacies shape the profession and the sartorial performances of professionalism that are named authentic to it. In her essay "Labor and Looking 'Professional,'" Autumn Whitefield-Madrano notes: "Looking professional means sending a set of signals that amount to looking like one belongs in the professional class: not laborers."[1] Whitefield-Madrano

---

1. Autumn Whitefield-Madrano, "Labor and Looking 'Professional,'" *The New Inquiry*, February 19, 2016, https://thenewinquiry.com/blog/labor-and-looking-professional/.

proceeds to explore how one's labor, as well as the labor of others, are vital to the creation and sustenance of this look.[2]

Why does "looking professional," itself a kind of survival strategy, hinge so often on a distancing from the reality of labor and a sharp social division between the "professional" and the "laborer"? What are the consequences of refusing this imperative? Fashion, as a lived creative practice, can sometimes present the possibility of imaginary material spaces, through which librarians might exercise creativity and agency in their self-expression. Fashion can push back on ideas of professionalism and "what a librarian looks like" and even prefigure new worlds and realities (as documented by librarian-curated blogs like *Librarian Wardrobe*).[3] Nonetheless, the words *library* and *librarian* perform a particular role in the language of fashion. These words are often employed like adjectives, most frequently in phrases like *librarian chic*. Used sartorially, these words conjure a host of fantasies and imperatives about who librarians are, how they are recognized, and what labors they perform. These fantasies and imperatives center class-privileged white women as the default visible stewards of librarianship and the space of the library.

To explore the imagery of white femininity in sartorial representations of the library, I will closely examine designer Orla Kiely's London Fashion Week show *Library for Fall 2015* as a point of departure, looking at video documentation of the show alongside contemporaneous criticism. In *Library*, the fashion models (the overwhelming majority of them white) move through a fictive library tableau, at turns reading, browsing shelves, shushing audience members, and posing in Kiely's latest line of dresses, skirts, cardigans, coats, and accessories. I will investigate what the aesthetic choices for this show reveal about a persistent investment in white womanhood that courses through so many depictions of librarians. I will also consider what it means that Kiely cites as her "muse" for the show Ali McGraw's leading role in the 1970

---

2. Ibid.

3. *Librarian Wardrobe*, last accessed October 31, 2016, http://librarianwardrobe.com.

film *Love Story*, in which McGraw plays a young white woman studying at Radcliffe College in the late 1960s.[4] I will focus on three aesthetic qualities that resurface in *Library* and the conversations around them: nostalgia, cuteness, and as Kiely describes it, "geek chic."[5] What do these aesthetics suggest when the profession, in the contexts of both the United States and United Kingdom where Kiely lives and works, has such a long history of excluding and silencing people of color, from routinely racist hiring structures to colonial conventions in cataloging and classification systems like the Library of Congress Classification System (which Emily Drabinski identifies as "rooted in historical structures of white supremacy")?[6] For whom can these aesthetics, as deployed in *Library*, most easily connote an authentic and affirming space? For whom are they produced?

Kiely presented *Library* at London Fashion Week for Autumn/ Winter 2015. The show itself took place in February 2015, in keeping with the tradition of major fashion weeks anticipating their respective forthcoming seasons. The circulation of video and still images from *Library* through web-based publishing platforms likely gave the show a significantly larger audience than those who gathered in the room for the original show. I rely on these images and video footage, as well as the responses to *Library* from fashion journalists and other commentators, in my analysis of *Library*'s circuits. As such, I hope to think through the expression of style in Kiely's *Library*, guided by Sianne Ngai's consideration of style as ways of perceiving an object rather than merely the "objective" qualities existing in the object. Ngai presents a compelling

---

4. Video Fashion News, *VF NEWS: Orla Kiely- Fall 2015- London Fashion Week- Runway & Designer Interview* (Getty Images, 2015), http://www.gettyimages.com/detail/video/orla-kiely-tells-a-preppy-love-story-for-fall-2015-and-news-footage/479561212.

5. Ibid.

6. Freeda Brook, Dave Ellenwood, and Althea Eannace Lazzaro, "In Pursuit of Antiracist Social Justice: Denaturalizing Whiteness in the Academic Library," *Library Trends* 64, no.2 (2015): 246-84, doi: 10.1353/lib.2015.0048; Emily Drabinski, "Teaching the Radical Catalog," in *Radical Cataloging: Essays at the Front*, ed. K. R. Roberto (Jefferson, NC: McFarland, 2008), 198.

case for attending to aesthetics in an analysis of whiteness, writing that aesthetic categories "are not for all this in the least bit abstruse but part of the daily texture of social life, central at once to our vocabulary for sharing and confirming our aesthetic experiences with others."[7]

The British Fashion Council video for the show opens with signage defining the space through textual cues: a sign marked "Notices: Orla Kiely Autumn/Winter 2015" opens the film, followed by a close-up of another sign marked "Entrance" that defines the place where models enter the library. This is quickly followed by a sign that demarcates the organization of books in the imagined library space: it reads "Mathematics A-Z." Together, these signs are not insignificant; in the fantasy space of the library, they impart verisimilitude by gesturing towards the signage one might find in an "authentic" academic library. At the same time, they approach these conventions with some creative license: for instance, a sign labeled "Existentialism" marks one section of bookshelves. In their demarcation of spatial boundaries, these signs also mark linguistic and epistemological boundaries—in Kiely's *Library*, English is the default language, and an Anglocentric and Eurocentric scheme of disciplines organizes materials (even when these disciplines are playfully reconfigured).

As models enter the library space in sequence, their navigation of the space both conforms to and defies the linear trajectory of a more traditional runway walk. The first model filmed entering the library space is filmed browsing the stacks, selecting a book, and subsequently taking it to a table to read. Others follow suit. The camera lingers on individuals as they read during this portion of the film. This moment of the performance creates a mood of interiority, perhaps inviting the viewer to wonder about the models' experiences of reading and to ask after what is not explicitly shown.

Not long after, the film shifts to a more conventional runway sequence, showing models entering the stage through the marked entrance and

7. Sianne Ngai, "Our Aesthetic Categories," *PMLA* 125, no.4 (October 2010), 952, doi: 10.1632/pmla.2010.125.4.948.

proceeding towards the stacks. These are presented as a curious mélange of backdrops, with a black and white facsimile of books on shelves, and sections with print books and magazines that the models retrieve from the shelves to read. The film ends by showing models walking single file, circumnavigating the room, passing stacks, ascending and descending stairs, and exiting the stage through the designated exit door.[8]

Though this film offers a relatively brief glimpse into the world of Kiely's *Library*, the show's reception extends its impact across time and space. For commentary on Kiely's work, we may first turn to Kiely herself. Named the "Queen of Print" by British newspaper *The Guardian*, her approach to pattern in clothing and home decoration has been described as "instantly recognizable."[9] In an interview during 2015's London Fashion Week, Kiely commented on the vision and inspiration for her Autumn/Winter collection and the *Library* show: "That's the idea, back to university. They're great years, you know, and it was a bit of geek chic but also looking at maths and geometry for our print. We're all about color…" and later, "I've always loved *Love Story* and Ali McGraw, so that was kind of our muse for the season."[10]

Let us pause for a moment to consider these words. The invocation of "back to university" suggests a reference to a previous lived experience for the designer. Referring to this time of higher education as "great years, you know," invites the interviewer (and by extension, the audience) to identify with this memory—but whose memory, we may ask. The final pronouncement of Ali McGraw in the film *Love Story* as "muse" maps this nostalgia onto a fictionalized time and space. Suddenly, a particular and personal lived experience melds with a presumed collective one, which is in turn confirmed by the 1970 film.

---

8. "Orla Kiely AW15 at London Fashion Week," YouTube video, 3:50, posted by British Fashion Council, February 21, 2015, https://www.youtube.com/watch?v=xr5ICGSu-FE.

9. Charlotte Abrahams, "My Space: Orla Kiely, Designer," *The Guardian*, May 9, 2009, https://www.theguardian.com/lifeandstyle/2009/may/10/ola-kiely-designer.

10. Video Fashion News, *VF NEWS*.

If we take a closer look at *Love Story* and the film's leading actor, Ali McGraw, as Kiely's "muse," we may start to ask some questions about how whiteness creates identifications across time and place, and how white femininity structures the fantasy of *Library* as one both fantastical and real, impossible yet supported by detail.

In *Love Story*, the protagonist Jenny, played by McGraw, is a white woman studying music as an undergraduate at Radcliffe College in Massachusetts. In one of the film's opening scenes, the moment when Jenny and her future lover Oliver first meet, Jenny is working at the circulation desk at the Radcliffe Library. Oliver, a Harvard student and son of a millionaire, demands access to a book, and Jenny confronts him about using Radcliffe's library when he has access to the more plentiful wealth and resources of Harvard's collections. It's notable that right away, this opening scene draws some attention to class struggles and gender oppression in American higher education. In her iconic role, Ali McGraw portrays a working class white woman studying at an Ivy League school, and this situates her character's whiteness in a specific way. Throughout the film, people of color are rarely shown, much less mentioned. The whiteness of the Ivy League in the 1970s (and before, and since) is furthermore never explicitly named or challenged, even as class and gender receive some attention.[11]

What does all of this mean for the nostalgia with which *Library* is performed? The *Dictionary of Race, Ethnicity, and Culture* locates the roots of the word "nostalgia" in the ancient Greek *nostos*—"voyage, return, and more particularly, return to one's country," and *algos*—"pain, suffering, affliction."[12] The *Oxford English Dictionary* offers as one definition "sentimental imagining or evocation of a period of the past."[13] Both time and place are significant to the sense of longing, mourning, and

---

11. *Love Story*, directed by Arthur Hiller. (1970; Hollywood, CA: Paramount, 2007), DVD.

12. Umberto Melotti, "Nostalgia (Homesickness)," in *Dictionary of Race, Ethnicity, and Culture*, ed. Guido Bolaffi, Raffaele Bracalenti, and Peter Braham (London: Sage UK, 2003), 210, doi: 10.4135/9781446220375.n162.

13. *Oxford English Dictionary*, 3rd ed., s.v. "nostalgia."

return staged in *Library*. It will be useful to take both time and space into account to identify how whiteness is marked in Kiely's show.

The pace of *Library* can perhaps be characterized as both time sensitive and leisurely. Models enter the stage with controlled, gradual pacing and movement. They also perform the visit to the library as slow, careful, and intentional—remarkably unruffled by the stressful demands of student and/or library worker life. As seen on film, this sense of slowness is also most certainly mediated by the camera, which lingers on individual models as they, in turn, linger in the act of reading.

In viewing the library at this pace, certain absences come into view. For one, the absence of acknowledgment of the library worker. In some photographs of the show, a model is shown seated at an information desk, stamping books and flanked by a shelf of titles labeled "References"; presumably, this model is "performing" as a library worker in the show. Otherwise, library workers are rendered invisible in this imaginary library. Kiely's *Library* circumvents the reality of the librarian's labor. Furthermore, so much of library labor is traditionally spatially segregated from public view: processing and cataloging materials, shelving these materials, cleaning and maintaining spaces, and facilitating use of library resources by visitors, among other work. The romanticized narrative of the white woman librarian leaves no room for library workers of color (many of whom work in positions that are not labeled as "librarian"). Another parallel comes to the surface here: the material labor of making clothes, so often done by women of color, which is routinely rendered invisible in the world of high fashion, where "creative work" is attributed to the designer.[14]

Style is not a given in a fashion show; it is produced through the reception that precedes, surrounds, and follows the show. Likewise,

---

14. Thuy Linh N. Tu, *The Beautiful Generation: Asian Americans and the Cultural Economy of Fashion* (Durham, NC: Duke University Press, 2011). Fashion studies scholar Thuy Linh Tu has written extensively on how intimacies and affiliations between Asian American fashion designers and Asian American garment workers complicate and trouble simplified dichotomies of labor and creativity, most notably in her book The Beautiful Generation. Tu's analysis inspires my own here.

the spatial dimension of the show has its own process of production. Alicia Kuhl proposes a framework for delineating three different kinds of space in fashion shows. Kuhl writes:

> Space is always socially constructed; that means that space as such can only then be experienced when humans have formed, built, entered, or lived in it, experienced something in it, or talked about it and so made it recognizable and endowed it with meaning. In terms specific to the fashion show it has to be differentiated between three types of space: the *place*, the *location*, and the so-called *imaginary space*. In the moment of its staging, all three merge to form the space of the fashion show.[15]

Kuhl goes on to clarify that place refers to a geographic area, broadly, while location narrows to a more concrete point within place, and imaginary place gestures toward that which is represented.[16] I would add to this framework a consideration of *time* in all three kinds of space. Following this framework, *Library's* three spaces could be named as follows: Place = London (specifically, London Fashion Week, 2015). Location = Soho Vinyl Factory, indoor space, February 21, 2015. Imaginary Space = The Orla Kiely Library, set vaguely in the late 1960s, in an Anglophone and likely British or North American place, also anticipating the fall and winter seasons of 2015.

The nostalgia evoked in *Library* finds its resonance in coverage of the show, where the language of fashion calls upon an assumed sense of shared sartorial history. In an article in *Vogue UK*, Lauren Milligan declares, "Orla Kiely's USP [unique selling proposition] is nostalgia," elaborating the salient details of the Autumn/Winter collection pieces: "Her muted Seventies palette, familiar prints and heritage fabrics evoke a comfortable sense of childhood: the mini skirts that Sixties school-girls longed to wear; the luxurious fabrics that chic women sported in the Seventies; even the swishing lengths of your mother's skirt in the

---

15. Alicia Kuhl, "Framing 'Saints and Sinners.' Methods of Producing Space in Fashion Shows," in *Aesthetic Politics in Fashion*, ed. Elke Gaugele (Vienna: Sternberg Press, 2014), 117-18.

16. Ibid., 118.

Eighties."[17] These descriptions seem to beckon the reader into identification and memory, in particular, the reference to "your mother's
skirt in the Eighties." The references to comfort, longing, and luxury
take in the paradoxical sweep of nostalgia as tied, on one hand, to the
familiar and, on the other hand, to the distant or longed for. Who is
invited to slip into this shared reverie and nod with recognition? Perhaps, for readers who weren't yet born in the '60s, or didn't remember
the clothes of the '60s in the same way, a sense of vicarious memory
might happen through exposure to artifacts of popular culture such
as movies and television shows (but do all, or even most, readers have
access to this, or desire this identification?). The easy historicization
of fashion across decades, with no regard to variant forms and styles
across geography, among other factors, assumes a default reading subject who shares these identifications and desires. Perhaps the language
could function to produce such desires in the reader where they didn't
previously exist. In either case, the fantasy of white nostalgia imparts a
sense of history and aspiration in the show, and in turn creates an idea
of the "ideal" reader/viewer.

In asking what ideas of white femininity the nostalgia of *Library* sum-
mons, we might also ask after its absences and omissions. What does it
mean that the historical era most strongly evoked by the show, the late
1960s and early 1970s, was also an era marked by a range of pivotal global
social movements led by people of color (among them struggles against
colonialism, racial apartheid, patriarchy, and homophobia)? That these
movements had a particularly pronounced impact on college campus
life in both the United States and United Kingdom urges the question:
why aren't there traces of these histories in the space of Kiely's *Library*?

The configuration of nostalgia and memory making in *Library* can
tell us something about whiteness in its more contemporary iterations.
In "The Distributions of Whiteness," Roderick Ferguson calls upon the
formative theorizing of W. E. B. Du Bois to characterize whiteness as "a

---

17. Lauren Milligan, "Orla Kiely Autumn/Winter 2015-16 Ready-To-Wear,"
Vogue UK, last accessed October 31, 2016, http://www.vogue.co.uk/fashion/
autumn-winter-2015/ready-to-wear/orla-kiely.

fundamentally and stubbornly antiredistributive formation."[18] Ferguson's essay explores what the author sees as a "new mode of whiteness," one that newly avows its own whiteness *and* acknowledges difference and "diversity," but nonetheless refuses to cede any of its power or to fight for structural changes that would dismantle white supremacy.[19] This new whiteness seems self-aware, even able to laugh at itself, but it refuses to undo the racist social order.[20] In her blog post "Progressive Racism," Sara Ahmed considers this contemporary form of whiteness as she writes, "racism progresses through institutions (courts, knowledge, manners) that are understood as progressive. So racism is justified *as* progressive, although the word 'racism' would never appear *because* of this justification (as if to say: it is not racism it is progress)."[21] The library functions as one of those spaces understood as progressive, through which racism progresses; conversely, the library also functions as a space of what Ahmed names "conservation," enacting racism through the maintenance of its own historically racist structure.[22]

So, what does this have to do with Kiely's *Library*? By offering up a scene of a '60s/'70s era academic library, virtually bereft of people of color, Kiely creates a fantasy library space that is selectively sealed from history, only allowing in the parts that would be "comfortable" to the white viewer/consumer. Perhaps, it could be argued, this is necessary to sell clothes; perhaps to do otherwise would be exploitative. Still, the tenacity with which *Library* clings to a class-privileged white femininity as default subjecthood has consequence. And it is telling that the imagined library functions as a space in which such whiteness is so thoroughly normalized that it strikes its viewers as *nostalgically* familiar. As Minh-Ha Pham writes:

---

18. Roderick A. Ferguson, "The Distributions of Whiteness," *American Quarterly* 66, no. 4 (December 2014): 1106, doi: 10.1353/aq.2014.0064.

19. Ibid., 1102.

20. Ibid., 1101.

21. Ahmed, Sara, "Progressive Racism," *feministkilljoys* (blog), May 30, 2016, https://feministkilljoys.com/2016/05/30/progressive-racism/.

22. Ibid.

Fashion, like so many other things associated primarily with women, may be dismissed as trivial, but it shapes how we're read by others, especially on the levels of gender, class and race. In turn, how we're read determines how we are treated, especially in the workforce – whether we are hired, promoted and respected, and how well we are paid. That most ordinary and intimate of acts, getting dressed, has very real political and economic consequences.[23]

Pham goes on to elaborate how these consequences of fashion affect women of color in particular, who are limited by racist stereotypes that can, in turn, cast some of us as "out of control" or, alternately, "easily controllable."[24] This creates a pressure around self-fashioning to "diminish racial difference."[25] The dizzying navigation of these misogynist, racist, classist, homophobic, and transphobic projections that are variously experienced by library workers affects how certain bodies are allowed to move through institutional spaces. For library workers of color especially, moving through library spaces without the privilege of being white all too often means being racialized as interlopers and outsiders, out of place and incongruous with our surrounding space. As Ahmed writes, "the body that causes their discomfort (by not fulfilling an expectation of whiteness) is the one who must work hard to make others comfortable. You have to pass by passing your way through whiteness, not by becoming white, but by minimizing the signs of difference. I have called this labor 'institutional passing.'"[26] How does one strategically navigate the normative white womanhood that is privileged in the dominant representations of libraries and librarians? And who is allowed, or encouraged, to do so?

As a second aesthetic quality that resurfaces in Kiely's show, cuteness delineates a particular kind of white femininity: a kind positioned as

---

23. Minh-Ha T. Pham, "If the Clothes Fit," *Ms*, Fall 2011, 39.

24. Ibid., 41.

25. Ibid..

26. Sara Ahmed, *On Being Included: Racism and Diversity in Institutional Life* (Durham, NC: Duke University Press, 2012), 41.

both unthreatening and endearing. Of all the words deployed in cover-age of *Library*, *cute* abounds with frequency. For instance: "Orla Kiely makes deeply cute clothes"; "we were dewey-eyed as they browsed the library in cute blouses with bows"; "cute co-ords"; "cute shoulder bags with chunky 'OK' appliques."[27] As a descriptor applied to very specific articles of clothing and accessories, cute zooms the viewer's gaze onto the objects, the pieces of fashion, that help define the show's style. It might be hard to determine exactly what "cute" even means, as broadly and variously as the adjective gets deployed. In her book *Our Aesthetic Categories,* Ngai characterizes cuteness as at once a "way of aestheticizing powerlessness" and a "commodity aesthetic" that seems to promise a more basic, intimate connection between people and their commodities.[28] Ngai also writes of the cute as a powerful force, inspir-ing a desire for care to be given to that which is deemed cute.[29] This approach to the aesthetics of cuteness can usefully prompt us to ask: rather than focusing on what cuteness is, what does cuteness *do?* The cuteness of Kiely's *Library* places demands on its audience, compelling us to see whatever is associated with it as cute, to view the clothes and accessories on display as well as the subjects displaying them as cute. Cuteness also compels the viewer to place value on the cute, as worthy of care, protection, and desire. If whiteness can be seen as cute, then it can be cast as unthreatening and devoid of its power to inflict violence. Cuteness, along with nostalgia, serves to normalize whiteness in Kiely's

27. Luke Leitch, "Orla Kiely Fall 2015 Ready-to-Wear Fashion Show," *Vogue*, February 22, 2015, vogue.com/fashion-shows/fall-2015-ready-to-wear/orla-kiely; She and Hem, "London Fashion Week AW15: Orla Kiely," *She and Hem*, February 27, 2015, http://sheandhem.co.uk/2015/02/27/london-fashion-week-aw15-orla-kiely; Hayley Leaver, "London Fashion Week: Orla Kiely," *The London Word*, February 22, 2015, http://www.thelondonword.com/2015/02/london-fashion-week-orla-kiely; Gemma Cartwright, "Orla Kiely's Autumn/Winter Clarks Shoe Collection Is Out Now!," *POPSUGAR Fashion UK*, September 14, 2015, http://www.popsugar.co.uk/fashion/Orla-Kiely-AutumnWinter-2015-Collection-Clarks-Shoes-36918398.

28. Adam Jasper and Sianne Ngai, "Our Aesthetic Categories: An Inter-view with Sianne Ngai," *Cabinet*, Fall 2011, http://www.cabinetmagazine.org/issues/43/jasper_ngai.php.

29. Ibid.

Library; the packaging reinforces the ways that these aesthetics familiarize and protect whiteness.

Geek chic works in counterpoint to the aesthetic of cuteness in *Library*. Curiously, it arises prominently in Kiely's own description of her creations, as she references "our geek chic girl" who "does mix it up a bit, so she doesn't mind a bit of sparkle with her mohair sweater," suggesting an innovative, adventurous approach to fashion (perhaps Kiely is referring partly to her own "geek chic" sensibilities here).[30] Sarah Waldron's coverage of *Library* takes this trope a step further by designating an archetype: Miss Priss.[31] She maps the sartorial re-emergence of the prissy—once "meaning fussy, prim, straight-laced, unnecessarily studious," but in 2015 having "found new relevance"—across the Fall collections of several designers, among them Kiely.[32] Waldron moves the lens outward from clothes to larger social trends by declaring that "being a geek or a priss has never been so cool."[33] She links this coolness to the emergence of educational programs like Women Who Code. This new valence of so-called "geek chic" style situates its subject as intelligent, and her style as reflecting this intelligence.

At first glance this might seem novel, but a closer look reveals a recurrent trope of white femininity (and white feminism) at play here—the notion of the "exceptional" (read: elite) woman as style icon. If Miss Priss's style reads as "smart," what does this imply about other sartorial choices that would be read under a white gaze as less than, or not, smart? All too often, the framing of certain kinds of dress and bodily comportment as "smart," associated with success, intelligence, and status, reinforces dichotomies that end up perpetuating misogyny, femmephobia, racism, classism, and ableism. Further, even within the apparent valuing of the so-called "cool" new iteration of "geek chic," the style

---

30. Video Fashion News, *VF NEWS*.

31. Sarah Waldron, "Prissy is Not an Insult in the Fashion World," *Irish Times*, October 20, 2015, http://www.irishtimes.com/life-and-style/fashion/prissy-is-not-an-insult-in-the-fashion-world-1.2391972.

32. Ibid.

33. Ibid.

is not spared from misogynistic readings, as evidenced in Luke Leitch's *Vogue* piece, where Leitch writes: "The models, all gray-stockinged, pottered back and forth between the shelves, sometimes giggling as they skimmed mathematics textbooks (unlikely) and sometimes staring passionately at the pages of 1969 editions of *Vogue* (entirely plausible)."[34] Here, "smartness" or "geekiness" is an aesthetic that the white woman librarian or library denizen wears, while the fashion critic presumes to know the extent of her cognition and imagination.

Ruth Frankenberg's work on the intersections of white privilege and gender help to illuminate the particular ways that whiteness manifests itself in *Library*. In "The Mirage of an Unmarked Whiteness," she writes of whiteness as "crosscut by a range of other axes of relative advantage and subordination; these do not erase or render irrelevant race privilege, but rather inflect or modify it."[35] Insisting on a careful reading of race, which Frankenberg calls "process rather than thing," means attending to the ways that people can be racialized through gender, gendered through racialization.[36] It also means noting how "whiteness is in a continual state of being dressed and undressed, or marking and cloaking."[37] This suggests that whiteness is not always, or even mostly, explicitly named as "white": it appears in cyphers and codes. Whiteness is also not necessarily "invisible" to everyone—Frankenberg considers, for instance, the ways that whiteness is all too visible for subjects who do not experience the privilege of being racialized as white.[38] The frequently repeated notion that whiteness is invisible itself presumes an optic position securely within whiteness, but what about perspectives of librarians of color?

---

34. Leitch, "Orla Kiely Fall 2015 Ready-to-Wear Fashion Show."

35. Ruth Frankenberg, "The Mirage of an Unmarked Whiteness," in *The Making and Unmaking of Whiteness*, ed. Birgit Brander Rasmussen (Durham, NC: Duke University Press, 2001,) 72–96.

36. Ibid.

37. Ibid.

38. Ibid.

Hope Olson and Melodie Fox's "Essentialism and Care in a Female-Intensive Profession" critiques traditional strategies within library and information science and studies (LIS) for addressing what have been framed as "women's issues."[39] Their work opens up crucial space for questioning the limits of essentialism, what they describe as the "invariable and fixed whatness of an identity," as a feminist strategy; this essentialism, as Fox and Olson write, "suspends women in the status quo like an insect in amber."[40] In exploring the uses of an ethic of care rooted in justice for feminist librarian activism, the authors ask, "what kind of action can we take to reassert ourselves?"[41] This question curiously suggests an insider group that identifies as "we" without really exploring the difference and intersectionality that constitutes this "we" (or considering whom the "we" has historically excluded). Fox and Olson thus fall short of addressing the whiteness that persists in what they characterize as a "female-intensive profession," even as their critiques of essentialism anticipate new avenues of analysis.

How might LIS scholarship inform new library imaginaries that resist patriarchal white scripts of the profession? Works by Nicole Pagowsky, Erica DeFrain, and Ayanna Gaines engage the histories and legacies of gendered stereotypes of librarians, while Maria Accardi's *Feminist Pedagogy in Library Instruction* explores praxis deeply.[42] Scholarship in LIS that

---

39. Hope A. Olson and Melodie Fox, "Essentialism and Care in a Female-Intensive Profession," in *Feminist and Queer Information Studies Reader*, ed. Rebecca Dean and Patrick Keilty (Sacramento, CA: Litwin Books, 2013), 48.

40. Ibid, 49.

41. Ibid, 55.

42. Nicole Pagowsky and Erica DeFrain, "Ice Ice Baby: Are Librarian Stereotypes Freezing Us out of Instruction?" *In the Library with the Lead Pipe* (June 2014), http://www.inthelibrarywiththeleadpipe.org/2014/ice-ice-baby-2; Ayanna Gaines, "That's Women's Work: Pink-Collar Professions, Gender, and the Librarian Stereotype," in *The Librarian Stereotype: Deconstructing Perceptions and Presentations of Information Work*, ed. Nicole Pagowsky and Miriam Rigby (Chicago: Association of College and Research Libraries, 2014), 85–130; Maria T. Accardi, *Feminist Pedagogy for Library Instruction* (Sacramento, CA: Library Juice Press, 2013) .

engages race *with* gender, along with multiple vectors of identity and oppression, complicates and deepens these analyses. Gina Schlesselman-Tarango has uncovered tropes of white womanhood used in LIS to enact white supremacy within the profession and as part of a broader United States nationalist project.[43] April Hathcock's critique of white-led "diversity" initiatives in LIS engages critical whiteness studies to trace the enactment of whiteness in librarianship at large—she begins with a working definition of whiteness as "a theoretical concept that can extend beyond the realities of racial privilege to a wide range of dominant ideologies based on gender identity, sexual orientation, class, and other categories."[44] Hathcock also maps out concrete resistance to these structures of whiteness.[45] Fobazi Ettarh has brought an ever-relevant reading of Kimberlé Crenshaw's vital theory of intersectionality to readers in the LIS world, looking at how axes of identity and oppression intersect in libraries.[46] The anthology *Where are All the Librarians of Color?* makes vital space for personal narrative and critical analysis around the experiences of academic librarians of color.[47] Library literature, itself so historically white, needs even more interventions like these (though truly, this paragraph is a far-from-comprehensive representation of critical work already circulating in the field).

In Kiely's *Library*, a sartorial and spatial fantasy of a library draws on nostalgia and, given its positioning as a Fashion Week Show, an anticipated futurity to solidify the iconic place of white femininity in

---

43. Gina Schlesselman-Tarango, "The Legacy of Lady Bountiful: White Women in the Library," *Library Trends* 64, no. 4 (2016): 667–86, doi: 10.1353/lib.2016.0015.

44. April Hathcock, "White Librarianship in Blackface: Diversity Initiatives in LIS," *In the Library with the Lead Pipe* (October 2015), http://www.inthelibrarywiththeleadpipe.org/2015/lis-diversity/.

45. Ibid.

46. Fobazi Ettarh, "Making a New Table: Intersectional Librarianship," *In the Library with the Lead Pipe* (July 2014), http://www.inthelibrarywiththeleadpipe.org/2014/making-a-new-table-intersectional-librarianship-3/.

47. Rebecca Hankins and Miguel Juarez, eds., *Where are All the Librarians of Color? The Experiences of People of Color in Academia* (Sacramento, CA: Library Juice Press, 2016).

the imagined library. Fantasies produced and sustained by fashion are powerful in informing reality and in creating the aesthetic of "professionalism" that has so often limited who can steward the space of the library. With this in mind, it is also important to consider resistant imaginings of fashion, resistant spaces of pleasure, expression, and embodiment that could challenge and explode popular understandings of what a library worker or library user "looks like" and to whom the library belongs. Library workers of color, including gender nonbinary people of color and women of color (trans and cis), are creating these spaces every day. In addition to *Librarian Wardrobe*, readers might also look to projects like *Of Another Fashion,* a digital archive co-created by people of color exploring histories of US-based women of color in fashion, as well as *dapperQ*, a blog highlighting fashion and style by and for trans, gender non-conforming, and queer people, as sites that represent fashion intentionally resistant to scripts of whiteness.[48] Perhaps most importantly, we who care about and work in libraries could commit ourselves to refashioning the library. We could work to undo white supremacist structures that control and police library spaces and the people that move through them.

Bibliography

Abrahams, Charlotte. "My Space: Orla Kiely, Designer." *The Guardian*, May 9, 2009. http://www.theguardian.com/lifeandstyle/2009/may/10/ola-kiely-designer.

Accardi, Maria T. *Feminist Pedagogy for Library Instruction*. Sacramento, CA: Library Juice Press, 2013.

Ahmed, Sara. *On Being Included: Racism and Diversity in Institutional Life*. Durham, NC: Duke University Press, 2012.

---

48. Minh-Ha Pham, "Of Another Fashion," accessed October 31, 2016, http://ofanotherfashion.tumblr.com/?og=1; "dapperQ," *dapperQ*, accessed October 31, 2016, http://www.dapperq.com/.

————. "Progressive Racism." *feministkilljoys* (blog), May 30, 2016. https://feministkilljoys.com/2016/05/30/progressive-racism/.

British Fashion Council. "Orla Kiely AW15 at London Fashion Week." YouTube video, 3:50. Posted February 21, 2015. https://www.youtube.com/watch?v=xr5ICGSu-FE.

Brook, Freeda, Dave Ellenwood, and Althea Eannace Lazzaro. "In Pursuit of Antiracist Social Justice: Denaturalizing Whiteness in the Academic Library." *Library Trends* 64, no. 2 (2015): 246–84. doi:10.1353/lib.2015.0048.

Cartwright, Gemma. "Orla Kiely's Autumn/Winter Clarks Shoe Collection Is Out Now!" *POPSUGAR Fashion UK*, September 14, 2015. http://www.popsugar.co.uk/fashion/Orla-Kiely-AutumnWinter-2015-Collection-Clarks-Shoes-36918398.

dapperQ. Accessed June 1, 2016. http://www.dapperq.com/.

Drabinski, Emily. "Teaching the Radical Catalog." In *Radical Cataloging: Essays at the Front*, edited by K. R. Roberto, 198-205. Jefferson, NC: McFarland, 2008.

Ettarh, Fobazi. "Making a New Table: Intersectional Librarianship" *In the Library with the Lead Pipe* (July 2014). http://www.inthelibrarywiththeleadpipe.org/2014/making-a-new-table-intersectional-librarianship-3/.

Ferguson, Roderick A. "The Distributions of Whiteness." *American Quarterly* 66, no. 4 (December 2014): 1101–06, doi: 10.1353/aq.2014.0064.

Frankenberg, Ruth. "The Mirage of an Unmarked Whiteness." In *The Making and Unmaking of Whiteness*, edited by Birgit Brander Rasmussen, 72–96. Durham, NC: Duke University Press, 2001.

Gaines, Ayanna. "That's Women's Work: Pink-Collar Professions, Gender, and the Librarian Stereotype." In *The Librarian Ste-*

reotype: Deconstructing Perceptions and Presentations of Information Work, edited by Nicole Pagowsky and Miriam Rigby, 85–130. Chicago: Association of College and Research Libraries, 2014.

Hankins, Rebecca, and Miguel Juarez, eds. *Where are All the Librarians of Color? The Experiences of People of Color in Academia.* Sacramento, CA: Library Juice Press, 2016.

Hathcock, April. "White Librarianship in Blackface: Diversity Initiatives in LIS" *In the Library With the Lead Pipe* (October 2015). http://www.inthelibrarywiththeleadpipe.org/2015/lis-diversity/.

Jasper, Adam, and Sianne Ngai. "Our Aesthetic Categories: An Interview with Sianne Ngai." *Cabinet*, Fall 2011. http://www.cabinetmagazine.org/issues/43/jasper_ngai.php.

Kuhl, Alicia. "Framing 'Saints and Sinners.' Methods of Producing Space in Fashion Shows." In *Aesthetic Politics in Fashion*, edited by Elke Gaugele, 113–26. Vienna: Sternberg Press, 2014.

Leaver, Hayley. "London Fashion Week: Orla Kiely." *The London Word*, February 22, 2015. http://www.thelondonword.com/2015/02/london-fashion-week-orla-kiely/.

Leitch, Luke. "Orla Kiely Fall 2015 Ready-to-Wear Fashion Show." *Vogue*, February 22, 2015. http://www.vogue.com/fashion-shows/fall-2015-ready-to-wear/orla-kiely.

Librarian Wardrobe. Accessed October 31, 2016. http://librarian-wardrobe.com.

Love Story. DVD. Directed by Arthur Hiller. 1970. Hollywood, CA: Paramount Pictures, 2007.

Melotti, Umberto. "Nostalgia (Homesickness)." In *Dictionary of Race, Ethnicity and Culture*, edited by Guido Bolaffi, Raffaele Bracalenti and Peter Braham, 210. London: SAGE Publications, 2003. doi: 10.4135/9781446220375.n162.

Milligan, Lauren. "Orla Kiely Autumn/Winter 2015-16 Ready-To-Wear." *Vogue UK*, accessed October 31, 2016. http://www.vogue.co.uk/fashion/autumn-winter-2015/ready-to-wear/orla-kiely.

Ngai, Sianne. *Our Aesthetic Categories: Zany, Cute, Interesting.* Cambridge, MA: Harvard University Press, 2012.

———. "Our Aesthetic Categories." *PMLA* 125, no.4 (October 2010): 948-58, doi: 10.1632/pmla.2010.125.4.948.

Olson, Hope A., and Melodie Fox. "Essentialism and Care in a Female-Intensive Profession." In *Feminist and Queer Information Studies Reader*, edited by Rebecca Dean and Patrick Keilty, 48–61. Sacramento, CA: Litwin Books, 2013.

Pagowsky, Nicole, and Erica DeFrain. "Ice Ice Baby: Are Librarian Stereotypes Freezing Us out of Instruction?" *In the Library With the Lead Pipe* (June 2014). http://www.inthelibrarywiththeleadpipe.org/2014/ice-ice-baby-2/.

Pham, Minh-Ha. Of Another Fashion. Accessed October 31, 2016. http://ofanotherfashion.tumblr.com/?og=1.

———. "If the Clothes Fit." *Ms*, Fall 2011.

Schlesselman-Tarango, Gina. "The Legacy of Lady Bountiful: White Women in the Library." *Library Trends* 64, no. 4 (September 13, 2016): 667–86, doi: 10.1353/lib.2016.0015.

She and Hem. "London Fashion Week AW15: Orla Kiely." *She and Hem*, February 27, 2015. http://sheandhem.co.uk/2015/02/27/london-fashion-week-aw15-orla-kiely/.

Tu, Thuy Linh N. *The Beautiful Generation: Asian Americans and the Cultural Economy of Fashion.* Durham, NC: Duke University Press, 2011.

Video Fashion News. *VF NEWS: Orla Kiely - Fall 2015 - London Fashion Week - Runway & Designer Interview.* Getty Images, 2015. http://www.gettyimages.com/detail/video/orla-kiely-tells-a-preppy-love-story-for-fall-2015-and-news-foot-age/479561212.

Waldron, Sarah. "Prissy is Not an Insult in the Fashion World."
    Irish Times, October 20, 2015. http://www.irishtimes.com/
    life-and-style/fashion/prissy-is-not-an-insult-in-the-fashion-world-1.2391972.

Whitefield-Madrano, Autumn. "Labor and Looking 'Professional.'"
    The New Inquiry, February 19, 2016. http://thenewinquiry.
    com/blogs/the-beheld/labor-and-looking-professional/.

Chapter 7

WHITE FEMINISM AND DISTRIBUTIONS OF POWER IN ACADEMIC LIBRARIES

Megan Watson

Introduction

> I urge each one of us here to reach down into that deep place of knowledge inside herself and touch that terror and loathing of any difference that lives there. See whose face it wears. –Audre Lorde, *Sister Outsider*

Academic libraries and librarians routinely tout a commitment to diversity and inclusivity, as evidenced by numerous initiatives related to hiring, retention, and equity.[1] Despite these efforts, whiteness continues to define and distinguish the profession due to a variety of barriers found along the entire timeline of a typical professional career.[2] The few

---

1. Association of College and Research Libraries, "Diversity Standards: Cultural Competency for Academic Libraries (2012)," last accessed April 16, 2016, http://www.ala.org/acrl/standards/diversity; Association of Research Libraries, "Initiative to Recruit a Diverse Workforce (IRDW)," last accessed April 16, 2016, http://www.arl.org/leadership-recruitment/diversity-recruitment/initiative-to-recruit-a-diverse-workforce-irdw; Charlene Maxey-Harris, *Diversity Plans and Programs*, SPEC Kit 319 (Washington, DC: Association of Research Libraries, 2010).

2. Freeda Brook, Dave Ellenwood, and Althea Eannace Lazzaro, "In Pursuit of Antiracist Social Justice: Denaturalizing Whiteness in the Academic Library," *Library Trends* 64, no. 2 (2015): 246–84, doi:10.1353/lib.2015.0048;

students of color who enter Library and Information Science (LIS) programs face a whitewashed curriculum with little integration of culturally relevant topics or equity-oriented discussions.[3] The emphasis on conformity and erasure of difference continues throughout the formal hiring process, from opaque expectations of cultural "fit" and behavior to the perpetuation of recruitment programs (such as fixed-term diversity residencies) offering opportunity for the price of precarity.[4] Once employed, academic librarians of color encounter microaggressions and other types of stereotyping and silencing tactics, leading to high rates of attrition and an increasingly homogeneous workforce ascending into leadership positions.[5] The end result is a doggedly stagnant profession

Angela Galvan, "Soliciting Performance, Hiding Bias: Whiteness and Librarianship," *In the Library with the Lead Pipe* (June 2015), http://www.inthelibrarywiththeleadpipe.org/2015/soliciting-performance-hiding-bias-whiteness-and-librarianship/; April Hathcock, "White Librarianship in Blackface: Diversity Initiatives in LIS," *In the Library with the Lead Pipe* (October 2015), http://www.inthelibrarywiththeleadpipe.org/2015/lis-diversity/; Myrna Morales, Em Claire Knowles, and Chris Bourg, "Diversity, Social Justice, and the Future of Libraries," *portal: Libraries and the Academy* 14, no. 3 (2014): 439–51, doi:10.1353/pla.2014.0017; Jennifer Vinopal, "The Quest for Diversity in Library Staffing: From Awareness to Action," *In the Library with the Lead Pipe* (January 2016), http://www.inthelibrarywiththeleadpipe.org/2016/quest-for-diversity/.

3. Nicole A. Cooke, Miriam E. Sweeney, and Safiya Umoja Noble, "Social Justice as Topic and Tool: An Attempt to Transform an LIS Curriculum and Culture," *Library Quarterly* 86, no. 1 (2016): 107–24, doi:10.1086/684147; Lori S. Mestre, "Librarians Working with Diverse Populations: What Impact Does Cultural Competency Training Have on Their Efforts?" *Journal of Academic Librarianship* 36, no. 6 (2010): 479–88, doi:10.1016/j.acalib.2010.08.003.

4. Galvan, "Soliciting Performance, Hiding Bias"; Juleah Swanson et al., "Why Diversity Matters: A Roundtable Discussion on Racial and Ethnic Diversity in Librarianship," *In the Library with the Lead Pipe* (July 2015), http://www.inthelibrarywiththeleadpipe.org/2015/why-diversity-matters-a-roundtable-discussion-on-racial-and-ethnic-diversity-in-librarianship/.

5. Jaena Alabi, "Racial Microaggressions in Academic Libraries: Results of a Survey of Minority and Non-Minority Librarians," *Journal of Academic Librarianship* 41, no. 1 (2015): 47–53, doi:10.1016/j.acalib.2014.10.008; Brook et al., "In Pursuit of Antiracist Social Justice;" Nicole A. Cooke, "Pushing Back from the Table: Fighting to Maintain My Voice as a Pre-Tenure Minority Female in the White Academy," *Polymath: An Interdisciplinary Arts and Sciences Journal* 4, no. 2 (2014): 39–49, https://ojcs.siue.edu/ojs/index.php/polymath/article/view/2934/1000; Deborah A. Curry, "Your Worries Ain't

and a growing body of literature grappling with the perplexing but persistent problem of diversity in the field.[6]

By focusing on demographics, however, "we deflect attention away from genuinely liberatory struggles" and shirk our "obligation as human beings to examine the systems of oppression and domination that we have created and in which we are complicit."[7] Many note reluctance on the part of libraries and librarians to confront the ways whiteness characterizes our profession as a whole and our diversity efforts in particular, effectively replicating the inequitable and oppressive power dynamics of society at large.[8] This chapter analyzes academic libraries' practices through the lens of white feminism, a brand of feminist praxis defined by the exclusion of the bodies and concerns of women of color. After reviewing white feminism within mainstream feminist movements, I will explore the ways our institutions' grounding in white feminist thinking directs the flow of power and influence, shapes decision-making processes and norms, and limits our capacity for substantive change by reinforcing white supremacy and cultural hegemony within our organizations. Finally, I will offer an alternative theoretical approach and related

Like Mine: African American Librarians and the Pervasiveness of Racism, Prejudice and Discrimination in Academe," in *Racial and Ethnic Diversity in Academic Libraries: Multicultural Issues*, ed. Deborah A. Curry, Susan Griswold Blandy, and Lynne M. Martin, *Reference Librarian*, 45/46 (Binghamton, NY: The Haworth Press, 1994), 299–311; Joyce K. Thornton, "African American Female Librarians: A Study of Job Satisfaction," *Journal of Library Administration* 33, no. 1–2 (2001): 141–64, doi:10.1300/J111v33n01_10; Vinopal, "The Quest for Diversity."

6. Ibid.

7. Mandy Henk, "Mandy Henk's Hikuwai Event: What Is Critical Librarianship?," *Library Juice* (blog), April 21, 2016, http://libraryjuicepress.com/blog/?p=5252.

8. Hathcock, "White Librarianship in Blackface"; Christina Neigel, "LIS Leadership and Leadership Education: A Matter of Gender," *Journal of Library Administration* 55, no. 7 (2015): 521–34, doi:10.1080/01930826.2015.1076307; Vinopal, "The Quest for Diversity"; Gina Schlesselman-Tarango, "The Legacy of Lady Bountiful: White Women in the Library," *Library Trends* 64, no. 4 (Spring 2016): 667–86, doi:10.1353/lib.2016.0015; Shinjoung Yeo and James R. Jacobs, "Diversity Matters? Rethinking Diversity in Libraries," *Counterpoise* 10, no. 1/2 (Winter 2006): 78–80, http://freegovinfo.info/files/diversity_counterpoise.pdf.

strategies designed to inspire deeper, self-critical reflection and identify new paths toward a truly transformative model of social justice.

The Origins and Evolution of White Feminism

The emergence of first-wave feminist activism in the United States was embedded in the struggle for (white) women's suffrage and rooted in racist ideology.[9] As the first wave made way for the second wave in the 1960s and '70s, the concept of "white feminism" as a distinct philosophy and set of practices solidified. Black and woman of color feminists such as Barbara Smith, Cherríe Moraga, and Audre Lorde argued that mainstream women's movements (typified by organizations such as National Organization for Women [NOW] and NARAL Pro-Choice America) perpetuated racism and classism by failing to acknowledge or address the roles whiteness and white privilege play in the struggle for gender equality.[10] White feminism maintains and reproduces white supremacy by focusing on the concerns of middle- and upper-class white women, disregarding the oppression faced by women of color along the axes of race, class, and sexual orientation and actively excluding and silencing activists who push back against what bell hooks called feminism's

---

9. Jessie Daniels, "Trouble with White Feminism: Racial Origins of U.S. Feminism," February 18, 2014, *Racism Review*, http://www.racismreview.com/blog/2014/02/18/trouble-with-white-feminism/; bell hooks, *Ain't I a Woman: Black Women and Feminism* (New York: Routledge, 2015), 159-75.

10. Combahee River Collective, "The Combahee River Collective Statement," in *Home Girls: A Black Feminist Anthology*, ed. Barbara Smith (New York: Kitchen Table: Women of Color Press, 1978), 272–82; hooks, *Ain't I a Woman*; Gloria T. Hull, Patricia Bell Scott, and Barbara Smith, eds., *All the Women Are White, All the Blacks Are Men, But Some of Us Are Brave: Black Women's Studies* (New York: The Feminist Press at the City University of New York, 1982); Audre Lorde, *Sister Outsider: Essays and Speeches*, Rev. ed. (Berkeley, CA: Crossing Press, 2007); Cherríe Moraga and Gloria Anzaldúa, eds., *This Bridge Called My Back: Writings by Radical Women of Color* (New York: Kitchen Table: Women of Color Press, 1983); Barbara Smith, ed., *Home Girls: A Black Feminist Anthology* (New York: Kitchen Table: Women of Color Press, 1983); Elizabeth V. Spelman, *Inessential Woman: Problems of Exclusion in Feminist Thought* (Boston, MA: Beacon Press, 1988).

"party line."[11] It is important to note that white feminism refers to the partisan framework underlying an individual or group's feminist praxis rather than the racial background of the individual or group themselves. Under this construction, not all white women are "white feminists"; however, one must also concede that most "white feminists" are, in fact, white women.[12]

The stance that "relations between women and men, rather than class or ethnicity, provided the primary site of oppression" was central to the second-wave white feminist agenda.[13] Betty Friedan's groundbreaking call-to-arms, *The Feminine Mystique*, exemplifies this approach.[14] Focusing on the problems facing (white) stay-at-home mothers, Friedan is silent regarding the systemic subjugation of women of color, forced by economic circumstances to work long hours outside the home for low pay.[15] Within second-wave feminist circles, white women's priorities (e.g., workplace discrimination as it affects the upwardly mobile, reproductive freedom within the bounds of heterosexual, monogamous relationships, etc.) serve as stand-ins for *all* women's priorities and hijack the movement's cultural and legislative agendas.[16] Issues of importance to women of color, such as generational poverty, lack of educational opportunity, immigration status, domestic violence, and housing discrimination, were summarily minimized and dismissed. As Kimberlé Crenshaw argues,

---

11. bell hooks, *Feminist Theory: From Margin to Center* (New York: Routledge, 2015), 9; Lorde, *Sister Outsider*, 40-123; Maria Lugones, *Pilgrimages/Peregrinajes: Theorizing Coalition against Multiple Oppressions* (Lanham, MD: Rowman & Littlefield, 2003).

12. Cate Young, "This Is What I Mean When I Say 'White Feminism,'" *BattyMamzelle* (blog), January 10, 2014, http://battymamzelle.blogspot.com/2014/01/This-Is-What-I-Mean-When-I-Say-White-Feminism.html.

13. Amanda D. Lotz, "Communicating Third-Wave Feminism and New Social Movements: Challenges for the Next Century of Feminist Endeavor," *Women & Language* 26, no. 1 (Spring 2003): 2.

14. Betty Friedan, *The Feminine Mystique* (New York: Norton, 1963).

15. hooks, *Feminist Theory*, 1-3.

16. Aimee M. Carrillo Rowe, "Locating Feminism's Subject: The Paradox of White Femininity and the Struggle to Forge Feminist Alliances," *Communication Theory* 10, no. 1 (2000): 64, doi:10.1111/j.1468-2885.2000.tb00179.x; hooks, *Ain't I a Woman*, 160-61.

"women of color are differently situated in the economic, social, and political worlds. When reform efforts undertaken on behalf of women neglect this fact, women of color are less likely to have their needs met than women who are racially privileged."[17] White feminists view their activism through the lens of what Adrienne Rich called "white solipsism," the perhaps unintentional but nonetheless nefarious tendency to "think, imagine, and speak as if whiteness described the world."[18] As Barbara Smith noted, "the percentage of white feminists who are concerned about racism is still a minority of the movement, and even within this minority those who are personally sensitive and completely serious about formulating an *activist* challenge to racism are fewer still."[19]

The consequences of white feminism's single-minded fixation on white women's issues fall disproportionately on women of color, who "become 'other,' the outsider whose experience and tradition is too 'alien' to comprehend."[20] Excluded from decision-making processes and subject to essentializing discourse depicting the struggles of women of color as inevitable or natural, the cultural norms and legislative advancements championed by second-wave feminists primarily benefited white women.[21] Feminists of color (many of whom developed new political constructs such as Third World feminism, womanism, and Xicanisma) responded by creating their own agendas, communities, and spaces, devising new epistemologies and modes of praxis independent of those operating in mainstream feminist movements.[22] Such inter-group coali-

---

17. Kimberlé Crenshaw, "Mapping the Margins: Intersectionality, Identity Politics, and Violence against Women of Color," *Stanford Law Review* 43, no. 6 (1991): 1250, doi:10.2307/1229039.

18. Adrienne Rich, *On Lies, Secrets, and Silence: Selected Prose 1966-1978* (New York: W. W. Norton & Co., 1979).

19. Smith, *Home Girls*, xxxiv.

20. Lorde, *Sister Outsider*, 117.

21. hooks, *Feminist Theory*, 97-100.

22. Combahee River Collective, *The Combahee River Collective Statement*; Patricia Hill Collins, *Black Feminist Thought: Knowledge, Consciousness, and the Politics of Empowerment*, 2nd ed. (New York: Routledge, 2000); Alethia Jones and Virginia Eubanks, eds., *Ain't Gonna Let Nobody Turn Me Around: Forty Years of Movement Building with Barbara Smith* (Albany, NY: SUNY Press, 2014).

tion building, however, did not negate or diminish the need to break through white feminists' "massive silence" and continue calling out their racist traditions.[23] Audre Lorde, speaking at an academic conference in 1979, pointedly queried her audience: "If white American feminist theory need not deal with the differences between us, and the resulting difference in our oppressions, then how do you deal with the fact that the women who clean your houses and tend your children while you attend conferences on feminist theory are, for the most part, poor women and women of color?"[24] Such confrontations led many white feminists to accuse black and woman of color feminists of needlessly sowing discord, frustrating efforts to cultivate alliances and concentrate power. Distilling the issue, hooks states that, for white feminists, "identifying oneself as oppressed freed one from being an oppressor. To a very grave extent such thinking prevented white feminists from understanding and overcoming their own sexist-racist attitudes toward black women. They could pay lip-service to the idea of sisterhood and solidarity between women but at the same time dismiss black women."[25]

Second-wave white feminists' unwillingness to self-educate and take action to forge more inclusive, multi-issue coalitions eventually led to the emergence of a new mainstream movement. Third-wave feminism, initially coined by Rebecca Walker in a 1992 *Ms.* article, promised a more heterogeneous, equitable approach centering the voices of and issues affecting marginalized women, particularly women of color and the LGBTQIA+ community.[26] Embracing Crenshaw's framework of intersectionality, which addresses how different dimensions of identity (race, gender, class, etc.) intersect to produce different experiences of oppression, third-wave feminists infuse their politics with the understanding that one's identities governs one's access to power.[27] While

---

23. Hull et al., *All Women are White*, 158.

24. Lorde, *Sister Outsider*, 112.

25. hooks, Ain't I a Woman, 9.

26. Rebecca Walker, "Becoming the Third Wave," *Ms.*, February 1992.

27. Kimberlé Crenshaw, "Demarginalizing the Intersection of Race and Sex: A Black Feminist Critique of Antidiscrimination Doctrine, Feminist Theory

third-wave feminism is hardly a single, cohesive movement, the flawed principles of white feminism continue to enact a powerful (if coded) influence over its ethics and activism. This white feminism evolved from the second wave's flagrant disregard of issues of race and difference into a more insidious form of "loving, knowing ignorance."[28] The central paradox Mariana Ortega outlines is white feminists' sympathy toward the "other's" struggle and ability to parrot the discourse of anti-racism without the courage to question long-held assumptions or engage wholeheartedly with the lived experiences of women of color.[29] The continued universalization of white women's reality is further shaded by an obfuscating arrogance, a "self-congratulatory reflection about how far we have come as white feminists who recognize difference within feminism."[30]

Recently, white feminism has come under the influence of neoliberalism, the broad set of ideas and practices applying free market rationality and competitive individualism to other social locations and contexts. Neoliberal feminism made its formal debut with the publication of Sheryl Sandberg's 2013 memoir *Lean In*, which the author evasively labels as "sort of a feminist manifesto."[31] In white feminism's twenty-first century iteration of *The Feminine Mystique*, Sandberg expresses a vision of women's liberation that disregards complex issues of race and class to promote an individualistic approach to corporate success cloaked in the "wrapping paper of feminism."[32] Her focus on personal transformation

and Antiracist Politics," *University of Chicago Legal Forum* (1989): 139–67, http://chicagounbound.uchicago.edu/uclf/vol1989/iss1/8; Crenshaw, "Mapping the Margins," 1241; Lotz, "Communicating Third-Wave Feminism," 3.

28. Mariana Ortega, "Being Lovingly, Knowingly Ignorant: White Feminism and Women of Color," *Hypatia* 21, no. 3 (2006): 56-74, doi:10.1353/hyp.2006.0034.

29. Ibid.

30. Jill Blackmore, "'The Other Within': Race/Gender Disruptions to the Professional Learning of White Educational Leaders," *International Journal of Leadership in Education* 13, no. 1 (2010): 46, doi:10.1080/13603120903242931.

31. Sheryl Sandberg, *Lean In: Women, Work, and the Will to Lead* (New York: Alfred A Knopf, 2013), 9.

32. bell hooks, "Dig Deep: Beyond Lean In," *The Feminist Wire*, October 28,

operates under the assumption that "the struggle for racial equality—just like the feminist revolution—has, in some sense, already occurred, been successful and is, consequently, a thing of the past."[33] Recalling mainstream second-wave feminism, this neoliberal feminism is narrowly focused on the problems of cisgender, heterosexual, able-bodied, middle- and upper-class white women, whitewashing the adversity facing women of color and other marginalized populations (though, like many third-wave white feminists, Sandberg does briefly acknowledge the limitations of her experience).[34] Again, gender is identified as the primary site of oppression, with race, class, and other axes of identity merely an afterthought. The significant shift from earlier mainstream women's movements lies in neoliberal feminism's disavowal of coalition building in favor of personal transformation and individual responsibility, "reorient[ing] women away from conceptions of solidarity and towards their own *particular development*."[35] As Aimee Carrillo Rowe argues, "the unnamed experience of racial privilege through which White women often secure institutional mobility may incline White women to buy into racist and color-blind myths of meritocracy, the American dream, and individual exceptionalism."[36]

Rich's white solipsism thus matures into what Stephanie Shields notes is "not unwillingness to see privilege, but unthinkingness, a kind of taken-for-granted state."[37] These "sincere fictions" help white feminists avoid their residual fear of plurality and circumvent the guilt they feel if and when confronted by the stark differences between their experiences

2013, http://www.thefeministwire.com/2013/10/17973/.

33. Catherine Rottenberg, "The Rise of Neoliberal Feminism," *Cultural Studies* 28, no. 3 (2014): 428, doi:10.1080/09502386.2013.857361.

34. Ibid., 418-37.

35. Ibid., 426.

36. Carrillo Rowe, "Locating Feminism's Subject," 69.

37. Stephanie A. Shields, "Waking Up to Privilege: Intersectionality and Opportunity," in *Presumed Incompetent: The Intersections of Race and Class for Women in Academia*, ed. Gabriella Gutiérrez y Muhs, Yolanda Flores Niemann, and Carmen G. Gonzalez (Logan, UT: Utah State University Press, 2012), 29–39.

and those of women of color.[38] White feminists may be willing to recognize the *negative* impact of racism on the lives of women of color but
unable or unwilling to understand the *positive* impact of racism on the
lives of white women. When racism is addressed, the context is cerebral,
approached from a safe intellectual distance with little in the way of
meaningful contemplation.[39] As such, hooks notes, "the contemporary
feminist call for sisterhood, the radical white woman's appeal to black
women and all women of color to join the feminist movement, is seen
by many black women as yet another expression of white female denial
of the reality of racist domination, of their complicity in the exploitation
and oppression of black women and black people."[40]

White Feminism and Power in Academic Libraries

Academic libraries and librarians are prone to white feminist inter-
pretations of social justice due to the hegemonic context in which they
operate. White, patriarchal authority remains the dominant influence
in academia and is replicated in ways that appear normal and benign.[41]
Diane Gusa outlines the stifling effect of whiteness in higher education
through her framework of White Institutional Presence, the means

---

38. Eduardo Bonilla-Silva, *Racism Without Racists: Color-Blind Racism and the
Persistence of Racial Inequality in America*, 4th ed. (Lanham, MD: Rowman & Lit-
tlefield, 2014), 2; Ortega, "Being Lovingly, Knowingly Ignorant," 66; Shields,
"Waking Up to Privilege," 29.

39. Rich, *On Lies, Secrets, and Silence*, 281.

40. bell hooks, *Teaching to Transgress: Education as the Practice of Freedom* (New
York: Routledge, 1994).

41. Blackmore, "The Other Within," 45-61; Isabel Espinal, "A New
Vocabulary for Inclusive Librarianship: Applying Whiteness Theory to Our
Profession," in *The Power of Language/El Poder de La Palabra: Selected Papers
from the Second REFORMA National Conference*, ed. Lillian Castillo-Speed
(Englewood, CO: Libraries Unlimited, 2001), 131–49; Galvan, "Soliciting Per-
formance, Hiding Bias"; Hathcock, "White Librarianship in Blackface;" Todd
Honma, "Trippin' Over the Color Line: The Invisibility of Race in Library
and Information Studies," *InterActions: UCLA Journal of Education and Information Studies* 1, no. 2 (2005): 1–26, http://escholarship.org/uc/item/4nj0w1mp;
Yeo and Jacobs, "Diversity Matters," 78-80.

through which white processes, epistemologies, and norms are maintained and reinforced in institutions.[42] Freeda Brook, Dave Ellenwood, and Althea Lazzaro apply Gusa's principles to academic libraries in particular, highlighting the ways unquestioned adherence to these norms alienates those who don't fit into the dominant paradigm and leads to further homogenization of the workforce.[43] Further complicating matters is the increasingly powerful influence of neoliberalism in our organizations,[44] driving an approach to social justice that "adopts a commodified diversity management more in line with capitalist market relations than emancipatory anti-racist struggles."[45] As in activist spaces, white feminism finds a foothold in these institutions, with their commitment to equity on one hand and misplaced fidelity to whiteness on the other. Below, I chart the means by which white feminism regulates access to power and influence, directs and limits decision making, and constrains meaningful change in academic libraries.

White feminist thinking is readily apparent in the LIS literature around gender equity and leadership, reflecting and affecting the ways power is understood within the field. Much of the research concerning the advancement of women speaks to a persistent gender divide without acknowledging or fully addressing the role race and other axes of oppression play.[46] By using the term "women" while in fact writing only of

---

42. Diane Lynn Gusa, "White Institutional Presence: The Impact of Whiteness on Campus Climate," *Harvard Educational Review* 80, no. 4 (2010): 464–90, doi:10.17763/haer.80.4.p5j483825u110002.

43. Brook et al., "In Pursuit of Antiracist Social Justice," 251-52.

44. Chris Bourg, "The Neoliberal Library: Resistance is Not Futile," *Feral Librarian* (blog), January 16, 2014, https://chrisbourg.wordpress.com/2014/01/16/the-neoliberal-library-resistance-is-not-futile/; Karen P. Nicholson, "The McDonaldization of Academic Libraries and the Values of Transformational Change," *College & Research Libraries* 76, no. 3 (2015): 328–38, doi:10.5860/crl.76.3.328.

45. Honma, "Trippin' Over the Color Line," 11.

46. Kathleen DeLong, "Career Advancement and Writing about Women Librarians: A Literature Review," *Evidence Based Library and Information Practice* 8, no. 1 (2013): 59–75, doi:10.18438/b8cs4m; Marta Mestrovic Deyrup, "Is the Revolution Over? Gender, Economic, and Professional Parity in Academic Library Leadership Positions," *College & Research Libraries* 65, no. 3

white women, this research erases the experiences of women of color and other librarians whose reality conflicts with the standard narrative.[47] White women's progress is deceptively framed as a triumph for all women, leading some authors to float the argument that parity has, in fact, been achieved.[48] Save a passing mention of people of color and other marginalized populations, these studies, explicitly or implicitly, present the inclusion of such groups as outside the scope of their inquiry.[49] Employing de-raced "women" as a frame of reference suggests that the increase in white women in leadership positions is actually evidence of libraries' successful commitment to diversity.[50] Christine Williams, who in 1992 coined the term "glass escalator" to describe the phenomenon of men holding a disproportionately high number of leadership roles in women-dominated professions, critiqued her own lack of intersectional understanding and analysis nearly twenty years later, suggesting the "glass escalator" concept be retired.[51] Further critical examination of this literature is necessary if we are to effectively "interrogate the silences through which White supremacy is (re)produced."[52]

(May 2004): 242–50, doi:10.5860/crl.65.3.242; Bertie Greer, Denise Stephens, and Vicki Coleman, "Cultural Diversity and Gender Role Spillover: A Working Perspective," *Journal of Library Administration* 33, no. 1/2 (2001): 125–40, doi:10.1300/J111v33n01_09; Neigel, "LIS Leadership and Leadership Education," 521–34, doi: 10.1080/01930826.2015.1076307; Betty J. Turock, "Women and Leadership," *Journal of Library Administration* 32, no. 3–4 (2001): 115–37, doi:10.1300/J111v32n03_08.

47. Carrillo Rowe, "Locating Feminism's Subject," 69-70; Shields, "Waking Up to Privilege," 29-39.

48. Blackmore, "The Other Within," 50; Deyrup, "Is the Revolution Over," 249.

49. Deborah R. Hollis, "Affirmative Action or Increased Competition," *Journal of Library Administration* 27, no. 1–2 (1999): 51, doi:10.1300/J111v27n01_05.

50. Suzanne Hildenbrand, "Library Feminism and Library Women's History: Activism and Scholarship, Equity and Culture," *Libraries & Culture* 35, no. 1 (Winter 2000): 56; Hollis, "Affirmative Action or Increased Competition," 71.

51. Christine L. Williams, "The Glass Escalator, Revisited Gender Inequality in Neoliberal Times," *Gender & Society* 27, no. 5 (2013): 609–29, doi:10.1177/0891243213490232.

52. Carrillo Rowe, "Locating Feminism's Subject," 66.

The inadequate and misleadingly sunny picture painted by the literature occludes the very real barriers women of color face as they endeavor
to move into leadership roles. Academic libraries and librarians expect
their leaders to exemplify (or at least conform to) the dominant culture,
asking leadership candidates to effectively and imperceptibly perform
whiteness.[53] These expectations demand significant emotional labor as
one struggles to assume a compliant but compelling academic persona
in order to earn credibility and authority within a community skeptical
of one's presence.[54] Debra Harley argues that African American women
are perceived as the "maids of academe," called to be "advocates for
black issues, translators of black culture, navigators of a patriarchal and
racial minefield, community liaison, and conduits for others' problems"
while perpetually remaining "under surveillance to make sure that they
do not pose a threat to the status quo."[55] As Jacqueline Jones Royster says
of her faculty experience, "I face what I call the power and function of
deep disbelief."[56] Diversity-related service and research responsibilities,
halfheartedly supported and disproportionately assigned to librarians
of color, contribute to the sense of being "overextended, underval-
ued, and underappreciated."[57] As institutions marginalize and devalue
said responsibilities, they perpetuate the perception that the individuals
engaged in this labor belong on the lower rungs of the hierarchal ladder.[58] As in white feminist activism, race work is second tier and must be

---

53. Hathcock, "White Librarianship in Blackface"; Vinopal, "The Quest for
Diversity."

54. Cooke, "Pushing Back from the Table," 39-49; Galvan, "Soliciting Performance, Hiding Bias."

55. Debra A. Harley, "Maids of Academe: African American Women Faculty at Predominately White Institutions," *Journal of African American Studies*
12, no. 1 (March 2008): 24, doi: 10.1007/s12111-007-9030-5.

56. Jacqueline Jones Royster, "When the First Voice You Hear Is Not Your
Own," *College Composition and Communication* 47, no. 1 (February 1996): 34,
doi:10.2307/358272.

57. Honma, "Trippin' Over the Color Line," 13-19; Mestre, "Librarians
Working with Diverse Populations," 486; Harley, "Maids of Academe," 19–36.

58. Sara Ahmed, "The Language of Diversity," *Ethnic and Racial Studies* 30,
no. 2 (2007): 235, doi:10.1080/01419870601143927.

undertaken in ways that minimize white discomfort. Assuming power, then, becomes a matter of overcoming the hindrance of underrated professional labor and attempting to replicate the dominant culture of an institution that prefers individuals of the dominant race and gender.[59]

Effective leadership continues to be defined in typically masculine terms, despite increasing gender parity and a significant body of research extolling the benefits of non-normative decision-making practices.[60] Historically, women were perceived as fundamentally deficient in terms of talent and skills, a shortfall to be overcome only through extraordinary individual effort.[61] To find success at higher organizational levels, women were expected to assume the management styles characteristic of white men, and white women could rely on their whiteness to earn them conditional access to such methods.[62] Sexist stereotyping and gendered expectations persist, with women required to conform to the amorphous ideal of the "right kind of female leader."[63] The traits of said female leader comprise a mixture of (white) male qualities such as assertiveness, confidence, and decisiveness tempered by (white) female characteristics such as kindness, empathy, and deference.[64] Each is grounded in either the denial or expression of emotion, both of which are not only gendered but racialized.[65] While white women in leadership are perceived negatively for assuming the white male qualities enumerated above, women of color adopting these characteristics are at risk

---

59. Blackmore, "The Other Within," 54; Brook et al., "In Pursuit of Antiracist Social Justice," 265.

60. Blackmore, "The Other Within," 47-50; Jill Blackmore, "A Feminist Critical Perspective on Educational Leadership," *International Journal of Leadership in Education* 16, no. 2 (2013): 139–54, doi:10.1080/13603124.2012.754057.

61. Turock, "Women and Leadership," 120.

62. Neigel, "LIS Leadership and Leadership Education," 521-34; Turock, "Women and Leadership," 121-22.

63. Jessica Olin and Michelle Millet, "Gendered Expectations for Leadership in Libraries," *In the Library with the Lead Pipe* (November 2015), http://www.inthelibrarywiththeleadpipe.org/2015/libleadgender/.

64. Ibid.

65. Blackmore, "A Feminist Critical Perspective," 149.

of being presumed angry, troublesome, or even dangerous.[66] This sets a nefarious trap, denying women of color access to positions of power and undermining their management practices as a result of being perceived as not just "bossy," but threatening. The repercussions of failing to fit into this narrow space and assimilate into a culture emphasizing conformity limit the possibilities for transformative decision making that could address root inequities. White women who successfully overcome negative perceptions of their leadership abilities, on the other hand, are rewarded for making decisions that reinforce the status quo and reify what is known, comfortable, and safe. When presented with challenging situations, these library leaders opt instead to "alter some portion of this system while leaving the larger structures of domination intact."[67] Furthermore, white women in positions of power enjoy the privilege of "being the one who decides which woman of color gets to be let in the club, being able to speak for women of color, being able to feel that she is the one responsible for their salvation, and having the choice to see women of color or not."[68] A white feminist culture in libraries is invested in organizational inertia and encourages women of color to become "complicit in the very structures of their oppression" in order to succeed.[69] It continually reproduces itself, not only by circumscribing the types of decisions made, but by limiting who is empowered to make those decisions in the first place.

Though white women continue to be hindered by gender inequity in academic libraries, whiteness still enables them to access and wield hegemonic privilege and power.[70] Such access, paired with the belief that professional success is the result of individual hard work and merit, lends itself to white feminist neoliberal thinking.[71] As Deborah Hollis noted

---

66. Lorde, *Sister Outsider*; hooks, *Teaching to Transgress*.

67. Henk, "Mandy Henk's Hikuwai Event."

68. Ortega, "Being Lovingly, Knowingly Ignorant," 68.

69. Henk, "Mandy Henk's Hikuwai Event."

70. Carrillo Rowe, "Locating Feminism's Subject," 68-72.

71. DeLong, "Career Advancement," 65.

nearly two decades ago, "the 'good old boys' are turning into the 'good old girls,'"[72] and this continued concentration of whiteness at the top solidifies an institutional structure predicated on marginalizing, assimilating, and/or silencing the "other." White feminist leaders, for whom a commitment to social justice is an integral component of their cultivated progressive identity, use their authority to reinforce a professional culture that avoids or elides explicit discussions of race and racism.[73] Demands for such discussions make white feminists feel their character (rather than their behavior) and their leadership capabilities (rather than their specific actions) are under attack.[74] This enables continued avoidance of both personal and institutional discomfort and thwarts opportunities to unlearn deeply rooted biases and enact transformational institutional change.[75] By prioritizing "their personal advancements within the patriarchal structure of the institution over their alliances with women of color . . . white feminists are merely reproducing, indeed reinforcing, exploitative systems."[76] The pernicious effect of white feminism allows academic library leaders to trumpet a commitment to diversity without backing up those values through substantive action.

Resisting White Feminism

White librarians, particularly those in positions of leadership, are obligated to use their power to challenge white feminism in academic

---

72. Hollis, "Affirmative Action or Increased Competition," 50.

73. Sara Ahmed, "Progressive Racism," *feministkilljoys* (blog), May 30, 2016, https://feministkilljoys.com/2016/05/30/progressive-racism/.

74. Kenneth Jones and Tema Okun, "White Supremacy Culture," in *Dismantling Racism: A Workbook for Social Change Groups* (ChangeWork, 2001), http://www.cwsworkshop.org/PARC_site_B/dr-culture.html; nina de jesus, "The Problem with Nice White Ladies(tm)," *Satifice* (blog), October 4, 2014, https://epicfails.xyz/posts/2014-10-03-the-problem-with-nice-white-ladi-estm.html.

75. Irene H. Yoon, "The Paradoxical Nature of Whiteness-at-Work in the Daily Life of Schools and Teacher Communities," *Race Ethnicity and Education* 15, no. 5 (November 2012): 587–613, doi:10.1080/13613324.2011.624506.

76. Carrillo Rowe, "Locating Feminism's Subject," 76.

libraries, rather than relying on librarians of color to promote anti-racist practices.[77] In order to identify and dismantle systems of oppression and assume a truly intersectional feminist approach to social justice, white women must "get a critical handle on the meaning of 'whiteness' in their lives"[78] and "examine [their] role as women in the perpetuation and maintenance of systems of domination."[79] Additionally, libraries must transition from programs focused on patching up problem areas to initiatives that unflinchingly deconstruct the inequitable foundations upon which our work is built. In short, we must transform our culture, not simply our demographics, if we wish to become truly inclusive organizations.

In seeking salient alternatives we can turn to the movement created to resist and reject white feminism's hegemony: black feminism. While I cannot do justice to the full complexity of black feminist theory here, I will briefly outline a few key concepts as they appear in the work of two prominent black scholars and activists: Patricia Hill Collins and Barbara Smith. An essential belief they share is the inextricable connectedness of individual experiences and institutional systems. In her formative work, *Black Feminist Thought: Knowledge, Consciousness, and the Politics of Empowerment*, Collins outlines two approaches to power. The first details the "relationship linking oppression and activism, where groups with greater power oppress those with lesser amounts."[80] The second "views [power] not as something that groups possess, but as an intangible entity that circulates within a particular matrix of domination and to which individuals stand in varying relationships."[81] The collective

---

77. Chris Bourg, "The Unbearable Whiteness of Librarianship," *Feral Librarian* (blog), March 4, 2014, https://chrisbourg.wordpress.com/2014/03/03/the-unbearable-whiteness-of-librarianship/; Morales et al., "Diversity, Social Justice, and the Future of Libraries," 439–51; Vinopal, "The Quest for Diversity."

78. hooks, *Teaching to Transgress*, 104.

79. bell hooks, *Talking Back: Thinking Feminist, Thinking Black* (New York: Routledge, 1989), 20.

80. Collins, *Black Feminist Thought*, 274.

81. Ibid.

approach enables the formation of "group-based standpoints that . . . can foster the type of group solidarity necessary for resisting oppressions," while the individual approach "emphasize[s] how domination and resistance shape and are shaped by individual agency." These two seemingly distinct perspectives, she argues, are not "competing" but "complementary," and in fact "neither is sufficient without the other."[82]

Accordingly, Smith's feminism "challenges us all to forge effective alliances for social justice across difference because our futures are bound up in each other."[83] Throughout her writings she argues that black feminist theory and activism must address "key political principles" in concert with "individual behavior," paying "close attention to the particularity of lived experiences" in order to "deepen movement building."[84] While coalition development and collective action form the foundation from which to pursue meaningful institutional change, a black feminist ethic sees personal and institutional work as overlapping and intricately entangled, each sustaining and supporting the other. Smith cautions, however, that in order for those who "derive power from conforming to the status quo" (i.e. white women) to authentically engage in anti-racist activism, they must identify and excise the "dominant cultural messages of superiority" they have internalized.[85] The critical work of white women to come to terms with the advantages institutional racism and white supremacy bring to their lives is distinctly different from the individual work women of color must do to find empowerment through the lens of their lived experience. Personal confessions of privilege as a means of assuaging white guilt merely reproduce the individualistic fallacies of neoliberal white feminism.[86] Similarly, white women who approach social justice work through an institutional perspective alone

---

82. Ibid., 275.

83. Jones and Eubanks, *Ain't Gonna Let Nobody*, 6.

84. Ibid., 3-4.

85. Ibid., 6.

86. Ahmed, "Progressive Racism;" Andrea Smith, "The Problem with 'Privilege,'" *Andrea Smith's Blog*, August 14, 2013, https://andrea366.wordpress.com/2013/08/14/the-problem-with-privilege-by-andrea-smith/.

often fail to confront their individual culpability in, and responsibility for, the racist systems from which they benefit. White people in both scenarios, fancying themselves allies, undermine the connections across difference that could result in a radical reimagining of social systems, the invention of more equitable institutions, and the opportunity to "creat[e] that which we cannot now know."[87] "Revolution begins with the self, in the self," Toni Cade Bambara states, but as Collins reminds us, "while individual empowerment is key, only collective action can effectively generate the lasting institutional transformation required for social justice."[88] In the space remaining, I will explore the interconnected personal and institutional strategies academic libraries and librarians may draw on to resist white feminist praxis and envision new ways of being and leading.

To begin addressing the structural racism embedded in their spaces, academic libraries must first name the problem and its underlying causes.[89] Ruth Frankenberg defines whiteness as "a set of cultural practices that are usually unmarked and unnamed," and Irene Yoon notes that "whiteness-at-work can be difficult to pinpoint because it is often a normative, unspoken assumption of how things are."[90] Thus, labeling whiteness within our spaces is essential to resisting its oppressive effects.[91] Framing the issue only in vague, neutralized, and de-raced language, such as *diversity*, *inclusion*, *pluralism*, etc., impedes our ability to take meaningful steps toward institutional change, painting the solution as a matter of acquiring positives (e.g., improving workforce diversity by hiring people of color) without addressing existing flaws. This mirrors

---

87. Smith, "The Problem with 'Privilege.'"

88. Toni Cade Bambara, "On the Issue of Roles," in *The Black Woman: An Anthology*, ed. Toni Cade Bambara (New York: Washington Square Press, 1970), 133; Collins, *Black Feminist Thought*, 290.

89. Vinopal, "The Quest for Diversity."

90. Ruth Frankenberg, *White Women, Race Matters: The Social Construction of Whiteness* (Minneapolis, MN: University of Minnesota Press, 1993), 1; Yoon, "The Paradoxical Nature of Whiteness at Work," 607.

91. Espinal, "A New Vocabulary," 131-49; Honma, "Trippin' Over the Color Line," 1-26.

a pattern within LIS leadership literature identifying the problem as a lack of people of color in leadership roles, "perpetuat[ing] the myth that the issue lies in the racialized or gendered embodiment of individuals or a particular social group, rather than in the structures, cultures and mythologies constituting dominant institutional and populist notions of leadership."[92] Diversity work within formal institutions is, by definition, inextricably entrenched within the hierarchical structures of privilege and oppression upon which those organizations are built.[93] Explicitly naming these structures and articulating at the institutional level an unequivocal stance that racism is real, present, and actively operating within our spaces is crucial if we hope to dismantle them.

Labeling underlying issues is a necessary step toward uprooting white feminism's effect on our recruitment and retention practices, both in terms of how they are normalized institutionally and enacted interpersonally. As Choo and Ferree note, organizations often find it "easier to include multiply-marginalized groups than to analyze the relationships that affect them intersectionally," contributing to the continual reproduction of hostile work cultures that keep or push marginalized individuals out.[94] Critically deconstructing hiring processes in order to identify expectations grounded in whiteness and develop new, holistic means of evaluating candidates enables libraries and librarians to avoid perpetuating narrow notions of "fit."[95] Retaining staff and clearing paths toward leadership opportunities requires thoughtful analyses of the institutional and interpersonal processes that erect opaque barriers and continue to alienate librarians of color. Academic libraries (and the white women who manage them) must consider how power remains

---

92. Blackmore, "The Other Within," 50.

93. Ahmed, "The Language of Diversity," 247-48.

94. Hae Yeon Choo and Myra Marx Ferree, "Practicing Intersectionality in Sociological Research: A Critical Analysis of Inclusions, Interactions, and Institutions in the Study of Inequalities," *Sociological Theory* 28, no. 2 (2010): 145, doi:10.1111/j.1467-9558.2010.01370.x.

95. Galvan, "Soliciting Performance, Hiding Bias;" Hathcock, "White Librarianship in Blackface."

concentrated with members of the dominant group and reenvision the means by which professional capital is earned. Service and research expectations in particular must be rethought to value diversity-focused work equally while also committing to distribute this labor amongst all librarians equitably. As in other communities committed to social justice, inclusion is not enough; internal and institutional transformation is necessary in order to prevent marginalized members from "disappearing through a trap door" before advancing beyond the entry level.[96] It is therefore "crucial to engage in and create space for dialog to challenge our consciousness and dominant ideas within the community – however difficult or uncomfortable this may be."[97]

Embracing discomfort and challenging norms that emphasize complacency and conformity is key to effectively curbing white feminist habits and practices.[98] A "cultural climate of avoidance" leads workers and leaders to fear difficult conversations and the organizational cracks that may be exposed as a result.[99] Anti-racist practice requires honest exploration of race and racism in our institutions.[100] Thoughtful professional development and training programs can provide a mediated space for such conversations and one potential site of meaningful change,[101] so long as their purpose is not simply to "minimize dysfunctional conflicts."[102] Such training must reach beyond promoting awareness to transforming

---

96. Williams, "The Glass Escalator, Revisited," 622.

97. Yeo and Jacobs, "Diversity Matters," 7.

98. Robin DiAngelo, "White Fragility," International Journal of Critical Pedagogy 3, no. 3 (2011): 54–70, https://libjournal.uncg.edu/index.php/ijcp/article/view/249; Yoon, "The Paradoxical Nature of Whiteness-at-Work," 587-613.

99. Carrillo Rowe, "Locating Feminism's Subject," 66.

100. Brook et al., "In Pursuit of Antiracist Social Justice," 248; hooks, Teaching to Transgress, 102.

101. Althea Eannace Lazzaro et al., "Cultural Competency on Campus: Applying ACRL's Diversity Standards," College & Research Libraries News 75, no. 6 (2014): 332–35, http://crln.acrl.org/content/75/6/332.short.

102. Greer et al., "Cultural Diversity," 136.

systems, as the former is insufficient to render genuine social justice.[103] In so doing, the focus can shift from race to whiteness and the ways the latter is sustained and reproduced in predominantly white settings. White women in particular must step outside the expectations and conventions of whiteness in order to "move beyond the most superficial aspects of social change" and "examine, undefensively, how Whiteness both privileges and contains them"[104] Centering whiteness as the source of institutional and interpersonal oppression may result in feelings of shame and stigma; indeed, as Rich noted, white women in academia often find it easier to tackle racism as an intellectual concept rather than to engage fully and emotionally with the lived experiences of women of color.[105] Pushing past this guilt is necessary to overcome "color-blind" ideologies and undo the racist thinking that hinders organizational diversity.[106] The work started in training projects can continue and expand through mentorship programs. While often recommended as an important retention measure for librarians of color,[107] mentoring should also be explored as a means of guiding white librarians to critically examine how whiteness shapes their behavior and their institutions, resist latent white feminist praxis, and imagine more equitable spaces.

Current library leaders must further engage in a "pedagogy of discomfort" if they are to divest of "conventional paradigms of domination."[108]

---

103. Blackmore, "A Feminist Critical Perspective," 147.

104. Lorde, Sister Outsider, 122; Carrillo Rowe, "Locating Feminism's Subject," 77.

105. Rich, *On Lies, Secrets, and Silence*, 281.

106. While "color-blind" racism, defined and developed by Eduardo Bonilla-Silva, is employed throughout the sociological literature, it can be and is interpreted as ableist. By using the term here, I seek to connect this thread to existing conversations in anti-racist activist and scholarly circles, rather than reproduce ableist discourse.

107. Melody Royster et al., "Mentoring and Retention of Minority Librarians," in *Where Are All the Librarians of Color? The Experiences of People of Color in Academia*, ed. Rebecca Hankins and Miguel Juárez (Sacramento, Calif.: Library Juice Press, 2015), 55–69.

108. Blackmore, "A Feminist Critical Perspective," 147; hooks, *Teaching to Transgress*, 105.

White feminists in leadership positions often seek to smooth over conflict and regulate emotional expression within the bounds of normative
whiteness.[109] In order to break up the homogeneous control of institutional power, it's necessary to embrace and even encourage interpersonal
conflicts that may arise during honest discussions of difference. Leaders
applying an anti-racist feminist framework acknowledge the privileging
structures that underpin their access to power and push beyond "symbolic and superficial soft multiculturalism" toward more "deliberative
democratic processes."[110] Fearless analyses of the marginalizing consequences of institutional privilege and oppression are an important
first step in building stronger coalitions dedicated to change. "Solidarity is not the same as support," however, and the former requires a
"sustained, ongoing commitment" to reimagining radically equitable
organizational structures.[111] To effectively transcend white feminism,
then, is to proactively relinquish power that's been unjustly disbursed,
an act that, though focused on institutional change, demands individual
sacrifice. Leaders need to question and dismantle hierarchical systems
that situate power and influence in the hands of a select few, those who,
more often than not, happen to look, sound, and act like them. White
women who are or hope to become library leaders must also be critical of a neoliberal, individualistic, white feminist thinking that paints
achievement as the result of merit rather than entrenched institutional
advantage. Rejecting these fictions and embracing opportunities for
collective decision making and coalition building lays the groundwork
for deeper understanding, stronger interpersonal alliances, and more
radically inclusive organizations.

---

109. Blackmore, "A Feminist Critical Perspective," 139-54.

110. Blackmore, "The Other Within," 58.

111. hooks, Feminist Theory, 67.

Conclusion

White feminist thought and practice in libraries amplifies pernicious inequities and continues the process of institutional exclusion by discounting race as a primary site of women's persecution and insisting that white women's experiences are universal. Recognizing "loving, knowing ignorance" and moving from awareness to action requires that white leaders "display the political will to shift organizational cultures, although this may mean feeling uncomfortable, and adopting bold and unpopular positions, while relinquishing their individual advantage."[112] Critically examining individual and institutional practices and building transformative coalitions with librarians of color empowers us to implement alternative ways of leading and distributing power. As Audre Lorde reminds us, "change means growth, and growth can be painful,"[113] but if we wish to transcend the limitations of a white feminist framework, we must recognize that our practices are not neutral and our good intentions are not good enough.

Bibliography

Ahmed, Sara. "The Language of Diversity." *Ethnic and Racial Studies* 30, no. 2 (2007): 235–56. doi:10.1080/01419870601143927.

———. "Progressive Racism." *feministkilljoys* (blog), May 30, 2016. https://feministkilljoys.com/2016/05/30/progressive-racism/.

Alabi, Jaena. "Racial Microaggressions in Academic Libraries: Results of a Survey of Minority and Non-Minority Librarians." *The Journal of Academic Librarianship* 41, no. 1 (2015): 47–53. doi:10.1016/j.acalib.2014.10.008.

---

112. Blackmore, "The Other Within," 58.
113. Lorde, *Sister Outsider*, 123.

Association of College and Research Libraries. "Diversity Standards: Cultural Competency for Academic Libraries (2012)." Accessed April 16, 2016. http://www.ala.org/acrl/standards/diversity.

Association of Research Libraries. "Initiative to Recruit a Diverse Workforce (IRDW)." Accessed April 16, 2016. http://www.arl.org/leadership-recruitment/diversity-recruitment/initiative-to-recruit-a-diverse-workforce-irdw#.VxJuQD-i-qB.

Blackmore, Jill. "A Feminist Critical Perspective on Educational Leadership." *International Journal of Leadership in Education* 16, no. 2 (2013): 139–54. doi:10.1080/13603124.2012.754057.

———. "'The Other Within': Race/Gender Disruptions to the Professional Learning of White Educational Leaders." *International Journal of Leadership in Education* 13, no. 1 (2010): 45–61. doi:10.1080/13603120903242931.

Bonilla-Silva, Eduardo. *Racism Without Racists: Color-Blind Racism and the Persistence of Racial Inequality in America*. 4th ed. Lanham, MD: Rowman & Littlefield, 2014.

Bourg, Chris. "The Neoliberal Library: Resistance is Not Futile." *Feral Librarian* (blog), January 16, 2014. https://chrisbourg.wordpress.com/2014/01/16/the-neoliberal-library-resistance-is-not-futile/.

———. "The Unbearable Whiteness of Librarianship." *Feral Librarian* (blog), March 4, 2014. https://chrisbourg.wordpress.com/2014/03/03/the-unbearable-whiteness-of-librarianship/.

Brook, Freeda, Dave Ellenwood, and Althea Eannace Lazzaro. "In Pursuit of Antiracist Social Justice: Denaturalizing Whiteness in the Academic Library." *Library Trends* 64, no. 2 (2015): 246–84. doi:10.1353/lib.2015.0048.

Cade Bambara, Toni. "On the Issue of Roles." In *The Black Woman: An Anthology*, edited by Toni Cade Bambara, 123–35. New York: Washington Square Press, 1970.

Carrillo Rowe, Aimee M. "Locating Feminism's Subject: The Paradox of White Femininity and the Struggle to Forge Feminist Alliances." *Communication Theory* 10, no. 1 (2000): 64–80. doi:10.1111/j.1468-2885.2000.tb00179.x.

Choo, Hae Yeon, and Myra Marx Ferree. "Practicing Intersectionality in Sociological Research: A Critical Analysis of Inclusions, Interactions, and Institutions in the Study of Inequalities." *Sociological Theory* 28, no. 2 (2010): 129–49. doi:10.1111/j.1467-9558.2010.01370.x.

Collins, Patricia Hill. *Black Feminist Thought: Knowledge, Consciousness, and the Politics of Empowerment.* 2nd ed. New York: Routledge, 2000.

Combahee River Collective. "The Combahee River Collective Statement." In *Home Girls: A Black Feminist Anthology*, edited by Barbara Smith, 272–82. New York: Kitchen Table: Women of Color Press, 1983.

Cooke, Nicole A. "Pushing Back from the Table: Fighting to Maintain My Voice as a Pre-Tenure Minority Female in the White Academy." *Polymath: An Interdisciplinary Arts and Sciences Journal* 4, no. 2 (2014): 39–49. https://ojcs.siue.edu/ojs/index.php/polymath/article/view/2934/1000.

Cooke, Nicole A., Miriam E. Sweeney, and Safiya Umoja Noble. "Social Justice as Topic and Tool: An Attempt to Transform an LIS Curriculum and Culture." *The Library Quarterly* 86, no. 1 (2016): 107–24. doi:10.1086/684147.

Crenshaw, Kimberlé. "Demarginalizing the Intersection of Race and Sex: A Black Feminist Critique of Antidiscrimination Doctrine, Feminist Theory and Antiracist Politics." *University of Chicago Legal Forum*, 1989, 139–67. http://chicagounbound.uchicago.edu/uclf/vol1989/iss1/8.

———. "Mapping the Margins: Intersectionality, Identity Politics, and Violence against Women of Color." *Stanford Law Review* 43, no. 6 (1991): 1241-99. doi:10.2307/1229039.

Curry, Deborah A. "Your Worries Ain't Like Mine: African American Librarians and the Pervasiveness of Racism, Prejudice and Discrimination in Academe." In *Racial and Ethnic Diversity in Academic Libraries: Multicultural Issues*, edited by Deborah A. Curry, Susan Griswold Blandy, and Lynne M. Martin, 299–311. Binghamton, NY: The Haworth Press, 1994.

Daniels, Jessie. "Trouble with White Feminism: Racial Origins of U.S. Feminism." *Racism Review*, February 18, 2014. http://www. racismreview.com/blog/2014/02/18/trouble-with-white-feminism/.

DeLong, Kathleen. "Career Advancement and Writing about Women Librarians: A Literature Review." *Evidence Based Library and Information Practice* 8, no. 1 (2013): 59–75. doi:10.18438/b8cs4m.

Deyrup, Marta Mestrovic. "Is the Revolution Over? Gender, Economic, and Professional Parity in Academic Library Leadership Positions." *College & Research Libraries* 65, no. 3 (May 2004): 242–50. doi:10.5860/crl.65.3.242.

DiAngelo, Robin. "White Fragility." *International Journal of Critical Pedagogy* 3, no. 3 (2011): 54–70. https://libjournal.uncg.edu/index.php/ijcp/article/view/249.

Espinal, Isabel. "A New Vocabulary for Inclusive Librarianship: Applying Whiteness Theory to Our Profession." In *The Power of Language/El Poder de La Palabra: Selected Papers from the Second REFORMA National Conference*, edited by Lillian Castillo-Speed, 131–49. Englewood, CO: Libraries Unlimited, 2001.

Frankenberg, Ruth. *White Women, Race Matters: The Social Construction of Whiteness*. Minneapolis, MN: University of Minnesota Press, 1993.

Friedan, Betty. *The Feminine Mystique*. New York: Norton, 1963.

Galvan, Angela. "Soliciting Performance, Hiding Bias: Whiteness and Librarianship." *In the Library with the Lead Pipe* (June 2015). http://www.inthelibrarywiththeleadpipe.org/2015/soliciting-performance-hiding-bias-whiteness-and-librarianship/.

Greer, Bertie, Denise Stephens, and Vicki Coleman. "Cultural Diversity and Gender Role Spillover: A Working Perspective." *Journal of Library Administration* 33, no. 1/2 (2001): 125–40. doi:10.1300/J111v33n01_09.

Gusa, Diane Lynn. "White Institutional Presence: The Impact of Whiteness on Campus Climate." *Harvard Educational Review* 80, no. 4 (2010): 464–90. doi:10.17763/haer.80.4.p5j483825u110002.

Harley, Debra A. "Maids of Academe: African American Women Faculty at Predominately White Institutions." *Journal of African American Studies* 12, no. 1 (March 2008): 19–36. doi:10.1007/s12111-007-9030-5.

Hathcock, April. "White Librarianship in Blackface: Diversity Initiatives in LIS." *In the Library with the Lead Pipe* (October 2015). http://www.inthelibrarywiththeleadpipe.org/2015/lis-diversity/.

Henk, Mandy. "Mandy Henk's Hikuwai Event: What Is Critical Librarianship?" *Library Juice* (blog), April 21, 2016. http://libraryjuicepress.com/blog/?p=5252.

Hildenbrand, Suzanne. "Library Feminism and Library Women's History: Activism and Scholarship, Equity and Culture." *Libraries & Culture* 35, no. 1 (Winter 2000): 51–65.

Hollis, Deborah R. "Affirmative Action or Increased Competition." *Journal of Library Administration* 27, no. 1–2 (1999): 49–75. doi:10.1300/J111v27n01_05.

Honma, Todd. "Trippin' Over the Color Line: The Invisibility of Race in Library and Information Studies." *InterActions: UCLA Journal of Education and Information Studies* 1, no. 2 (2005): 1–26. http://escholarship.org/uc/item/4nj0w1mp.

hooks, bell. *Ain't I a Woman: Black Women and Feminism.* New York: Routledge, 2015.

———. "Dig Deep: Beyond Lean In." *The Feminist Wire*, October 28, 2013. http://www.thefeministwire.com/2013/10/17973/.

―――. *Feminist Theory: From Margin to Center.* New York: Routledge, 2015.

―――. *Talking Back: Thinking Feminist, Thinking Black.* New York: Routledge, 2014.

―――. *Teaching to Transgress: Education as the Practice of Freedom.* New York: Routledge, 1994.

Hull, Gloria T., Patricia Bell Scott, and Barbara Smith, eds. *All the Women Are White, All the Blacks Are Men, But Some of Us Are Brave: Black Women's Studies.* New York: The Feminist Press at the City University of New York, 1982.

de jesus, nina. "The Problem with Nice White Ladies(tm)." *Satifice* (blog), October 4, 2014. https://epicfails.xyz/posts/2014-10-03-the-problem-with-nice-white-ladiestm.html.

Jones, Alethia, and Virginia Eubanks, eds. *Ain't Gonna Let Nobody Turn Me Around: Forty Years of Movement Building with Barbara Smith.* Albany, NY: SUNY Press, 2014.

Jones, Kenneth, and Tema Okun. "White Supremacy Culture." In *Dismantling Racism: A Workbook for Social Change Groups.* ChangeWork, 2001. http://www.cwsworkshop.org/PARC_site_B/dr-culture.html.

Lazzaro, Althea Eannace, Shardé Mills, Tami Garrard, Emily Ferguson, Megan Watson, and Dave Ellenwood. "Cultural Competency on Campus: Applying ACRL's Diversity Standards." *College & Research Libraries News* 75, no. 6 (2014): 332–35. http://crln.acrl.org/content/75/6/332.short.

Lorde, Audre. *Sister Outsider: Essays and Speeches.* Rev. ed. Berkeley, CA: Crossing Press, 2007.

Lotz, Amanda D. "Communicating Third-Wave Feminism and New Social Movements: Challenges for the Next Century of Feminist Endeavor." *Women & Language* 26, no. 1 (Spring 2003): 2-9.

Lugones, Maria. *Pilgrimages/Peregrinajes: Theorizing Coalition against Multiple Oppressions*. Lanham, MD: Rowman & Littlefield, 2003.

Maxey-Harris, Charlene. *Diversity Plans and Programs*. SPEC Kit 319. Washington, DC: Association of Research Libraries, 2010.

Mestre, Lori S. "Librarians Working with Diverse Populations: What Impact Does Cultural Competency Training Have on Their Efforts?" *The Journal of Academic Librarianship* 36, no. 6 (2010): 479–88. doi:10.1016/j.acalib.2010.08.003.

Moraga, Cherríe, and Gloria Anzaldúa, eds. *This Bridge Called My Back: Writings by Radical Women of Color*. New York: Kitchen Table: Women of Color Press, 1983.

Morales, Myrna, Em Claire Knowles, and Chris Bourg. "Diversity, Social Justice, and the Future of Libraries." *portal: Libraries and the Academy* 14, no. 3 (2014): 439–51. doi:10.1353/pla.2014.0017.

Neigel, Christina. "LIS Leadership and Leadership Education: A Matter of Gender." *Journal of Library Administration* 55, no. 7 (2015): 521–34. doi:10.1080/01930826.2015.1076307.

Nicholson, Karen P. "The McDonaldization of Academic Libraries and the Values of Transformational Change." *College & Research Libraries* 76, no. 3 (2015): 328–38. doi:10.5860/crl.76.3.328.

Olin, Jessica, and Michelle Millet. "Gendered Expectations for Leadership in Libraries." *In the Library with the Lead Pipe* (November 2015). http://www.inthelibrarywiththeleadpipe.org/2015/libleadgender/.

Ortega, Mariana. "Being Lovingly, Knowingly Ignorant: White Feminism and Women of Color." *Hypatia* 21, no. 3 (2006): 56–74. doi:10.1353/hyp.2006.0034.

Rich, Adrienne. *On Lies, Secrets, and Silence: Selected Prose 1966-1978*. New York: W. W. Norton & Co., 1979.

Rottenberg, Catherine. "The Rise of Neoliberal Feminism." *Cultural Studies* 28, no. 3 (2014): 418–37. doi:10.1080/09502386.2013.857361.

Royster, Jacqueline Jones. "When the First Voice You Hear Is Not Your Own." *College Composition and Communication* 47, no. 1 (1996): 29–40. doi:10.2307/358272.

Royster, Melody, David Schwieder, Ava Iuliano Brillat, and Lori Driver. "Mentoring and Retention of Minority Librarians." In *Where Are All the Librarians of Color? The Experiences of People of Color in Academia*, edited by Rebecca Hankins and Miguel Juárez, 55–69. Sacramento, CA: Library Juice Press, 2015.

Sandberg, Sheryl. *Lean In: Women, Work, and the Will to Lead.* New York: Alfred A Knopf, 2013.

Schlesselman-Tarango, Gina. "The Legacy of Lady Bountiful: White Women in the Library." *Library Trends* 64, no. 4 (Spring 2016): 667–86. doi:10.1353/lib.2016.0015.

Shields, Stephanie A. "Waking Up to Privilege: Intersectionality and Opportunity." In *Presumed Incompetent: The Intersections of Race and Class for Women in Academia*, edited by Gabriella Gutiérrez y Muhs, Yolanda Flores Niemann, and Carmen G. Gonzalez, 29–39. Logan, UT: Utah State University Press, 2012.

Smith, Andrea. "The Problem with 'Privilege.'" *Andrea Smith's Blog*, August 14, 2013. https://andrea366.wordpress.com/2013/08/14/the-problem-with-privilege-by-andrea-smith/.

Smith, Barbara, ed. *Home Girls: A Black Feminist Anthology.* New York: Kitchen Table: Women of Color Press, 1983.

Spelman, Elizabeth V. *Inessential Woman: Problems of Exclusion in Feminist Thought.* Boston, MA: Beacon Press, 1988.

Swanson, Juleah, Ione Damasco, Isabel Gonzalez-Smith, Dracine Hodges, Azusa Tanaka, and Todd Honma. "Why Diversity Matters: A Roundtable Discussion on Racial and Ethnic Diversity in Librarianship." *In the Library with the Lead Pipe* (July 2015). http://www.inthelibrarywiththeleadpipe.org/2015/why-diversity-matters-a-roundtable-discussion-on-racial-and-ethnic-diversity-in-librarianship/.

Thornton, Joyce K. "African American Female Librarians: A Study of Job Satisfaction." *Journal of Library Administration* 33, no. 1–2 (2001): 141–64. doi:10.1300/J111v33n01_10.

Turock, Betty J. "Women and Leadership." *Journal of Library Administration* 32, no. 3–4 (2001): 115–37. doi:10.1300/J111v32n03_08.

Vinopal, Jennifer. "The Quest for Diversity in Library Staffing: From Awareness to Action." *In the Library with the Lead Pipe* (January 2016). http://www.inthelibrarywiththeleadpipe.org/2016/quest-for-diversity/.

Walker, Rebecca. "Becoming the Third Wave." *Ms.*, February 1992.

Williams, Christine L. "The Glass Escalator, Revisited Gender Inequality in Neoliberal Times." *Gender & Society* 27, no. 5 (2013): 609–29. doi:10.1177/0891243213490232.

Yeo, Shinjoung, and James R. Jacobs. "Diversity Matters? Rethinking Diversity in Libraries." *Counterpoise* 10, no. 1/2 (Winter 2006): 78–80. http://freegovinfo.info/files/diversity_counterpoise.pdf.

Yoon, Irene H. "The Paradoxical Nature of Whiteness-at-Work in the Daily Life of Schools and Teacher Communities." *Race Ethnicity and Education* 15, no. 5 (November 2012): 587–613. doi:10.1080/13613324.2011.624506.

Young, Cate. "This Is What I Mean When I Say 'White Feminism.'" *BattyMamzelle* (blog), January 10, 2014. http://battymamzelle.blogspot.com/2014/01/This-Is-What-I-Mean-When-I-Say-White-Feminism.html.

Chapter 8

WHO KILLED THE WORLD? WHITE MASCULINITY AND THE TECHNOCRATIC LIBRARY OF THE FUTURE

Rafia Mirza and Maura Seale

> There's the People Eater himself. Coming to count the cost.
> —*Capable, Mad Max: Fury Road*

The representation of libraries and librarians has historically been contested terrain. In the early twentieth century, librarians were understood to be performing the work "of a parent or teacher."[1] Like missionaries or Lady Bountiful,[2] librarians participated in "civilizing" and assimilating the tired, huddled masses into American democracy (as long as they could potentially become white). However, as we have argued previously,[3] as information technology became more central to librarianship in the

---

1. Mary Niles Maack, "Gender, Culture, and the Transformation of American Librarianship, 1890-1920," *Libraries & Culture* 33, no. 1 (1998): 53.

2. Gina Schlesselman-Tarango, "The Legacy of Lady Bountiful: White Women in the Library," *Library Trends* 64, no. 4 (2016): 667-86, doi: 10.1353/lib.2016.0015.

3. Maura Seale and Rafia Mirza, "Watchers, Punks, and Dashing Heroes: Representations of Male Librarians in Generation-X Mass Culture," in *Generation X Perspectives on Librarianship*, eds. Martin K. Wallace, Erik Sean Estep, and Rebecca Tolley-Stokes (Jefferson, NC: McFarland, 2010), 135-46.

1990s and 2000s, it incited a continuing existential crisis within the field, and librarians were increasingly represented as white men in mass culture. In the age of what Evgeny Morozov calls internet-centrism,[4] the figure of the white female librarian, simultaneously "civilizing" and serving patrons, has been replaced by the prophets of Silicon Valley, whose technological solutions will free us all to pursue life, liberty, and happiness.

The focus on technology as the solution to complex social problems (which Morozov refers to as *solutionism*) is central to technocratic ideology. Technocratic ideology is also characterized by its stance of impartial, apolitical rationality; technocrats are interested in efficiency, not politics, and believe technological fixes can be applied universally.[5] The ability to claim a position outside of politics, to claim rationality, has historically been the domain of white men. White masculinity is an unmarked identity and so can function as the universal norm.[6] Technocratic ideology, then, with its reliance on rationality and universality, and rejection of politics, is inextricably bound up in white supremacy and patriarchy.

As David Theo Goldberg has argued in *Racist Culture*,[7] notions of objectivity, rationality, and Enlightenment are at their foundation racialized, and since the eighteenth century have been consistently associated with and solely attributed to white, Western men.[8]

Technocratic ideology is inescapably bound up with white masculinity; it can only claim a position of neutrality and objectivity because

---

4. Evgeny Morozov, *To Save Everything, Click Here* (New York: Public Affairs, 2013).

5. Morozov, *To Save Everything, Click Here*.

6. When we say "white masculinity," we are referring to the social formation, not individual white men. White masculinity, as a social formation of dominance, recruits other forms of dominance and unmarkedness as well - Westernness, heterosexuality, cis-genderedness, and middle-classness.

7. David Theo Goldberg, *Racist Culture: Philosophy and the Politics of Meaning* (Cambridge: Blackwell, 1993).

8. nina de jesus, "Locating the Library in Institutional Oppression," *In the Library with the Lead Pipe* (September, 2014), http://www.inthelibrarywiththe-leadpipe.org/2014/locating-the-library-in-institutional-oppression/.

whiteness functions, as Richard Dyer notes, as the "human norm,"[9] and masculinity is similarly unmarked.[10] Dyer goes on to argue: "There is no more powerful position than that of being 'just' human. The claim to power is the claim to speak for the commonality of humanity."[11] Speaking from the position of unmarked, purportedly apolitical white masculinity, the unacknowledged ground of technocratic ideology, acts to uphold white supremacy and patriarchy.

Technocratic ideology and solutionism pervades discussions and representations of the future of libraries and librarians. Librarianship itself is and has historically been invested in whiteness[12] and notions of neutrality, objectivity, and rationality,[13] which is perhaps why tech-

---

9. Richard Dyer, *White* (London: Routledge, 1997), 1.

10. Todd W. Reeser, *Masculinities in Theory: An Introduction* (Chichester, England: Wiley-Blackwell, 2010).

11. Dyer, *White*, 2.

12. Angela Galvan, "Soliciting Performance, Hiding Bias: Whiteness and Librarianship," *In the Library with the Lead Pipe* (June 2015), http://www.inthelibrarywiththeleadpipe.org/2015/soliciting-performance-hiding-bias-whiteness-and-librarianship/; Jennifer Vinopal, "The Quest for Diversity in Library Staffing: From Awareness to Action," *In the Library with the Lead Pipe* (January 2016), http://www.inthelibrarywiththeleadpipe.org/2016/quest-for-diversity/; April Hathcock, "White Librarianship in Blackface: Diversity Initiatives in LIS," *In the Library with the Lead Pipe* (October 2015), http://www.inthelibrarywiththeleadpipe.org/2015/lis-diversity/; Freeda Brook, Dave Ellenwood, and Althea Eannace Lazzaro, "In Pursuit of Antiracist Social Justice: Denaturalizing Whiteness in the Academic Library," *Library Trends* 64, no. 2 (2015), 246-284, doi: 10.1353/lib.2015.0048; Todd Honma, "Trippin' Over the Color Line: The Invisibility of Race in Library and Information Studies," *InterActions: UCLA Journal of Education and Information Studies*, 1, no. 2 (2005), 1-26, http://escholarship.org/uc/item/4nj0w1mp; Gina Schlesselman-Tarango, "Critical Whiteness Studies for Academic Librarianship: Problems and Possibilities" (presentation, Canadian Association of Professional Librarians [CAPAL], Ottawa, May 31, 2015), http://scholarworks.lib.csusb.edu/library-publications/27.

13. Chris Bourg, "Never Neutral: Libraries, Technology, and Inclusion," *Feral Librarian* (blog), January 29, 2015, https://chrisbourg.wordpress.com/2015/01/28/never-neutral-libraries-technology-and-inclusions; de jesus, "Locating the Library in Institutional Oppression"; Barbara Fister, "Admitting Our Agendas," *Library Babel Fish* (blog), August 29, 2013, https://www.insidehighered.com/blogs/library-babel-fish/admitting-our-agendas; Nicole Pagowsky and Niamh Wallace, "Black Lives Matter! Shedding Library Neutrality Rhetoric for Social Justice," *College & Research Libraries News* 76, no. 4 (2015), 196-214, http://crln.acrl.org/content/76/4/196; Jessica Critten,

nocratic ideology and solutionism has resonated so strongly within librarianship, particularly within discussions of the future of libraries and librarians. This connection with technocratic ideology and white masculinity is exemplified in the American Library Association's (ALA) recently launched initiative, Libraries Transform, and specifically with the Trend Library produced by the Center for the Future of Libraries. The Trend Library offers simplistic solutions to the complex problem of the future of libraries and librarians. It offers solutions that ahistorically insist on their universal applicability; obscure race, class, gender, sexuality, disability, and other axes of difference; reify technology, social change, and the future; and actively hide the inequities of the social world. In short, the Trend Library offers technocratic solutions embedded in white masculinity. Moreover, the technological fixes promoted by the Trend Library reinforce existing neoliberal tendencies within librarianship.[14]

The Future of Libraries

In May 2014, the ALA officially launched the Center for the Future of Libraries, which has three main tasks: "Identify emerging trends relevant to libraries and the communities they serve; Promote futuring and innovation techniques to help librarians and library professionals shape their future; Build connections with experts and innovative thinkers

---

"'The One Language That Has Eaten All Others': Evidence-based Practice in the Neoliberal Library," (presentation, Critical Librarianship and Pedagogy Symposium, Tucson, February 25, 2016); Maura Seale, "Compliant Trust: The Public Good and Democracy in the ALA's 'Core Values of Librarianship,'" *Library Trends* 64 no. 3 (2016), 585–603, doi: 10.1353/lib.2016.0003.

14. For discussion of neoliberalism within libraries, see Nathaniel F. Enright, "The Violence of Information Literacy: Neoliberalism and the Human as Capital" in *Information Literacy and Social Justice: Radical Professional Praxis*, eds. Lua Gregory and Shana Higgins (Sacramento: Library Juice Press, 2013): 15-38; Karen Nicholson, "The McDonaldization of Academic Libraries and the Values of Transformational Change," *College & Research Libraries* 76, no. 3 (2015): 328-38, doi: 10.5860/crl.76.3.328. See also the work of John Buschman, for example, *Libraries, Classrooms, and the Interests of Democracy: Marking the Limits of Neoliberalism*. (Lanham, MD: Scarecrow Press, 2012). For a theorization of neoliberalism as ideology, see Wendy Brown, *Undoing the Demos: Neoliberalism's Stealth Revolution* (Cambridge: MIT Press, 2015).

to help libraries address emerging issues."[15] The largest section of the website is the Trend Library, which was officially introduced in a February 2015 *American Libraries* article.[16] The webpage explains, "the Center for the Future of Libraries works to identify trends relevant to libraries and librarianship. This collection is available to help libraries and librarians understand how trends are developing and why they matter. Each trend is updated as new reports and articles are made available. New trends will be added as they are developed."[17] The twenty-one trends are classified and color coded into the following categories: society, technology, education, environment, politics and government, economics, and demographics. Each trend includes a bibliography, primarily consisting of stories from news and technology websites. Because the Center for the Future of Libraries was created by the ALA, it can be understood as an official view; its Trend Library, combined with the broader ALA initiative, Libraries Transform,[18] is probably the most thorough articulation of the dominant vision of the future of libraries.

The Libraries Transform initiative, the Center for the Future of Libraries, and the Trend Library participate in what Morozov has called "internet-centrism," which is characterized by "epochalism" or "the firm conviction that we are living through unique, revolutionary times, in which the previous truths no longer hold, everything is undergoing profound change, and the need to 'fix things' runs as high as ever," and "[u]nfolding trends are perceived to be so monumental and inevitable that all resistance seems futile."[19] At the same time "internet-centrism" views technology as "fixed and permanent, perhaps even ontological—'the

---

15. "Center for the Future of Libraries," *American Library Association*, last accessed May 28, 2016, http://www.ala.org/transforminglibraries/future.

16. Miguel Figueroa, "Forecasting the Future of Libraries 2015," *American Libraries Magazine*, February 26, 2015, https://americanlibrariesmagazine.org/2015/02/26/forecasting-the-future-of-libraries-2015/.

17. "Trends | Libraries Transform," *American Library Association*, last accessed May 15, 2016, http://www.ala.org/transforminglibraries/future/trends.

18. "Libraries Transform," *American Library Association*, last accessed May 16, 2016, http://www.ala.org/transforminglibraries/.

19. Morozov, *To Save Everything, Click Here*, 15-16, 36.

Internet' just is and it always will be."[20] It "is believed to possess an inherent nature, a logic, a teleology, and that nature is rapidly unfolding in front of us."[21] It possesses agency, is inevitable, fundamentally disconnected from the past, and exists outside of history. This logic pervades the Trend Library, in which technologies are frequently described as engaging in action and having agency.[22] Changes "will" occur, and the present is consistently depicted in terms of rupture, disruption, innovation, and progress.

Internet-centrism undergirds technological solutionism, which recasts "all complex social situations either as neatly defined problems with definite, computable solutions or as transparent and self-evident processes that can be easily optimized."[23] The Trend Library of the Center for the Future of Libraries thus casts the uncertain future of libraries as something that can be solved by studying and individually responding to the various trends it has collected. The complexity of and differences between libraries are dissolved by summoning technology and the future. The Trend Library presents solutions without articulating the problems that these solutions purportedly address. This forecloses discussion of what these problems might be, what solutions might be

---

20. Ibid., 21-22. Other recent critics of solutionism/technological determinism include Kentaro Toyamo, *Geek Heresy: Rescuing Social Change from the Cult of Technology* (New York: Public Affairs, 2015); Jaron Lanier, *Who Owns the Future?* (New York: Simon and Schuster, 2013), and David Golumbia, *The Cultural Logic of Computation* (Cambridge: Harvard University Press, 2009).

21. Morozov, *To Save Everything, Click Here*, 24.

22. For example, technologies "have fundamentally changed young people," "have introduced new conveniences," "require the supply of more and more personal information," "displace or eliminate many middle-class jobs," drive "new categories of work," and provide "limitless opportunities." "Digital Natives," *American Library Association*, last accessed May 16, 2016, http://www.ala.org/transforminglibraries/future/trends/digitalnatives; "Privacy Shifting," *American Library Association*, last accessed May 16, 2016, http://www.ala.org/transforminglibraries/future/trends/privacy; "Income Inequality," *American Library Association*, last accessed May 16, 2016, http://www.ala.org/transforminglibraries/future/trends/incomeinequality; "Connected Learning," *American Library Association*, last accessed May 16, 2016, http://www.ala.org/transforminglibraries/future/trends/connectedlearning.

23. Morozov, *To Save Everything, Click Here*, 5.

most appropriate, and indeed, what the future of libraries should or could be. The website instead declares what the future will be, because technological change is inevitable.

One of the main dangers of solutionism is that "the quick fixes it peddles do not exist in a political vacuum. In promising almost immediate and much cheaper results, they can easily undermine support for more ambitious, more intellectually stimulating, but also more demanding reform projects."[24] It is embedded in technocratic ideology, which assumes that it is objective and neutral. The Trend Library might claim to be dispassionately predicting the future, but it does indeed have an ideology. It embraces an apolitical, ahistorical, technocratic perspective that sees technology as the solution to complex social, political, and economic problems.[25] Indeed, while the Trend Library gestures towards the importance of politics and government in its trend classification system, no trends are actually designated as belonging to that category. Morozov explicitly connects technocratic ideology and solutionism to the Enlightenment and the scientism that followed.

Invisible Labor

This unspoken investment in white masculinity is emphasized in the Trend Library's treatment of labor. In the Trend Library, only certain types of labor are understood to be important. For example, the language describing the Maker Movement is unremittingly positive: "Makers take advantage of the availability of new technology and traditional craft tools, improved communication between community members, and new pathways to the marketplace" and "see opportunities to develop important new skills, including design, programming, media creation, website development, and entrepreneurship."[26] Making not only involves

---

24. Ibid., 9.

25. Ibid., 136-37.

26. "Maker Movement," *American Library Association*, last accessed July 3, 2016, http://www.ala.org/transforminglibraries/future/trends/makers.

quantitative and digital skills, but also entrepreneurship and innovation, all of which are seen as positive forces within solutionism. The individual, entrepreneurial worker is the default within the Trend Library. This worker moves to the city in order to find "more opportunities for employment and pathways to higher personal success."[27] As robots inevitably enter the workplace, these are the workers that "will be free to focus on higher level and creative tasks."[28] They will innovate, monetize, and leverage. They are the individualistic entrepreneurs of Silicon Valley, disproportionately male and disproportionately white.[29]

The types of work valued in the Trend Library are the types of technology and information work disproportionately performed by white men. Emotion and care work, reproductive labor, service, maintenance work, and manual labor are disproportionately seen as feminized labor and "non-skilled" service labor. This type of "non-skilled" labor, often associated with people whose identities have less social capital due to the intersections of oppression around gender and racial identities, is not seen as relevant to the future of libraries.[30] Nor is the type of

---

27. "Urbanization," *American Library Association*, last accessed November 1, 2016, http://www.ala.org/transforminglibraries/future/trends/urbanization.

28. "Robots," *American Library Association*, last accessed November 1, 2016, http://www.ala.org/transforminglibraries/future/trends/robots.

29. Lauren Britton, "Power, Access, Status: The Discourse of Race, Gender, and Class in the Maker Movement," *Technology & Social Change Group*, March 18, 2015, http://tascha.uw.edu/2015/03/power-access-status-the-discourse-of-race-gender-and-class-in-the-maker-movement/; Hope A. Jahren, "She Wanted to Do Her Research. He Wanted to Talk 'Feelings,'" *New York Times*, March 4, 2016, http://www.nytimes.com/2016/03/06/opinion/sunday/she-wanted-to-do-her-research-he-wanted-to-talk-feelings.html; Nitasha Tiku, "This Is Why There Aren't Enough Women In Tech," *Valleywag*, August 29, 2013, http://valleywag.gawker.com/this-is-why-there-arent-enough-women-in-tech-1221929631; Melissa Villa-Nicholas, "The Invisible Information Worker: Latinas in Telecommunications," in *The Intersectional Internet: Race, Sex, Class and Culture Online*, eds. Safiya Umoja Noble and Brendesha M. Tynes (New York: Peter Lang, 2016), 195-214.

30. Andrew Russell and Lee Vinsel, "Innovation Is Overvalued. Maintenance Often Matters More," *Aeon*, accessed April 7, 2016, https://aeon.co/essays/innovation-is-overvalued-maintenance-often-matters-more; Debbie Chachra, "Why I Am Not a Maker," *The Atlantic*, January 23, 2015, http://www.the-atlantic.com/technology/archive/2015/01/why-i-am-not-a-maker/384767/.

low-wage and often precarious work done in fast casual restaurants or the so-called sharing economy, both of which are cataloged in the Trend Library. Libraries, which share resources, are equated with Uber, which enriches (white male) shareholders while relying on precarious, low-wage work lacking legal protections.[31] The Trend Library notes that sharing systems such as Uber rely "heavily on trust, which social technologies help advance through publicly shared feedback, reviews, comments, and connections,"[32] but it fails to note that these systems incorporate the inequities of the social world, such as racial prejudice,[33] and that systems based on popularity tend to work against diversity and inclusion.[34] When this ideal worker enters a fast casual restaurant, it is as a consumer, not an employee. When this worker opens the Uber app, it is to arrange for a pickup, not the start of a long night of driving. This does not matter, however, as Uber or Lyft drivers are not included in this vision of the future "entrepreneurial" worker. The Trend Library

---

31. The "sharing economy" (at times more appropriately referred to as the "gig economy") is a term which itself elides the labor that is occurring.

32. "Sharing Economy," *American Library Association*, last accessed May 16, 2016, http://www.ala.org/transforminglibraries/future/trends/sharing economy.

33. Nancy Leong, "The Sharing Economy Has a Race Problem," *Salon*, November 2, 2014, http://www.salon.com/2014/11/02/the_sharing_economy_has_a_race_problem/; Shankar Vedantam, "#AirbnbWhileBlack: How Hidden Bias Shapes The Sharing Economy," *NPR*, April 26, 2016, http://www.npr.org/2016/04/26/475623339/-airbnbwhileblack-how-hidden-bias-shapes-the-sharing-economy. See also Matthew Reidsma, "Algorithmic Bias in Library Discovery Systems," MatthewReidsma.com, March 11, 2016, https://matthew.reidsrow.com/articles/173; Safiya Noble, "Google Search: Hyper-Visibility as a Means of Rendering Black Women and Girls Invisible," *InVisible Culture: An Electronic Journal for Visual Culture*, no. 19 (2013), n.p. http://ivc.lib.rochester.edu/google-search-hyper-visibility-as-a-means-of-rendering-black-women-and-girls-invisible/; Lauren Kirchner, "When Discrimination Is Baked Into Algorithms," *The Atlantic*, September 6, 2015, http://www.theatlantic.com/business/archive/2015/09/discrimination-algorithms-disparate-impact/403969/; Michael Brennan, "Can Computers Be Racist? Big Data, Inequality, and Discrimination," *Ford Foundation*, November 18, 2015, http://www.fordfoundation.org/ideas/equals-change-blog/posts/can-computers-be-racist-big-data-inequality-and-discrimination/ for broader discussions of the racial and other biases embedded in algorithms.

34. Morozov, *To Save Everything, Click Here*, 178.

pays more attention to the potential labor of drones and robots than to
workers of color, women workers, low-wage workers, the unemployed,
and those who cannot work.

If the labor of white women and people of color[35] is not visible in the
Trend Library, it is because the emphasis on technology actively obscures
the labor behind that same technology. This includes the mining for
metals used in computer components in the Democratic Republic of
Congo and Mongolia,[36] the assembly of computers and other devices
in China,[37] the filtering of social media performed by workers in the
Philippines,[38] the technical support provided by call center workers in

---

35. The phrase "women and people of color" can be problematic as it
erases women of color from the category of women. We are using the phras-
ing "white women and people of color" throughout this paper to describe
those groups that are often marginalized by white patriarchy, while acknowledging differences between those groups. See Yolanda Flores Niemann, "The
Problem with the Phrases 'Women and Minorities' and 'Women and People
of Color'," *University Press of Colorado & Utah State University Press*, September
22, 2015, http://upcolorado.com/about-us/blog/item/2843-the-problem-
with-the-phrases-women-and-minorities-and-women-and-people-of-color.

36. Jay Greene, "Digging for Rare Earths: The Mines Where iPhones Are
Born." *CNET*, September 26, 2012, http://www.cnet.com/news/digging-
for-rare-earths-the-mines-where-iphones-are-born/; Nick Heath, "How
Conflict Minerals Funded a War That Killed Millions, and Why Tech Giants
Are Finally Cleaning up Their Act," *TechRepublic*, March 23 2014, http://
www.techrepublic.com/article/how-conflict-minerals-funded-a-war-that-
killed-millions; "'This Is What We Die For:' Human Rights Abuses in the
Democratic Republic of the Congo Power the Global Trade in Cobalt,"
Amnesty International, January 19 2016, https://www.amnesty.org/en/docu-
ments/afr62/3183/2016/en/; Jennifer Brea, "Your Computer Is Killing
the Congo," *The Root,* May 28, 2009, http://www.theroot.com/articles/cul-
ture/2009/05/your_computer_is_killing_the_congo.html.

37. Joel Johnson, "1 Million Workers. 90 Million iPhones. 17 Suicides. Who's
to Blame?" *Wired*, February 28, 2011, http://www.wired.com/2011/02/
ff_joelinchina; "Something's Not Right Here: Poor Working Conditions Persist at Apple Supplier Pegatron," *China Labor Watch*, October 22,
2015, http://www.chinalaborwatch.org/report/109; Aditya Chakrabortty,
"The Woman Who Nearly Died Making Your iPad," *The Guardian*, August
5, 2013, http://www.theguardian.com/commentisfree/2013/aug/05/
woman-nearly-died-making-ipad.

38. Sarah T. Roberts, "Commercial Content Moderation: Digital Laborers'
Dirty Work" in *The Intersectional Internet: Race, Sex, Class and Culture Online*, eds.
Safiya Umoja Noble and Brendesha M. Tynes (New York: Peter Lang, 2016)
147-60; Adrian Chen, "The Laborers Who Keep Dick Pics and Beheadings

India and the Philippines,[39] the disposal and recycling of technological equipment in China and Ghana,[40] and so on.[41] Technology recycling is briefly mentioned in the Internet of Things trend, but not the men and women who perform it: "the manufacturing of new enabled devices means that older devices will be displaced and disposed of and, potentially worse, a whole host of devices will enter a technology upgrade cycle (planned obsolescence) to which they might never previously have belonged, further contributing to cycles of disposal."[42] Once again, technology acquires agency and inevitability and human actors disappear. The environmental consequences of digital technologies (e.g., electricity use, resource extraction, server farms[43]) and the ways in which those contribute to climate change are summoned and then accepted as inevitable through the rhetorical construction of the future as known and unchanging.[44] Similarly, the environmental impact of making is

Out of Your Facebook Feed," *Wired*, October 23, 2014, http://www.wired.com/2014/10/content-moderation/.

39. Vikas Bajaj, "A New Capital of Call Centers," *New York Times*, November 25, 2011, http://www.nytimes.com/2011/11/26/business/philippines-over-takes-india-as-hub-of-call-centers.html.

40. Jay Akbar, "Africa's Electronic Graveyards Where the World's 'E-Waste' Ends up." *Daily Mail Online*, April 23, 2015, http://www.dailymail.co.uk/news/article-3049457/Where-computer-goes-die-Shocking-pictures-toxic-electronic-graveyards-Africa-West-dumps-old-PCs-laptops-microwaves-fridges-phones.html; Ivan Watson, "China: The Electronic Wastebasket of the World," *CNN*, May 30, 2013, http://www.cnn.com/2013/05/30/world/asia/china-electronic-waste-e-waste/; Jacopo Ottaviani, "E-Waste Republic: Discarded Electronics and Ghana's Environmental Conundrum," *Spiegel Online*, April 11, 2016, http://www.spiegel.de/international/tomorrow/electronic-waste-in-africa-recycling-methods-damage-health-and-the-environment-a-1086221.html.

41. Christian Fuchs provides a Marxist analysis of most of these examples in *Digital Labour and Karl Marx* (New York: Routledge, 2014).

42. "Internet of Things," *American Library Association*, last accessed July 3, 2016, http://www.ala.org/transforminglibraries/future/trends/IoT.

43. Ingrid Burrington, "The Environmental Toll of a Netflix Binge," *The Atlantic*, December 16, 2015, http://www.theatlantic.com/technology/archive/2015/12/there-are-no-clean-clouds/420744/.

44. Toyamo, *Geek Heresy*, 23.

completely avoided.[45] But the consequences of resource extraction and climate change will likely have a much more significant impact on groups that are already marginalized: the poor, politically disempowered, and systematically oppressed.[46]

It is not expected that a website dealing with the future of libraries would speak to each of these issues, but it is also no accident that the labor generally performed by white men in the United States is valorized while other forms of labor—forms that are necessary and undergird the technology solutions advanced by the Trend Library, forms that are most often performed by people of color, women, and workers in non-Western countries—are invisible or erased. It is no accident that environmental issues around technology are made invisible, nor is it a mistake that none of the trends is connected to politics. The Trend Library adopts the universal stance of white masculinity, which is able to avoid the messiness of the social world and the perceived biases of politics, via the neutrality and objectivity of technocratic solutions.

The Trend Library is pervaded by the language of benefits, opportunity, innovation, and progress; it appears to be a truly fortuitous time for libraries. But where are librarians? The Trend Library generally takes its subject to be libraries and only briefly mentions librarians, save for this prediction: "Library workers may increasingly seek opportunities to unplug, be reflective, or quietly focus on specific work activities—and this may be a challenge in a culture that does not provide opportunities for that type of work time."[47] This frames reflective or quiet work

---

45. Lyndsey Gilpin, "The Dark Side of 3D Printing: 10 Things to Watch," *TechRepublic*, March 5, 2014, http://www.techrepublic.com/article/the-dark-side-of-3d-printing-10-things-to-watch/.

46. There are several book-length treatments of the lifecycle and environmental impact of digital technologies and devices. See Elizabeth Grossman, *High Tech Trash: Digital Devices, Hidden Toxics, and Human Health* (Washington: Island Press, 2006); Jennifer Gabrys, *Digital Rubbish: A Natural History of Electronics* (Ann Arbor: University of Michigan Press, 2011); and Elizabeth Woyke, *The Smartphone: Anatomy of an Industry* (New York: The New Press, 2014).

47. "Unplugged," *American Library Association Center for the Future of Libraries: Trends*, last accessed July 3, 2016, http://www.ala.org/transforminglibraries/future/trends/unplugged.

as already inevitably gone, rather than as minimized and devalued by policies implemented by specific companies and organizations with particular ends in mind, such as fewer employees doing increasingly more work. This is reinforced in the Fast Casual trend; if libraries must emphasize their "affordability" and "value" to patrons,[48] if library workers are the functional equivalent of Chipotle employees,[49] what does this imply about library work, library workers' salaries and benefits, and library workers' skills, abilities, and knowledge? By ignoring librarians and library workers in favor of technology, the Trend Library valorizes the work of library administration and information technology, areas dominated by white men, while devaluing the service, care, maintenance, and manual labor that is at the core of libraries' everyday functioning but is dominated by lower-earning white women and people of color.

Although the Trend Library is just one version—albeit an authoritative and influential one—of the future of libraries, its unacknowledged reliance on white masculinity pervades other discussions of libraries. Referring to libraries as "platforms" evokes the white masculinity of Silicon Valley and technocratic ideology, prioritizes monetization, and obscures library resources that are low- or non-technological."[50] "Unbundling," which is a core precept of the educational technology community,[51] has also been pushed within librarianship. If what libraries need is a collection of skills, offered just-in-time at the lowest possible cost, then a disruptive or innovative solution might be something similar to either Amazon's Mechanical Turk or Uber. Day-to-day service work can be performed by paraprofessional staff similar to workers

---

48. "Fast Casual," *American Library Association Center for the Future of Libraries: Trends*, last accessed July 3, 2016, http://www.ala.org/transforminglibraries/future/trends/fastcasual.

49. Who should also be paid a living wage and receive benefits.

50. Shannon Mattern, "Library as Infrastructure," *Places Journal*, June 9, 2014, https://placesjournal.org/article/library-as-infrastructure/.

51. Mara Sapon-Shevin, "Inclusive Education, High Stakes Testing and Capitalist Schooling," *Monthly Review*, July 1, 2011, http://monthlyreview.org/2011/07/01/inclusive-education-high-stakes-testing-and-capitalist-schooling/..

employed in fast casual restaurants, while high-paying technological and administrative work can be performed by "full-stack librarians." The idea of the "full-stack librarian," which emerged from the notion of the "full-stack programmer,"[52] "is a generalist who uses the full range of resources available *to position the library as an educational technology*."[53] The technology work performed by the full-stack librarian is implicitly coded as white and male in contrast to the emotional labor of traditional (female) librarians.

The devaluation of librarianship by positioning it as "traditional" and ignoring it in discussions of the future of libraries is also tied to technocratic ideology and white masculinity. "Traditional" librarianship, which emphasizes service, emotional labor, and interpersonal interaction, is overdetermined as feminine and is devalued within technocratic ideology. In the future envisioned by the Trend Library, there are no reference services or instruction, for example. Reference is a key point of contact with patrons, but it is not innovative or efficient. The focus on efficiency, the rhetorical move from "reference librarians" to "access engineers,"[54] and the use of chatbots presuppose that reference is universally unnecessary.[55] The use of student or paraprofessional staff might be more cost efficient for the library, but it is also exploitative since those employees generally do not receive recognition or additional compensation.[56] Although library instruction has thus far avoided the standardization of K-12 education and indeed tends to be fairly cost efficient as it primarily consists of one-shot sessions, there is a continual

---

52. O'Reilly Media, "Developers Need to Broaden Their Range," *Forbes*, April 11, 2014, http://www.forbes.com/sites/oreillymedia/2014/04/11/full-stack-developer-is-a-tall-order-bordering-on-unicorn-territory/.

53. Steven Bell, "What to Expect From a 'Full Stack' Librarian," *EdSurge News*, December 16, 2015, https://www.edsurge.com/news/2015-12-16-what-to-expect-from-a-full-stack-librarian. Emphasis added.

54. David S. Nolen, "Reforming or Rejecting the Reference Desk: Conflict and Continuity in the Concept of Reference," *Library Philosophy and Practice*, May 12, 2010, http://www.webpages.uidaho.edu/~mbolin/nolen.htm.

55. Ibid.

56. Christopher Magee and Michael Perini, "The Blended Desk and Its Consequences on Collaboration," *Collaborative Librarianship* 6, no. 3 (2014): 127.

push (in the Trend Library and elsewhere) for technological interventions to replace even that small amount of interaction between librarians and patrons: tutorials, library guides, badges, FAQs, flipped learning, connected learning, and gamification.[57] These are often framed as more convenient or appealing for patrons, but they embody technocratic ideology in their technological and universalizing solution to the complex social problem of education.

Despite various initiatives sponsored by the ALA, Association of College & Research Libraries (ACRL), and other professional organizations, the Master of Library Science (MLS) degree has begun to be seen as of limited utility—library science is of the past while information technology is the future. Academic libraries in particular hire individuals lacking the degree for librarian positions,[58] and the focus on "functional specialists" in recent discussions of liaison librarianship may reinforce this practice.[59] Again, the solution is cast as technological. "Functional specialist" generally refers to expertise in some sort of digital technology: digital humanities, digital scholarship, data, user experience, interface design, and so on. The degree is devalued through the adjunctification of academic librarians, the outsourcing of public librarians, the replacement of librarians with student or paraprofessional employees, and by erasing librarians from the future of libraries, as the Trend Library does. Each of these examples promotes technocratic ideology, and by replacing the emotional labor, everyday work, manual labor, and maintenance performed by white women and people of color with the new shininess of innovation, reiterates white masculinity.[60] Each of these examples also reinscribes neoliberal ideology through their unquestioning adoption of

---

57. Karen Nicholson, "Badging, Information Literacy, and Academic Capitalism" (presentation, Critical Librarianship and Pedagogy Symposium, Tucson, AZ, February 26, 2016); "Center for the Future of Libraries."

58. Bell, "What to Expect From a 'Full Stack' Librarian."

59. Janice M. Jaguszewski and Karen Williams, "New Roles for New Times: Transforming Liaison Roles in Research Libraries," August 2013, http://www.arl.org/publications-resources/2893-new-roles-for-new-times-transforming-liaison-roles-in-research-libraries.

60. Russell and Vinsel, "Innovation Is Overvalued. Maintenance Often Matters More."

ideas such as short-term results, the demands of the market, just-in-time services, return-on-investment (ROI), and efficiency.

The emotional labor of women and the physical labor of people of color are necessary to the smooth functioning of both society and libraries, but it is consistently ignored in discussions and representations of the future of libraries. Instead, these texts uncritically embrace technocratic ideology, white masculinity, and neoliberalism. As Miriam Posner notes, "when we choose not to invest in our own infrastructure, we choose not to articulate a different possible version of the world."[61] When we look to Silicon Valley to explain the future of libraries, we give up our ability to actively shape it ourselves.

Conclusion: The Green Place

Mad Max: Fury Road, the film from which this chapter's epigraph is drawn, is a dystopic vision of a world following environmental catastrophe. In accounting for such destruction, it is revealed that the characters Immortan Joe, the People Eater, and the Bullet Farmer are "killing everyone and everything." In our reading of the film, Immortan Joe embodies white patriarchy, and the Bullet Farmer, war. The People Eater, who is always counting the costs, symbolizes capitalism. In seeking to determine, as one character puts it, "who killed the world," viewers are prompted to consider not only the destructive consequences of patriarchy, but also the ways in which emancipatory, resistant spaces might be carved out—indeed, one of the film's protagonists, Furiosa, and a band of women attempt to escape to the Green Place, a land free from the destructive impact of patriarchy and environmental collapse. However, there is no escape from the destruction that white patriarchy causes and while the Vuvalini or Many Mothers can briefly live apart, their Green Place is also eventually contaminated. The Vuvalini, Furiosa,

---

61. We follow Russell and Vinsel and consider infrastructure to be the often invisible structures and labor that make "innovation" possible. Miriam Posner, "Money and Time," *Miriam Posner's Blog*, March 14, 2016, http://miriamposner.com/blog/money-and-time/.

and the Wives must reclaim the Citadel in order to survive. Calling upon this film, then, seemed a fitting way to frame our discussion of white masculinity and the future of librarianship, as well as the need to center a humanistic vision of our future, rather than a technocratic vision.[62]

The ALA's Center for the Future of Libraries and its Trend Library propose objective, universal, technocratic solutions to the problem of the future of libraries, but those solutions are ultimately bound up with, rely on, and privilege white masculinity. Those solutions are also, perhaps unsurprisingly, embedded in neoliberalism—the dominant ideology of our political present. Technocratic visions of the future of libraries aspire to a world outside of politics and ideology, to the unmarked space of white masculinity, but such visions are embedded in multiple layers and axes of privilege. They elide the fact that technology is not benevolently impartial but is subject to the same inequities inherent to the social world. They hide the physical and emotional labor of the precariat, who are frequently gendered, racialized, or otherwise marginalized, behind discourses of freedom, progress, and the disruptive potential of the digital. It is not the irrationality of politics that foils these utopian projects, but rather the weight of history.

When librarians utilize this rhetoric uncritically we erase differences, ignore power, and legitimate the voices of the privileged. Shannon Mattern suggests that libraries can be "spaces of exception" as well as the spaces for the entrepreneurship demanded by neoliberal policies, but in order for this to happen, "the library needs to know how to read itself as a social-technical-intellectual infrastructure."[63] There are no ideologically pure positions, just as it turns out that there is no Green Place untouched by ecological disaster in Mad Max: Fury Road. But acknowledging that we are all embedded in systems of power and inequality allows for the possibility of critically analyzing and changing those systems. We are not arguing for an ideal version of librarianship that once existed

---

62. *Mad Max: Fury Road*, directed by George Miller. (2015; Burbank, CA: Warner Home Video, 2015), DVD.

63. Mattern, "Library as Infrastructure." Emphasis in original.

and to which we must return, but rather for an historical and situated understanding of librarianship and technology, and the ways in which they intersect with dominant conceptions of white masculinity.

Bibliography

Akbar, Jay. "Africa's Electronic Graveyards Where the World's 'E-Waste' Ends up." *Daily Mail Online*, April 23, 2015. http://www.dailymail.co.uk/news/article-3049457/Where-computer-goes-die-Shocking-pictures-toxic-electronic-graveyards-Africa-West-dumps-old-PCs-laptops-microwaves-fridges-phones.html.

Bajaj, Vikas. "A New Capital of Call Centers." *New York Times*, November 25, 2011. http://www.nytimes.com/2011/11/26/business/philippines-overtakes-india-as-hub-of-call-centers.html.

Bell, Steven. "What to Expect From a 'Full Stack' Librarian." EdSurge, December 16, 2015. https://www.edsurge.com/news/2015-12-16-what-to-expect-from-a-full-stack-librarian.

Brea, Jennifer. "Your Computer is Killing the Congo." *The Root*, May 28, 2009. http://www.theroot.com/articles/culture/2009/05/your_computer_is_killing_the_congo.html.

Brennan, Michael. "Can Computers Be Racist? Big Data, Inequality, and Discrimination." *Ford Foundation*, November 18, 2015. http://www.fordfoundation.org/ideas/equals-change-blog/posts/can-computers-be-racist-big-data-inequality-and-discrimination/.

Britton, Lauren. "Power, Access, Status: The Discourse of Race, Gender, and Class in the Maker Movement." *Technology & Social Change Group*, March 18, 2015. http://tascha.uw.edu/2015/03/power-access-status-the-discourse-of-race-gender-and-class-in-the-maker-movement/.

Bourg, Chris. "Never Neutral: Libraries, Technology, and Inclusion."
    Feral Librarian (blog), January 29, 2015. https://chrisbourg.
    wordpress.com/2015/01/28/never-neutral-libraries-technol-
    ogy-and-inclusion/.

Brook, Freeda, Dave Ellenwood, and Althea Eannace Lazzaro. "In
    Pursuit of Antiracist Social Justice: Denaturalizing Whiteness
    in the Academic Library." *Library Trends* 64, no. 2 (2015):
    246-84. doi: 10.1353/lib.2015.0048.

Brown, Wendy. *Undoing the Demos: Neoliberalism's Stealth Revolution.*
    Cambridge, MA: MIT Press, 2015.

Burrington, Ingrid. "The Environmental Toll of a Netflix Binge."
    The Atlantic, December 16, 2015. http://www.theatlantic.
    com/technology/archive/2015/12/there-are-no-clean-
    clouds/420744/.

Buschman, John. *Libraries, Classrooms, and the Interests of Democracy:
    Marking the Limits of Neoliberalism.* Lanham, MD: Scarecrow
    Press, 2012.

"Center for the Future of Libraries." *American Library Association*,
    accessed May 28, 2016. http://www.ala.org/transforminglib-
    raries/future.

Chachra, Debbie. "Why I Am Not a Maker." *The Atlantic*, January
    23, 2015. http://www.theatlantic.com/technology/ar-
    chive/2015/01/why-i-am-not-a-maker/384767/.

Chakrabortty, Aditya. "The Woman Who Nearly Died Making Your
    iPad." *The Guardian*, August 5, 2013. http://www.theguard-
    ian.com/commentisfree/2013/aug/05/woman-nearly-died-
    making-ipad.

Chen, Adrian. "The Laborers Who Keep Dick Pics and Beheadings
    Out of Your Facebook Feed." *Wired*, October 23, 2014.
    http://www.wired.com/2014/10/content-moderation/.

Critten Jessica. "The One Language That Has Eaten All Others': Evidence-based Practice in the Neoliberal Library." Presentation at "Critical Librarianship and Pedagogy Symposium," Tucson, AZ. February 25-26, 2015.

"Connected Learning." *American Library Association*, accessed May 16, 2016. http://www.ala.org/transforminglibraries/future/trends/connectedlearning.

"The Distributed Librarian: Live, Online, Real-Time Reference." *American Libraries Magazine*, November 2000. https://americanlibrariesmagazine.org/the-distributed-librarianlive-online-real-time-reference/.

"Digital Natives." *American Library Association*, accessed May 16, 2016. http://www.ala.org/transforminglibraries/future/trends/digitalnatives.

Dyer, Richard. *White*. London: Routledge, 1997.

Enright, Nathaniel F. "The Violence of Information Literacy: Neoliberalism and the Human as Capital." In *Information Literacy and Social Justice: Radical Professional Praxis*, edited by Lua Gregory and Shana Higgins, 15-38. Sacramento, CA: Library Juice Press, 2013.

"Fast Casual." American Library Association, accessed May 16, 2016. http://www.ala.org/transforminglibraries/future/trends/fastcasual.

Figueroa, Miguel. "Forecasting the Future of Libraries 2015." *American Libraries Magazine*, February 26, 2015. https://americanlibrariesmagazine.org/2015/02/26/forecasting-the-future-of-libraries-2015/.

Fister, Barbara. "Admitting Our Agendas." *Library Babel Fish* (blog), August 29, 2013. https://www.insidehighered.com/blogs/library-babel-fish/admitting-our-agendas.

Fuchs, Christian. *Digital Labour and Karl Marx*. New York: Routledge, 2014.

Gabrys, Jennifer. *Digital Rubbish: A Natural History of Electronics*. Ann Arbor: University of Michigan Press, 2011.

Galvan, Angela. "Soliciting Performance, Hiding Bias: Whiteness and Librarianship." *In the Library with the Lead Pipe* (June 2015). http://www.inthelibrarywiththeleadpipe.org/2015/soliciting-performance-hiding-bias-whiteness-and-librarianship/.

Gilpin, Lyndsey. "The Dark Side of 3D Printing: 10 Things to Watch." *TechRepublic*, March 5, 2014. http://www.techrepublic.com/article/the-dark-side-of-3d-printing-10-things-to-watch/.

Goldberg, David Theo. *Racist Culture: Philosophy and the Politics of Meaning*. Cambridge, MA: Blackwell, 1993.

Golumbia, David. *The Cultural Logic of Computation*. Cambridge, MA: Harvard University Press, 2009.

Greene, Jay. "Digging for Rare Earths: The Mines Where iPhones Are Born." *CNET*, September 26, 2012. http://www.cnet.com/news/digging-for-rare-earths-the-mines-where-iphones-are-born/.

Grossman, Elizabeth. *High Tech Trash: Digital Devices, Hidden Toxics, and Human Health*. Washington DC: Island Press, 2006.

Hathcock, April. "White Librarianship in Blackface: Diversity Initiatives in LIS." *In the Library with the Lead Pipe* (October 2015). http://www.inthelibrarywiththeleadpipe.org/2015/lis-diversity/.

Heath, Nick. "How Conflict Minerals Funded a War That Killed Millions, and Why Tech Giants are Finally Cleaning up Their Act." *TechRepublic*, March 23, 2014. http://www.techrepublic.com/article/how-conflict-minerals-funded-a-war-that-killed-millions.

Honma, Todd. "Trippin' Over the Color Line: The Invisibility of Race in Library and Information Studies." *InterActions: UCLA Journal of Education and Information Studies* 1, no. 2 (2005): 1-26. http://escholarship.org/uc/item/4nj0w1mp.

"Income Inequality." *American Library Association*, accessed May 16, 2016. http://www.ala.org/transforminglibraries/future/trends/incomeinequality.

"Internet of Things." *American Library Association*, accessed July 3, 2016. http://www.ala.org/transforminglibraries/future/trends/IoT.

Jahren, Hope A. "She Wanted to Do Her Research. He Wanted to Talk 'Feelings." *New York Times*, March 4, 2016. http://www.nytimes.com/2016/03/06/opinion/sunday/she-wanted-to-do-her-research-he-wanted-to-talk-feelings.html.

Jaguszewski, Janice M., and Karen Williams. "New Roles for New Times: Transforming Liaison Roles in Research Libraries." *Association of Research Libraries*, 2013. http://www.arl.org/publications-resources/2893-new-roles-for-new-times-trans-forming-liaison-roles-in-research-libraries#.V3r7SI4nk01.

de jesus, nina. "Locating the Library in Institutional Oppression." *In the Library with the Lead Pipe* (September 2014). http://www.inthelibrarywiththeleadpipe.org/2014/locating-the-library-in-institutional-oppression.

Johnson, Joel. "1 Million Workers. 90 Million iPhones. 17 Suicides. Who's to Blame?" *Wired*, February 28, 2011. http://www.wired.com/2011/02/ff_joelinchina.

Kirchner, Lauren. "When Discrimination is Baked into Algorithms." *The Atlantic*, September 6, 2015. http://www.theatlantic.com/business/archive/2015/09/discrimination-algorithms-disparate-impact/403969/.

Lanier, Jaron. *Who Owns the Future?* New York: Simon and Schuster, 2013.

Leong, Nancy. "The Sharing Economy has a Race Problem." *Salon*, November 2, 2014. http://www.salon.com/2014/11/02/the_sharing_economy_has_a_race_problem/.

"Libraries Transform," *American Library Association*, accessed May 16, 2016. http://www.ala.org/transforminglibraries/.

Maack, Mary Niles. "Gender, Culture, and the Transformation of
American Librarianship, 1890-1920." *Libraries & Culture* 33,
no. 1 (1998): 51–61.

Mad Max: Fury Road. DVD. Directed by George Miller. Burbank,
CA: Warner Home Video, 2015.

Magee, Christopher, and Michael Perini. "The Blended Desk and Its
Consequences on Collaboration." *Collaborative Librarianship* 6,
no. 3 (2014): 124–29.

"Maker Movement." *American Library Association*, accessed May 16,
2016. http://www.ala.org/transforminglibraries/future/
trends/makers.

Mattern, Shannon. "Library as Infrastructure." *Places Journal,* June 9,
2014. https://placesjournal.org/article/library-as-infrastruc-
ture/.

Morozov, Evgeny. *To Save Everything, Click Here.* New York: Public
Affairs, 2013.

Nicholson, Karen. "Badging, Information Literacy, and Academic
Capitalism." Presentation at "Critical Librarianship and Pedagogy Symposium," Tucson, AZ, February 26, 2016.

———. "The McDonaldization of Academic Libraries and the Values of Transformational Change." *College & Research Libraries*
76, no. 3 (2015): 328-38. doi: 0.5860/crl.76.3.328.

Niemann, Yolanda Flores. "The Problem with the Phrases 'Women
and Minorities' and 'Women and People of Color.'" *University
Press of Colorado & Utah State University Press.* September 22,
2015. http://upcolorado.com/about-us/blog/item/2843-
the-problem-with-the-phrases-women-and-minorities-and-
women-and-people-of-color.

Noble, Safiya. "Google Search: Hyper-Visibility as a Means of Rendering Black Women and Girls Invisible." *InVisible Culture:
An Electronic Journal for Visual Culture*, no. 19 (2013). http://
ivc.lib.rochester.edu/google-search-hyper-visibility-as-a-
means-of-rendering-black-women-and-girls-invisible/.

Nolen, David S. "Reforming or Rejecting the Reference Desk: Conflict and Continuity in the Concept of Reference." Accessed May 15, 2016. http://www.webpages.uidaho.edu/~mbolin/nolen.htm.

O'Reilly Media. "Developers Need to Broaden Their Range." *Forbes*, April 11, 2014. http://www.forbes.com/sites/oreillymedia/2014/04/11/full-stack-developer-is-a-tall-order-bordering-on-unicorn-territory/.

Ottaviani, Jacopo. "E-Waste Republic." *Spiegel Online*, April 11, 2016. http://www.spiegel.de/international/tomorrow/electronic-waste-in-africa-recycling-methods-damage-health-and-the-environment-a-1086221.html.

Pagowsky, Nicole, and Niamh Wallace. "Black Lives Matter! Shedding Library Neutrality Rhetoric for Social Justice." *College & Research Libraries News* 76, no. 4 (2015): 196-214. http://crln.acrl.org/content/76/4/196.

Posner, Miriam. "Money and Time." *Miriam Posner's Blog*, March 14, 2016. http://miriamposner.com/blog/money-and-time/.

"Privacy Shifting." *American Library Association*, accessed May 16, 2016. http://www.ala.org/transforminglibraries/future/trends/privacy.

Reeser, Todd W. *Masculinities in Theory: An Introduction*. Chichester, England: Wiley-Blackwell, 2010.

Reidsma, Matthew. "Algorithmic Bias in Library Discovery Systems." March 11, 2016. https://matthew.reidsrow.com/articles/173.

Roberts, Sarah T. "Commercial Content Moderation: Digital Laborers' Dirty Work." In *The Intersectional Internet: Race, Sex, Class and Culture Online*, edited by Safiya Umoja Noble and Brendesha M. Tynes, 147-60. New York: Peter Lang, 2016.

"Robots," *American Library Association*, accessed November 1, 2016. http://www.ala.org/transforminglibraries/future/trends/robots.

Russell, Andrew and Lee Vinsel. "Innovation Is Overvalued. Maintenance Often Matters More." *Aeon*, April 7, 2016. https://
aeon.co/essays/innovation-is-overvalued-maintenance-
often-matters-more.

Sapon-Shevin, Mara. "Inclusive Education, High Stakes Testing and
Capitalist Schooling." *Monthly Review*, July 1, 2011. http://
monthlyreview.org/2011/07/01/inclusive-education-high-
stakes-testing-and-capitalist-schooling/.

Schlesselman-Tarango, Gina. "Critical Whiteness Studies for Academic Librarianship: Problems and Possibilities." Presentation, Canadian Association of Professional Librarians (CA-
PAL), Ottawa, May 31, 2015. http://scholarworks.lib.csusb.
edu/library-publications/27.

———. "The Legacy of Lady Bountiful: White Women in the Library." *Library Trends* 64, no. 4 (2016): 667-86. doi: 10.1353/
lib.2016.0015.

Schueller, Malini Johar. *Locating Race: Global Sites of Post-Colonial Citizenship*. Albany: SUNY Press, 2009.

Seale, Maura. "Compliant Trust: The Public Good and Democracy in
the ALA's 'Core Values of Librarianship.'" *Library Trends* 64,
no. 3 (2016): 585–603. doi: 10.1353/lib.2016.0003.

Seale, Maura, and Rafia Mirza. "Watchers, Punks, and Dashing He-
roes: Representations of Male Librarians in Generation-X
Mass Culture." In *Generation X Perspectives on Librarianship*, eds.
Martin K. Wallace, Erik Sean Estep, and Rebecca Tolley-
Stokes (Jefferson, NC: McFarland, 2010) 135-46.

"Sharing Economy." *American Library Association*, accessed May 16,
2016. http://www.ala.org/transforminglibraries/future/
trends/sharingeconomy.

"Something's Not Right Here: Poor Working Conditions Persist at
Apple Supplier Pegatron," *China Labor Watch*, October 22,
2015. http://www.chinalaborwatch.org/report/109.

"'This Is What We Die For:' Human Rights Abuses in the Democratic Republic of the Congo Power the Global Trade in Cobalt." *Amnesty International*, January 19, 2016. https://www.amnesty.org/en/documents/afr62/3183/2016/en/.

Tiku, Nitasha. "This is Why There aren't Enough Women in Tech." *Valleywag*, August 29, 2013. http://valleywag.gawker.com/this-is-why-there-arent-enough-women-in-tech-1221929631.

Toyamo, Kentaro. *Geek Heresy: Rescuing Social Change from the Cult of Technology*. New York: Public Affairs, 2015.

"Trends | Libraries Transform." *American Library Association*, accessed May 15, 2016. http://www.ala.org/transforminglibraries/future/trends.

"Unplugged." *American Library Association*, accessed May 16, 2016. http://www.ala.org/transforminglibraries/future/trends/unplugged.

"Urbanization," *American Library Association*, accessed November 1, 2016, http://www.ala.org/transforminglibraries/future/trends/urbanization.

Vedantam, Shankar. "#AirbnbWhileBlack: How Hidden Bias Shapes the Sharing Economy." *NPR*, April 26, 2016. http://www.npr.org/2016/04/26/475623339/-airbnbwhileblack-how-hidden-bias-shapes-the-sharing-economy.

Villa-Nicholas, Melissa. "The Invisible Information Worker: Latinas in Telecommunications." In *The Intersectional Internet: Race, Sex, Class and Culture Online*, edited by Safiya Umoja Noble and Brendesha M. Tynes, 195-214. New York: Peter Lang, 2016.

Vinopal, Jennifer. "The Quest for Diversity in Library Staffing: From Awareness to Action." *In the Library with the Lead Pipe* (January 2016). http://www.inthelibrarywiththeleadpipe.org/2016/quest-for-diversity/.

Watson, Ivan. "China: The Electronic Wastebasket of the World."
    CNN, May 30, 2013. http://www.cnn.com/2013/05/30/
    world/asia/china-electronic-waste-e-waste/.

Woyke, Elizabeth. *The Smartphone: Anatomy of an Industry.* New York:
    The New Press, 2014.

Chapter 9

THE WHITENESS OF PRACTICALITY

David James Hudson[1]

> We must focus less on ideas and more on action — getting things done.
> -James G. Neal, American Library Association president-elect (2017-18)[2]

From age eleven until I left for university, I lived three blocks down a quiet street from a small branch of the Ottawa Public Library. The first few years of my visits to the branch mostly resulted in piles of Asterix and Tintin comics, alongside hockey magazines, *National Geographic*, various editions of the *Guinness Book of World Records*, and the occasional copy of *Rolling Stone* (my mom often recounts that she and my dad were worried that I was not reading anything more substantial, even as the rest

---

1. Parts of this chapter are based on a keynote address given at the Critical Librarianship and Pedagogy Symposium on February 25th, 2016, at the University of Arizona. I'm grateful to the participants of the symposium for the valuable feedback they provided, as well as to Karen Nicholson and Lisa Baird for their help in working through early versions of these ideas. A special thanks is due to Gina Schlesselman-Tarango not only for her support throughout my development of these ideas and her careful editing work, but also for her patience with the delays that marked the process of this chapter's writing.

2. Neal's remarks were made as part of his address to the 2016 Charleston Conference during the "Libraries as Convener, Enabler, Distributor, Advocate, and Archive in the Future Knowledge Economy" plenary. See James G. Neal and Anja Smit, "Charleston Conference 2016 Thursday Plenary," Ustream video, 1:45:00, posted by "Charleston Conference," November 3, 2016, http://www.ustream.tv/recorded/92596956.

of the family were voracious readers). As I started to develop political consciousness through my mid to late teens, I gravitated towards more serious texts, including books on black liberation movements—Henry Hampton and Steve Fayer's *Voices of Freedom: An Oral History of the Civil Rights Movement from the 1950s Through the 1980s*, James Forman's *The Making of Black Revolutionaries*, and Hugh Pearson's *The Shadow of the Panther: Huey Newton and the Price of Black Power in America*.

For a time in this period, I had kept my awkward, inconsistent, frizzy hair twisted and knotted into short dreadlocks. After about a year, though, I tired of the upkeep the locks required, worrying further about a growing habit of anxiously fiddling with them and daydreaming instead of concentrating on homework. So I shaved them off. One day soon afterwards, I was in my beloved library branch checking out books with a kind librarian whom I quite liked; my brother had worked there as a page during high school, so the librarian knew me as "Ed's brother." As our conversation was ending, she commented that she was glad that I'd cut off my locks and that my now close-cropped hair was "much more civilized." Even as the library was a space in which I could explore germinal racial consciousness and find validation in extracurricular reading to counter the sense of racial alienation I felt among my peers, the building was also a space in which a sense of status quo utilitarianism tended to assert itself aggressively in racially coded ways—like innocuous comments on hair, implied alignments of dreadlocks with barbarism, valorizations of the orderly, the practical, the clean cut—the kind of haircut you can set your watch to.[3]

---

3. This latter image of clockwork haircuts is drawn from an episode of *The Simpsons* during which the character Grampa Simpson is shown in a flashback watching the 1969 Super Bowl. He comments disparagingly on the long hair of New York Jets quarterback Joe Namath, whose image is shown on the screen. When the opposing quarterback, Johnny Unitas of the Baltimore Colts, is shown, Simpson comments of the athlete's closely cropped short-back-and-sides hairstyle, "now, Johnny Unitas—there's a haircut you could set your watch to." See *The Simpsons*, season 7, episode no. 8, first broadcast November 19, 1995 on Fox, directed by David Silverman and written by Richard Appel and Dan Greaney.

Practicality more broadly operates as an imperative in our profession—a dearly-held value and an exhortation, an expectation inscribed into a thousand professional sites. This chapter raises critical questions about the racial politics of such an imperative: the focus of analysis is not on our commitment to prioritizing user needs, but rather on the operations of practicality as a dominant value. Turning as it does on relational exaltations of the practical and devaluations of the theoretical, the imperative to be practical is indeed truly hegemonic. It is not simply (or even chiefly) that institutional and organizational authorities are directly repressing attempts to do work understood to be theoretical. It is rather that our very expectations and assumptions about the practical character and value of our field subtly police the work we end up doing and supporting, the kind of questions we ask and conversations we have, our sense of what useful and appropriate conferences, publications, and research look like, and indeed our sense, more generally, of what useful and appropriate political interventions look like from the standpoint of our profession.

This chapter explores the implications of such hegemonic dynamics for anti-racist work in the library world. Where does the imperative that we be first and foremost practical in our library work intersect with the interests and violences of white supremacy? How could such a seemingly liberatory discourse—that we remain practical, focused on getting information to users with efficiency, committed to universalizing access—possibly be implicated in the dispossessive work of whiteness? Drawing on stories of theory and practice, of the world of libraries and beyond, of academia and beyond, of diversity and justice, of the normative and the unintelligible, of plain prose and deceptive violence, I suggest that there are answers to be found in the examination of whiteness's operations as an aggressively unmarked locus of power. Its self-effacing claims to self-evidence—and our field's perpetuation of its structures of material and epistemological violence—are left unchallenged as exaltations of practicality work to foreclose spaces in which we might confront white supremacy through interrogations of its complexities, practices of critique that do not always produce clear answers for the questions they pose. The foundational recourse to status quo languages and logics that, along with the disavowal of the unintelligible, underpins imperatives to practicality both reinforces the dominance of liberal racial politics in our field (under the sign of "diversity and inclusion") and obscures the ways in which such politics have themselves worked to entrench structures of white supremacy. We might craft alternate spaces of anti-racist critical practice in our field through purposeful challenges to such imperatives, through the recognition of the value of questions without answers and the value of language that pushes beyond common-sense meanings. We might also complement such work by unsettling the entrenched dualisms of theory and practice that animate such imperatives in the first place, by actively interrogating the assumptions about the location of intellectual life and critical analysis that underpins such dualisms, and by working to materially enact an anti-racism in the library world that hinges on translation across contexts of critical practice rather than the implicit dismissal of all understood to be impractical.

On Practicality Imperatives in Library Land

It is practicality in the popular sense of the word that is central to the library world. We organize and administer things. We develop systems and services, workflows and procedures, guides and frameworks. We identify technical problems and solutions. We emphasize efficiency, brevity, speed. We save the time of the user, to paraphrase Ranganathan's fourth law of library science.[4] No nonsense. *Get on with it so you can get it done.* Library service without friction, to repurpose Bill Gates's capitalist imagery.[5] I suspect even the most ardent critical theorist in library land rarely, if ever, responds to a simple directional question with an in-depth

---

4. S. R. Ranganathan, *The Five Laws of Library Science* (1931; repr., New Delhi: Ess Ess Publications, 2006), http://hdl.handle.net/2027/mdp .39015073883822.

5. Bill Gates, Nathan Myhrvold, and Peter Rinearson, *The Road Ahead* (New York: Viking, 1995).

lecture on the nuances of Frantz Fanon's *The Wretched of the Earth* and its implications for library-as-place.

But the imperative to be practical extends beyond the daily implementation of user services and organizational workflows. It shapes our intellectual work as well: we are to be pragmatic, solution-oriented professionals, not only when we are serving users, but also when we are undertaking scholarly inquiry. Library and information studies (LIS) education is dominated by "texts that solidify the use of technical and managerial language in LIS in the sense that they are basically how-to books, constantly referring to techniques, standards, principles, methods and rules."[6] Ours is a tradition, in Christine Pawley's words, "that uses managerial language as a matter of course and that pays almost exclusive attention to technical and administrative issues…we restrict ourselves to an instrumental, means-end range of concerns and language."[7] Concomitantly, "major areas of practice conduct a great deal of research that is pragmatic," write Gloria Leckie and John Buschman, "but highly uncritical."[8] Indeed, the vast majority of the intellectual output in our field, whether through presentations or writing, takes the form of positivist social science research, reflective case studies, standards, best practices, how-to guides and "cookbooks," and the like—work, in other words, that might be described as drawing on tangible, on-the-ground realities as subject matter and moving beyond questions to providing tangible, actionable answers.

The hegemony of such forms of intellectual output is shaped, at least in part, by the enshrinement of practicality demands in submission

---

6. Jack Anderson, "Information Criticism: Where is It?," *Progressive Librarian* no. 25 (Summer 2005): 16, http://www.progressivelibrariansguild.org/PL_Jnl/pdf/PL25_summer2005.pdf.

7. Christine Pawley, "Information Literacy: A Contradictory Coupling," *Library Quarterly* 73, no. 4 (2003): 443-44, doi:10.1086/603440.

8. Gloria Leckie and John Buschman, "Introduction: The Necessity for Theoretically Informed Critique in Library and Information Science," in *Critical Theory for Library and Information Science: Exploring the Social from Across the Disciplines*, ed. Gloria E. Leckie, Lisa M. Given, and John E. Buschman (Santa Barbara, CA: Libraries Unlimited, 2010), xii.

guidelines governing publication and presentation opportunities. A well-known journal of academic librarianship indicates in its submission guidelines that "above all, librarianship is a practiced discipline" and that the scholarship they are seeking to publish

- must be needed—in demand in individual institutions or broadly required elsewhere by other libraries—having intrinsic value and utility;
- must be used locally, and likely elsewhere, as an illustration of the value to the field of librarianship; and
- in short, must not be trivial.[9]

Another journal requires that all articles include a section called "Implications for Practice," in which authors articulate how the conclusions of their work "will impact practice."[10] Another journal still—one known to be open to critical theory—indicates an interest in "well written articles that have actionable solutions."[11] Similar examples abound from calls for conference presentations: presenters are encouraged, in the words of one call, to prepare "hands-on lessons and demonstrations (and/or practical takeaways)" so that participants can, in the words of another, "take home practical ideas/solutions."[12] In advising new professionals on how to develop a conference presentation, a 2011 primer-style article published in a fairly well-known Canadian journal of librarianship

---

9. "*portal: Libraries and the Academy*: Author Guidelines," *The Johns Hopkins University Press*, last accessed February 17, 2016, https://www.press.jhu.edu/journals/portal_libraries_and_the_academy/guidelines.html, para. 5–7.

10. "Submissions," *Journal of Librarianship and Scholarly Communication*, last accessed June 13, 2016, http://jlsc-pub.org/about/submissions, para. 39.

11. "Submission Guidelines," *In the Library with the Lead Pipe*, last accessed June 13, 2016, http://www.inthelibrarywiththeleadpipe.org/submission-guidelines, para. 5.

12. Jennifer Schwartz to ILI-L: The Information Literacy Instruction Discussion List, January 7, 2015, Call for Proposals: 14th Annual Information Literacy Summit — Deadline January 16th, 2015, http://lists.ala.org/sympa/arc/ili-l/2015-01/msg00015.html, para. 11; Brick and Click Symposium to ILI-L: The Information Literacy Instruction Discussion List, August 28, 2014, http://lists.ala.org/sympa/arc/ili-l/2014-08/msg00143.html, para. 4.

emphasizes that "conference committees are looking for sessions which contribute reliable or new knowledge in a particular area of librarianship and that *deliver concrete benefits to participants.*"[13] "Remember," the article continues, "organizations are investing a substantial amount of time and money in order to send delegates to a conference, and they will care about results. Your session should deliver education that leads to improved performance, improved services and improved results."[14]

The tacit narrative in such imperatives to practicality is that work understood to be theoretical—work concerned chiefly with foundational critique, work that does not focus on delivering measurable improvement in performance—is of little relevance to the library world. What is at work, in other words, is the well-worn binary dynamic of definition through exclusion: inasmuch as they are regulated by the reproduction of a popular conception of practice that is accorded exalted status, the physical and epistemological spaces we shape for intellectual work in LIS are also governed by the reproduction of popular conceptions of theory that is accorded devalued status. Such devaluations are at times quite explicit. The widely cited Association of College & Research Libraries (ACRL) report *The Value of Academic Libraries*, for example, takes time to acknowledge critique that situate the assessment movement within a broader context of the ever-intensifying corporatization of higher education:

> Those critical of the assessment movement say there is danger in adopting marketplace standards, rather than intellectual standards. Some point to the homogenizing effects of speedy and clear-cut measures of performance, believing it need not be inevitable that higher education adopt these corporate values and practices....Some go so far as to advocate that academics not even engage in designing appropriate performance

---

13. Tanya Lisa Rogoschewsky, "Developing a Conference Presentation: A Primer for New Library Professionals," *Partnership: The Canadian Journal of Library and Information Practice and Research* 6, no. 2, (2011): para. 5, emphasis mine.

14. Ibid., para. 22.

indicators, as that would be tacit endorsement, but instead use their ana-lytical and rhetorical skills to create counter narratives to these calls for accountability or call for alternative approaches to demonstrating value.[15]

While nominally "appreciated," however, such critiques are promptly dismissed as "impractical, given the realities we face today in our institutions."[16] Another recent conference call for proposals invites participants to "get real" with practical ideas for information literacy: "Librarians as scholars are bombarded with theory; however, it's time to get real! This year's conference is devoted to the mechanics of delivering effective and engaging information literacy instruction. Attendees will leave the conference with practical ideas to invigorate their programs."[17] Tacitly or explicitly, then, our hegemonic discourses of practicality are animated by a rough set of dualisms: practice is action, solutions, efficiency, the everyday, concreteness, reality; and theory is thinking, reflection, abstraction, problems, inapplicability, inefficiency. The theo-retical is definitionally disconnected from reality.[18]

Narratives of clarity often occupy a central place in our field's exaltation of practicality, with clear language serving as a marker of a professional commitment to efficient, solutions-oriented intellectual

---

15. Association of College and Research Libraries, *The Value of Academic Libraries: A Comprehensive Research Review and Report*, researched by Megan Oak-leaf (Chicago: Association of College and Libraries, 2010), http://www.ala.org/acrl/sites/ala.org.acrl/files/content/issues/value/val_report.pdf, 6-7.

16. Ibid., 7.

17. Janice A. Wilson to ILI-L: The Information Literacy Instruction Discus-sion List, January 15, 2015, Call for Session and Poster Proposals, http://lists.ala.org/sympa/arc/ili-l/2015-01/msg00079.html, para. 1.

18. Though there has certainly been an intensification of engagement with critical theory over the past few years, including conferences (for example, the Canadian Association of Professional Academic Librarians annual con-ference, the Gender and Sexuality in Information Studies Colloquium, the Critical Librarianship and Pedagogy Symposium, and the Social Justice and Libraries conference), journals (for example, *Journal of Radical Librarianship*, *Journal of Critical Library and Information Studies*, and *In the Library with the Lead Pipe*), regular #critlib and #radlibchat conversations on Twitter, and numer-ous individual publications. These have joined a handful of more established sites of critical engagement, such as *Progressive Librarian* and works published by Library Juice Press and Litwin Books.

work. Indeed, professional and scholarly communications venues regularly insist that all submissions be written in what's understood to be straightforward, everyday language. "Write in a style that is clear and concise," says one major journal.[19] Another indicates that submissions should use a "straightforward writing style, and [avoid] over-long or complex sentence structures."[20] Another journal still explicitly "values clarity and utility over formality,"[21] while yet another major journal advises that "clear, simple prose enhances the presentation of ideas and opinions."[22]

In this vein, imperatives to practicality more broadly might be said to rest on an appeal to shared frameworks—on shared languages, understandings, and conceptual foundations that in turn enable collective action. The exaltation of practicality certainly connects at some level, then, to our explicitly articulated commitment to access,[23] to a politics of inclusion that seeks to structure resources, services, and spaces so as to eliminate barriers for users. Imperatives to clarity thus pose a challenge to those normative rhetorics of intelligence that exalt institutionally-validated scholarly languages and that position linguistic complexity that conforms to such institutional norms as a sign of intellectual depth achieved by formal disciplinary specialization. To the extent that formal educational institutions might be understood to be oriented towards extending the interests of ruling classes, such challenges to the outward

---

19. "Guide for Authors [for *The Journal of Academic Librarianship*]," Elsevier, last accessed June 15, 2016, https://www.elsevier.com/journals/the-journal-of-academic-librarianship/0099-1333/guide-for-authors, para. 3.

20. "New Review of Academic Librarianship — Instructions for Authors," *Taylor & Francis Online*, last accessed June 15, 2016, http://www.tandfonline.com/action/authorSubmission?journalCode=racl20&page=instructions, para. 10.

21. "Article Guidelines," *Code4Lib Journal*, last accessed June 15, 2016, http://journal.code4lib.org/article-guidelines, para. 4.

22. "Instructions for Authors," *College & Research Libraries*, last accessed June 15, 2016, http://crl.acrl.org/site/misc/author.xhtml, para. 5.

23. "Core Values of Librarianship," *American Library Association*, June 29, 2004, www.ala.org/advocacy/intfreedom/statementspols/corevalues, para. 6.

complexity of institutionally-validated languages might themselves be understood to represent a challenge to domination.[24]

There are questions to be asked, however, about the pitfalls of practicality as a hegemonic value in professional politics of inclusion. From another angle, the mobilization of shared conceptual frameworks that underpins our professional imperative to practicality can be read as a foundational reliance on existing ways of knowing, on received languages, on common sense—and common sense is a deceptive ally in challenges to domination. It is difficult to undertake the slow, messy practice of unpacking foundational assumptions—and their material implication in the dispossessive violence of existing social, political, and economic arrangements—where one's environment is governed by expectations of efficiency, directness, brevity, speed. *Don't waste your time with questions for which there are no answers, with work that does not lead to improved productivity and measurable successes. Research is about results.* Research without the drag of disrupted conceptual bases. Research without friction.

It is difficult to explore the violence of status quo discourse where one's environment is governed by the exaltation of clarity, plain language, the everyday, the utilitarian transmission of content, the acceptance of normalcy as a basis for proceeding. Faced with such an imperative, what is one to do where the language that *is* plain and everyday is the language of domination—the language of daily epithets, to be sure, but also the language of occupations and settlements, of catastrophic pipeline projects, of a structure of profit inevitably dependent on labor exploitation?

On Whiteness, Normativity, and Language

Critical writing on race teaches us to be suspicious of claims to common sense; the denaturalization of racial difference and power—its

---

24. The narrative of postsecondary institutions as elite spaces of exclusion that maintain themselves as such through dense jargon has indeed been a recurring, if contested, feature of online critical librarianship discussions under the #critlib hashtag.

semiotics, its materiality—indeed remains a central feature of critical race analysis. Analysts of whiteness, accordingly, have long recognized that whiteness's dominative power resides, in crucial part, in its occupation of a space of unmarked normativity, its production as a "mythical norm," to use Audre Lorde's phrase:[25] white supremacy persists through an ability to assert its historical peculiarity and precarity as timeless, universal, and neutral.[26] Whiteness is, in this sense, standard(ized), unqualified, that which goes without saying, that which maintains structures of white supremacist domination through their presentation as self-evident, as simple, as plain. Such racializing work is relational, of course: the perpetuation of the standardized dominative space of white supremacy is itself impossible without the regulation of its internal orders and external borders through the violent (if contextually differential) delegitimization, exploitation, or elimination of non-white Others. The paving of racially unmarked roads (where it is undertaken, at least) is paid for by revenues generated by the fees and fines of a justice system that has, historically, itself been animated by narratives of black and brown criminality.[27] Perhaps more palatably, the racially unmarked "revitalized" downtown core—available to everyone, ostensibly—is made economically viable in part by the downward pressure on the real wages of a service sector supported disproportionately by the labor of black and brown working people, even as the "beautification" of such areas is also achieved through the eviction of inconvenient disorderly residents by police forces and, quite literally, by landlords. The official belonging of the racially unmarked (if tenuously multicultural) citizenry in a physically and economically secure Western nation-state is consolidated through

---

25. Audre Lorde, "Age, Race, Class, and Sex: Women Redefining Difference," in *Sister Outsider: Essays and Speeches* (Trumansburg, NY: Crossing Press, 1984), 116.

26. For a more detailed, critical overview of this central tenet of critical whiteness studies, see Steve Garner, *Whiteness: An Introduction* (New York: Routledge, 2007), 34–47.

27. Kriston Capps, "Why City Fees Keep Rising Instead of Taxes," *CityLab*, June 4, 2015, http://www.citylab.com/work/2015/06/why-city-fees-keep-rising-instead-of-taxes/394844/.

the perpetuation of non-white external threats—*border jumpers, terrorists* (homegrown or otherwise), an amalgam of brown enmity threatening to subvert *our way of life* (even as their mythologization does wonders for the security industrial complex and its contributions to gross domestic product). The production of massive resource extraction projects as drivers of racially unmarked economic growth turns on the ongoing colonization of indigenous land, on the elimination of indigenous sovereignty, of indigenous community, of indigenous life.[28] Whiteness, in other words, hinges on the physical and conceptual policing of the bounds of shared spaces of normalcy as they are inscribed territorially and corporeally both as a means of establishing its own ordered universality and as a means of (implicitly or explicitly) defining and delegitimizing the constitutive outside of disorderly particularity, of subjectivities marked as non-white and unintelligible in white supremacist social orders. In this respect, whiteness operates, in Homi Bhabha's words, as an "unsettled, disturbed form of authority" that must overcome "incommensurable differences"—namely, "the histories of trauma and terror that it must perpetrate and from which it must protect itself; the amnesia it imposes on itself; the violence it inflicts in the process of becoming a transparent and transcendent force of authority."[29]

Whiteness is thus the production of shared norms underwritten by physical and epistemological violence, a violence invisibilized as a

---

28. Paula Butler, *Colonial Extractions: Race and Canadian Mining in Contemporary Africa* (Toronto: University of Toronto Press, 2015); Marina Jimenez, "Mayan Families' Quest for Justice Against Canadian Mining Company HudBay," *Toronto Star*, June 20, 2016, https://www.thestar.com/news/world/2016/06/20/the-mayans-vs-the-mine.html; Winona LaDuke, *All Our Relations: Native Struggles for Land and Life* (Cambridge: South End Press; Minneapolis: Honor the Earth, 1999); Jody Porter, "Mercury Levels Still Rising Near Grassy Narrows First Nation, Report Says," *CBC News*, June 15, 2015, http://www.cbc.ca/news/canada/thunder-bay/mercury-levels-still-rising-near-grassy-narrows-first-nation-report-says-1.3109261; Leah Temper, "Unistoten Camp v. the PTP Pipeline, BC, Canada," *Environmental Justice Atlas*, May 9, 2016, https://ejatlas.org/conflict/unistoten-camp-v-the-ptp-pipeline-bc-canada; Traci Brynne Voyles, *Wastelanding Legacies of Uranium Mining in Navajo Country* (Minneapolis: University of Minnesota Press, 2015).

29. Homi K. Bhabha, "The White Stuff," *Artforum International* 36, no. 9 (May 1998): 21.

condition of governance (even as it may well be hypervisible to those whose dignity it assaults). "Here we touch on a well-rehearsed theme" Steve Garner observes: "the capacity of power to make itself appear natural and unquestionable."[30] Critiques of plain language advocacy emphasize that such self-concealing strategies of regimes of domination depend on the ongoing (re)production of linguistic self-evidence, on the curation of conceptual common sense. The exaltation of clarity is rooted in an assumption, then, that shared conceptual frameworks are politically neutral, an assumption that the languages and concepts that we've come to understand as ordinary and unremarkable are not part of the machinery of domination themselves. Judith Butler reminds us that "neither grammar nor style are politically neutral. Learning the rules that govern intelligible speech is an inculcation into normalized language…there is nothing radical about common sense."[31] Likewise, Trinh Minh-ha observes that "clarity is a means of subjection, a quality both of official, taught language and of correct writing, two old mates of power: together they flow, together they flower, vertically, to impose an order."[32] Domination would seem to wish to convince us that the expressed languages of its complex systems are actually not complex at all and are not about domination at all—that they are simple and common sensical and ordinary.

---

30. Garner, *Whiteness*, 35.

31. Judith Butler, *Gender Trouble*, 2nd ed. (New York: Routledge, 1999), xviii.

32. Trinh T. Minh-ha, *Woman, Native, Other: Writing Postcoloniality and Feminism* (Bloomington: Indiana University Press, 1989): 16–17. For additional critiques of clarity imperatives, see Christina Albrecht-Crane, "*Whoa*—Theory and Bad Writing," *Journal of Advanced Composition* 23, no. 4 (2003): 857–68, http://www.jaconlinejournal.com/archives/vol23.4/crane-whoa.pdf; Ian Barnard, "The Ruse of Clarity," *College Composition and Communication* 61, no. 3 (2010): 434–51; Henry Giroux, "Public Intellectuals, the Politics of Clarity, and the Crisis of Language," *State of Nature: An Online Journal of Radical Ideas* (April 2010), http://www.stateofnature.org/?p=5795; Patti Lather, "Troubling Clarity: The Politics of Accessible Language," *Harvard Educational Review* 66, no. 3 (1996): 525–45, doi:10.17763/haer.66.3.6qxv1p081102560g; and Donaldo Macedo,"Iintroduction," in *Pedagogy of the Oppressed*, by Paulo Freire, 30th anniversary ed. (New York: Continuum, 2005), 11–27.

The elimination, expulsion, and exploitation of languages cast as unintelligible and disorderly have long featured centrally as varied strategies in the maintenance of white supremacist orders. The elimination of indigenous languages and other forms of expression has consistently represented a key strategy in the genocide undertaken as a part of settler colonialism's violent erasure of disorderly elements in claims to the rightful ownership and ordering of *terrae nullius*. The overt profiling—and ejection—of travelers from flights in Anglo-Western territories for speaking or writing (what is presumed to be) Arabic is now a regular occurrence, steeped as it is in the same fear of unintelligible dark threats that makes investment in defense industry stocks a financially sound practice.[33] Music executives craft mainstream hip-hop for consumption

---

33. Patrick Condon, "Passengers May Be Sued in Imams' Removal," *Washington Post*, March 30, 2007, http://www.washingtonpost.com/wp-dyn/content/article/2007/03/30/AR2007033001266_pf.html; Lauren Gambino, "Southwest Airlines Criticized after Incidents Involving Middle Eastern Passengers," *The Guardian*, November 21, 2015, https://www.theguardian.com/us-news/2015/nov/21/southwest-airlines-muslim-middle-eastern-passengers; Christopher Leake and Andrew Chapman, "Mutiny as Passengers Refuse to Fly Until Asians are Removed," *Mail Online*, August 20, 2006, http://www.dailymail.co.uk/news/article-401419/Mutiny-passengers-refuse-fly-Asians-removed.html; Lizzie Parrie, "Security Scare Delays EasyJet Flight for Two Hours Because Schoolboy Saw Another Passenger 'Writing in Arabic,'" *The Daily Mail*, February 19, 2014, http://www.dailymail.co.uk/news/article-2563194/Security-scare-delays-EasyJet-flight-two-hours-schoolboy-saw-passenger-writing-Arabic.html; "Plane Brought Back to Gate at Logan Airport," *FOX25*, April 16, 2013, http://www.fox25boston.com/news/plane-brought-back-to-gate-at-logan-airport/140056602; Catherine Rampell, "Ivy League Economist Ethnically Profiled, Interrogated for Doing Math on American Airlines Flight," *Washington Post*, May 7, 2016, https://www.washingtonpost.com/news/rampage/wp/2016/05/07/ivy-league-economist-interrogated-for-doing-math-on-american-airlines-flight; Rachael Revesz, "Muslim Couple Kicked Off Delta Flight for 'Sweating', Saying 'Allah' and Texting," *The Independent*, August 4, 2016, http://www.independent.co.uk/news/world/americas/muslim-couple-kicked-off-delta-air-lines-plane-flight-attendant-uncomfortable-allah-sweating-texting-a7172591.html; Rachael Revesz, "Southwest Airlines Kicks Muslim Off a Plane for Saying 'Inshallah', Meaning 'God Willing' in Arabic," *The Independent*, October 6, 2016, http://www.independent.co.uk/news/world/americas/muslim-passenger-southwest-airlines-khairuldeen-makhzoom-arabic-phone-uncle-baghdad-cair-statement-a7347311.html; Liam Stack, "College Student is Removed from Flight After Speaking Arabic on Plane," *New York Times*, April 17, 2016, http://www.nytimes.com/2016/04/17/us/student-speaking-arabic-removed-southwest-airlines-plane.html.

by audiences largely made up of suburban white men—culture made saleable by its deployment of stock narratives of unruly blackness, including language presented as dangerous in its disorderliness. At the same time, plain language so often operates to sustain white supremacy through rhetorical sanitization. In a defense of Paulo Freire's *Pedagogy of the Oppressed* against critics who have dismissed the text as inaccessible, Donaldo Macedo points to the violence masked and extended through the integration into everyday parlance of seemingly unremarkable (and certainly racially unmarked) phrases like "collateral damage," "educational mortality," and "disadvantaged."[34] Similarly, the centuries-long, constantly shapeshifting violence of capitalism enacted disproportionately through the dispossession of non-white communities is absented through seemingly common-sense phrases like "tough economic climate" and "the real world." In the same newscasts and polite water-cooler conversations, protest of endemic state violence against black and brown communities is "civil unrest" and genocide is "racial conflict." Macedo notes that the sanitizing violence of such ostensibly commonplace phrases brings to mind Gayatri Spivak's comment that "plain prose cheats."[35] He follows this observation with an insightful amendment to Spivak's phrase: "I would go a step further and say, 'The call for plain prose not only cheats, it also bleaches.'"[36] Macedo's appended imagery here is notable in its duality: a chemical erasure through corrosion, as well as an enactment of whiteness.

On *Diverse Librarians*: The Deceptive Practicality of Common-Sense Phrasing

"Diversity" is the plain language of racial difference and power in the library world, the shared conceptual framework to which we turn

---

34. Macedo, "Introduction," 22.

35. Sara Danius, Stefan Jonsson, and Gayatri Chakravorty Spivak, "An Interview with Gayatri Chakravorty Spivak," *boundary* 2, 20, no. 2 (1993): 33, quoted in Macedo, "Introduction," 23.

36. Macedo, "Introduction," 23.

in attempts to make sense of the whiteness of the field. The figure of
the diverse librarian appears frequently within such discourse. One text
documents strategies for recruiting and retaining *ethnically/culturally diverse
librarians*.[37] Another notes that we often make the mistake of looking
to *diverse librarians* to meet the needs of *diverse users*,[38] while another still
reports that there are more *diverse librarians* these days, but also more
positions.[39] An institute for research in librarianship expresses emphatic
interest in applications from *ethnically diverse librarians*.[40] An American
Library Association program seeks to recruit *ethnically diverse* students
from high schools and colleges to careers in librarianship,[41] while a
pre-doctoral program at a library school seeks to remedy the shortage
of *culturally diverse* information professionals with advanced post-MLIS
training.[42] A ProQuest executive sees tremendous value in contributing
to the support of the group of *culturally diverse librarians* in the Spectrum
Scholarship Program.[43] The diverse librarian (in all its variations) is a
plain language figure, then, its denotative value—"diverse" for "non-
white"—generally accepted.

---

37. Charlene Maxey-Harris and Toni Anaya, *SPEC Kit 319: Diversity Plans and
Programs* (Washington, DC: Association of Research Libraries, 2010), http://
publications.arl.org/Diversity-Plans-and-Programs-SPEC-Kit-319, 11.

38. Ricardo Andrade and Alexandra Rivera, "Developing a Diversity-Competent Workforce: The UA Libraries' Experience," *Journal of Library Administration*
51, no. 7/8 (October 2011): 694, doi:10.1080/01930826.2011.60127

39. Marcia Smith-Woodard, "The Importance of Achieving Diversity in
Libraries," *Indiana Libraries* 31, no 1 (2012): 52, https://journals.iupui.edu/
index.php/IndianaLibraries/article/viewFile/2067/1946.

40. "Grant Proposal," *IRDL: Institute for Research Design in Librarianship*, last
accessed June 22, 2016, http://irdlonline.org/project-info/grant-proposal,
para. 24

41. "Discovering Librarianship: The Future is Overdue," *American Library
Association*, last accessed June 22, 2016, http://www.ala.org/offices/diversity/
imls.

42. "About," *Praxis*, last accessed June 22, 2016, http://polaris.gseis.ucla.
edu/cchu/praxis/about.htm.

43. "ProQuest Broadens Commitment to Spectrum Scholarship Program,"
ProQuest, June 25, 2014, http://www.proquest.com/about/news/2014/Pro-
Quest-Broadens-Commitment-to-Spectrum-Scholarship-Program.html.

At some level, such a corporate euphemism is about as laughable as the "ethnic food" aisle in the supermarket, providing a near perfect example of whiteness's operation as the racially unmarked norm. There's food—you know, regular food—and there's ethnic food—you know, the kind that comes from some specific place and culture, the kind for special occasions. There are librarians—you know, regular librarians—and there are diverse librarians—you know, the librarians who have diversity or, if we are to dispense with the euphemism, the librarians who have race. "There is no more powerful position than that of being 'just' human," writes Richard Dyer: "The claim to power is the claim to speak for the commonality of humanity. Raced people can't do that—they can only speak for their race. But non-raced people can, for they do not represent the interests of a race."[44] There is more at issue here than euphemism, then: the figure of the diverse librarian exemplifies a more fundamental displacement of the problem of racial power and difference onto non-white subjects in the library world. White subjects—library staff, user communities, and so on—are just human; but we culturally diverse subjects can only speak to the color line, to our special interests, as it were. Perhaps this is why we are always playing the race card, as the tired rhetoric of derailment would have it. *Such conversations are worth having sometimes, to be sure—but it's not the sort of thing one wishes to talk about all the time, is it?* Such dynamics of displacement, then, clearly serve white supremacy's interest in circumscribing the extent of racism, in casting racist violence as a series of localized, isolated incidents rather than a structure that governs virtually all aspects of our lives.

In its inscription of these familiar racial dynamics, the recurrence of the figure of the *diverse librarian* might well be said to represent a microaggression, a matter of interpersonal impropriety. But there is more at stake than personal anti-racist etiquette, than commitment and the conscious push to purge a phrase from professional discourse in place of a more direct naming of racial power and difference as matters that concern us all. Part of the challenge of developing spaces

---

44. Richard Dyer, *White* (New York: Routledge, 1997), 2.

for the confrontation of white supremacy from within the field lies in interrogating the more fundamental methodological assumptions and practices that underpin our discourse of racial power and difference. From this perspective, our field's reinscription of narratives of white normativity through the uncritical circulation of the seemingly innocuous trope of the *diverse librarian* is emblematic of our perpetuation of white supremacy through the uncritical circulation of the concept of diversity more broadly—its logics more than its lexicon—as our received anti-racist wisdom and timeless truth. As I have argued elsewhere, the ongoing hegemony of the diversity paradigm has been marked by a failure to interrogate the concept's fundamental premises as a racial politics—the premise that to be included is to have agency (as if racial inclusion, incorporation, cooptation have not long figured centrally into white supremacist formations[45]); the premise that heterogeneity is justice (as if multiracial spaces have not long been a feature of empire); the premise that racial difference is a discrete, ahistorical phenomenon that can easily be captured through demographic surveys and studies of racialized information behavior (as if our racialization is not an ongoing, always-already context-specific practice inevitably intertwined with white supremacy and its contestation); the premise that the reform of individual professionals and organizations towards cultural competence (or, if one prefers, anti-racist civility) and our organizations and profession towards demographic alignment with the nation is the only conceivable—or indeed ought to be our chief—goal in challenging white supremacy from within the field. Where left unsettled, such premises corrode the possibility of deeper interrogation of the structural character and complex, geo-historically varied operations of white supremacy as well as the ways in which we in the library world work to perpetuate it: racism is reduced to a standardized set of transgressive "race relations,"

---

45. Jodi Melamed, *Represent and Destroy: Rationalizing Violence in the New Racial Capitalism* (Minneapolis: University of Minnesota Press, 2011); Sunera Thobani, *Exalted Subjects: Studies in the Making of Race and Nation in Canada* (Toronto: University of Toronto Press, 2007); Patrick Wolfe, *Traces of History: Elementary Structures of Race* (New York: Verso, 2016).

to the maintenance of homogeneity by the exclusion of discrete (inter-changeable) racial subjects from library spaces through the misguided attitudes and behaviors of individuals and/or organizations.[46]

Diversity bleaches, in other words—as plain prose and received logic. Like the figure of the *diverse librarian*, diversity discourse more broadly extends contemporary white supremacist dynamics (if inadvertently) while obscuring the complex operations of such dynamics behind generally accepted and innocuous (or even progressive) conceptual frameworks. Diversity is the common-sense language of racial liberalism, the ready-to-wear, one-size-fits-all analytic available for the presumably simple, utilitarian task of transmitting anti-racism in the library world. *Stop talking, start doing.*[47]

The aim here, to paraphrase a point made by Ian Barnard,[48] is not to celebrate rhetorical density and abstraction as politically preferable, nor is it to demonize work understood to be clear and practical as auto-matically simplistic or regressive. It is rather to ask after the work that practicality does as an imperative. It is to invite consideration of the ways in which the hegemonic insistence on practicality, including calls to clarity, that animates our field serves to extend white supremacy by implicitly valorizing shared professional languages, assumptions, and methodologies as neutral vehicles for intellectual work that transcend white supremacy; and by tacitly reducing racism to an uncomplicated and timeless phenomenon that can be addressed pragmatically with no depar-ture from such frameworks. It is to suggest that we explore the tangled mess of aggressively self-effacing whiteness obscured by naturalized liberal languages of diversity and inclusion in our field. As a discourse, practicality renders theoretical engagement with such white supremacist

---

46. For a detailed elaboration of this argument, see David James Hudson, "On 'Diversity' as Anti-Racism in Library and Information Studies: A Cri-tique," *Journal of Critical Library and Information Studies* 1, no. 1 (2017).

47. This phrase is used as the title of Gregory L. Reese and Ernestine L. Hawkins's *Stop Talking, Start Doing! Attracting People of Color to the Library Profes-sion* (Chicago: American Library Association, 1999), a guide to the practice of recruitment and retention in the library world.

48. Barnard, "Ruse," 435.

complexities—and the critical departure from existing languages and foundational assumptions this requires—conceptually impermissible. As white supremacy's constantly shifting rhetorical figures and structures of material subordination extend beyond the bounds of the field, our anti-racist critique necessarily involves questions without immediate answers and therefore brings with it some level of unintelligibility. From the standpoint of hegemonic practicality imperatives, such non-sense is inaccessible, politically exclusivist in its assumed digression from the immediate aim of efficient access for a wide audience. From an anti-racist perspective, the rhetorical acrobatics are familiar: the minoritized work of challenging white domination is charged with divisiveness in its attempts to disrupt the aggressively enforced common-sense structures of racial power.

Challenging White Supremacy from within Library Land: Theory, Practice, Translation

The whiteness of practicality, then, is not a face-value formulation of neatly bounded, *a priori* elements—a color, a group, a demographic and a value, a predictable tendency, a cultural essence. It is not an assertion that "whites" are "more practical," nor a claim that all work popularly understood to be practical is solely and automatically complicit in upholding structures of white supremacist violence. Likewise, the whiteness of practicality is not an anti-racist acquittal of what is popularly understood to be theory: work that interrogates fundamental assumptions in abstract ways, that departs from received wisdom, that rejects plain prose may nevertheless perpetuate white domination, even if the questions posed by such work target structures of racial power and difference presumed to be hegemonic. "Simply arguing that theory displaces and breaks with structure and the establishment is to risk romanticizing an already territorialized space," writes Christa Albrecht-Crane: "An uncritical celebration and fetishization of theory's capacity to only disrupt risks placing us in an idealized, complacent, and complicit relationship with the state we so adamantly critique."[49] What we name theory may indeed "support the illusion that those institutionally situated as being 'in the know' truly are, and 'those who cannot understand' are 'legitimately excluded from understanding.'"[50]

Rather, the whiteness of practicality suggests that the exalted status of the practical in our field reproduces conditions through which whiteness sustains its dominative power by foreclosing spaces of critique in which the complex, ever-shifting dynamics of white supremacy might be confronted. If we are to deepen challenges to the whiteness of the field, then, it is crucial that we actively push back against imperatives to be practical, that we foster spaces that recognize the value of what is so often dismissed as "theory"—the value of questions without answers, of critique without actionable solutions, as well as the value of wrestling with difficult language and the value of the historical and political contexts, limits, and complicities of languages understood to be plain. And the recognition of such value must be more than notional: in this form, anti-racist work is a practice of shaping calls for submissions, tables of contents, and conference programs, of pushing back against the encroachment of dominant professional expectations in editorial practice and committee meetings, of advocacy to ensure that the work of critiquing normative structures of power without providing concrete, pragmatic service or policy recommendations is explicitly welcomed.

But challenges to the whiteness of practicality also require active recognition that conventional forms of scholarly communication do not represent the extent of anti-racist critique as such. As this suggests, we would do well to unsettle our assumptions about what theory and practice look like, about whose lives and labor are involved in each. At stake, indeed, are more deeply embedded assumptions about the intellectual lives of subordinated communities: the construction of theory as an elite, academic activity removed from the concrete realities of the everyday—*Enough with the theory! Let's get real!*—assumes that

---

49. Albrecht-Crane, "*Whoa*," 868.
50. Lather, "Troubling," 528.

subordinated communities do not engage in critical analyses that raise questions without immediate solutions, that subordinated communities do not reframe the world in unfamiliar language that disrupts received wisdom. Such mappings of theory/practice dualisms onto structures of power—the theoretical critique of the elite versus the lived experience and practice of ordinary people—are themselves implicated in insidious colonial narratives that cast the colonizer as mind and intellect, as white rationality, and the colonized as body and intuition, as the dark masses who, whether romanticized or demonized, appear as having only their experience and intuition—and certainly no critical faculties—through which to make sense of the world.

We would do well, indeed, to unsettle our assumption that theory and practice represent discrete phenomena with separate lives whose only meeting point might be in no-less binarizing formulations of praxis that hinge on combinations of elements—action plus reflection, theory plus practice—presumed to be distinct. Absented by such an assumption is the reality that those activities traditionally thought of as theory—thinking, speaking, writing abstract critiques of the fundamental assumptions that shape our worlds—are materially situated practices. Somewhere a scholar is preparing a manuscript on the poetry of Lucille Clifton while his child happily plays under the watch of a childcare provider, the cost of whose labor is paid without worry but the cost of whose living is a source of ongoing anxiety. Somewhere a Frantz Fanon scholar is spending grant money on addressing the built-in obsolescence of their laptop, the rare earth in the guts of which have been plundered from the ground in the new scramble for Africa;[51] the toxic skeletal remains of which will be shipped away out of sight, out of mind, to be dismantled by dispossessed, non-white hands in sacrifice zones for digital capitalism.[52] Somewhere a theorist of settler colonial economic formations is

---

51. Pádraig Carmody, *The New Scramble for Africa* (Malden, MA: Polity Press, 2011).

52. Adam Minter, "The Burning Truth Behind an E-Waste Dump in Africa," *Smithsonian.com*, January 13, 2016, http://www.smithsonianmag.com/science-nature/burning-truth-behind-e-waste-dump-africa-180957597/?no-ist.

falling asleep on the train en route to a precarious adjunct gig an hour and a half from home, the text of the conference proposal in their lap blurring like the landscape outside, their eyelids heavy from last night's shift at the café at which the hourly pay is more or less equivalent to that which they receive for teaching. Somewhere a mid-career scholar is arriving on campus for office hours more relaxed than they have been in years, buoyed by a mixture of validation and excitement after having read an article on white supremacy in classrooms led by non-white faculty, text on page relaxing muscles, jaw, and gut, thinning the dense cloud of alienation in a department in which indelicate phrases like "playing the race card" and "all lives matter" are replaced with more professional ones—like "you may be overreacting" and "try to adopt a student-centered approach." Scholarship, no matter how abstract its subject matter, is always already a material practice, a lived experience with complex, far-reaching physical entanglements.

Further absented is the anti-racist theoretical work that lives outside the academy and indeed outside research and writing. In *Teaching to Transgress*, bell hooks offers a story about the critical thinking, reflection, and analysis that helped her to negotiate her childhood struggles within the patriarchal structures of her home: "When I was a child, I certainly did not describe the processes of thought and critique I engaged in as 'theorizing.' Yet…the possession of a term does not bring a process or practice into being; concurrently one may practice theorizing without ever knowing/possessing the term, just as we can live and act in feminist resistance without ever using the word 'feminism.'"[53] Challenging the whiteness of practicality—making space for messy critiques of white supremacy that eschew pragmatic solutions—requires recognition of the theoretical work enacted through storytelling circles, through artistic performances, through protests, through forms of expression that elude easy classification. At some Black Lives Matter protests in Canada in the fall of 2014, for example, organizers encouraged non-black allies to attend, but asked that they situate themselves at the edge of the protests

---

53. bell hooks, *Teaching to Transgress* (New York: Routledge, 1994), 61–62.

and refrain from speaking to the media; black voices were purposefully centered in occupation of space and airtime. While this was not particularly controversial amongst those in attendance and was only one among many organizational details of the protests whose purpose was to draw attention to the deep structures of state violence against black communities in Canada, the physical centering of blackness became a focus of corporate media coverage, prompting backlash marked by the customary liberal narratives of reverse racism and racial unity.[54] By staging a public action in this way, then, the organizers theorized space, voice, and anti-racist solidarity in terms that departed sharply from mainstream liberal racial politics, the anti-racist plain languages of inclusion and heterogeneity. We would do well to recognize, in other words, that theory is material, theory is action, theory is practice.

Ultimately, the imperative to be practical in our field hinges on a deep (if somewhat paradoxical) individualism. In spite of overtones of inclusivity, it treats critical work as self-contained, suggesting that truly ethical work in the library world requires each of us to come up with complete sets of questions and complete sets of answers, to individually balance what is understood to be theory with what is understood to be practice, to ensure that our language is always going to be intelligible to everyone. We in the library world ought to understand that this is neither possible nor desirable, as so much of what we do points to the fact that all work is both necessarily incomplete and necessarily interdependent—the citation, the bibliography and its community of complicated absences, the shelf with more than one item, the marginalia and corporeal micro-residues (visible and invisible) left on magazines pulled through circulation, the reference interaction in which knowledge reveals itself to be created between subjects rather than springing forth *ex nihilo* as the stuff of individual genius. But the individualist myth of exhaustiveness is pervasive, even if it is persistently exhausting. Such

---

54. "Canadian Pro-Ferguson Rally Organizers Ask 'Whites' to Stay in Background," *Globe and Mail*, November 25, 2014, http://www.theglobeandmail.com/news/national/canadian-pro-ferguson-rally-organizers-ask-whites-to-stay-in-background/article21781408.

tiresome individualism is, of course, profoundly entangled with white-ness, serving as an animating force in well-worn colonial narratives of race: the unhinged white loner as mass shooter, as contrasted with the terrorist motivated by collective cultural allegiance; the intrepid white explorer "discovering" the land through economic enterprise; the dark masses of migrants threatening to flood the white nation's border, con-tainable only through mass detention, expulsion, or assimilation; the dispossession of a black single mother read as black cultural pathology. More specifically, it aligns epistemologically with the individualism of liberal racial politics: racism as an attribute of individuals, anti-racism as self-work, the problem and solution collocated and self-contained.

Perhaps the unsettling of the whiteness of practicality, then, in part brings with it a move to accept the messy collectivity of challenges to structures of white supremacy from within our field. What if our racial politics included meaningful treatment of racial identity not as an individual attribute that remains static from cradle to grave, but as constantly and relationally reproduced and redefined through disposses-sion and resistance within structures of white supremacy in which we are all implicated (albeit differentially so)? What if we accepted that the complexities of contemporary white supremacist formations are such that no one of us could possibly account for all its violent acrobatics and shapeshifts—including those enacted by the library world—or possibly achieve complete, transcendent solutions? And what if we reminded ourselves that being in critical community as such requires trusting that we do not have to do everything ourselves (even if we do have to do something)? What if we recognized that our anti-racism thus requires work across different contexts, both within our field and beyond it, with the understanding that we might learn from critical analysis wherever it takes place and without the assumption of scholarly origins? Such interdependence and transcontextual movement are perhaps a reminder that critical work is always a practice of translation, always already a practice of adjusting how we speak, depending on the environment we are in and our negotiation of the limits of its plain prose—and what could be more practical than that?

Bibliography

"About." *Praxis*. Accessed June 22, 2016. http://polaris.gseis.ucla. edu/cchu/praxis/about.htm.

Albrecht-Crane, Christina. "Whoa—Theory and Bad Writing." *Journal of Advanced Composition* 23, no. 4 (2003): 857–68. http://www. jaconlinejournal.com/archives/vol23.4/crane-whoa.pdf.

Anderson, Jack. "Information Criticism: Where is It?" *Progressive Librarian* 25 (Summer 2005): 12–22. http://www.progres-sivelibrariansguild.org/PL_Jnl/pdf/PL25_summer2005.pdf.

Andrade, Ricardo, and Alexandra Rivera. "Developing a Diversity-Competent Workforce: The UA Libraries' Experience." *Journal of Library Administration* 51, no. 7/8 (October 2011): 692–727. doi:10.1080/01930826.2011.60127.

"Article Guidelines." *Code4Lib Journal*, accessed June 15, 2016. http:// journal.code4lib.org/article-guidelines.

Association of College and Research Libraries. *The Value of Academic Libraries: A Comprehensive Research Review and Report*. Re-searched by Megan Oakleaf. Chicago: Association of College and Libraries, 2010. http://www.ala.org/acrl/sites/ala.org. acrl/files/content/issues/value/val_report.pdf.

Barnard, Ian. "The Ruse of Clarity." *College Composition and Communica-tion* 61, no. 3 (2010): 434–51.

Bhabha, Homi K. "The White Stuff." *Artforum International* 36, no. 9 (May 1998): 21–22, 24.

Butler, Judith. *Gender Trouble*. 2nd ed. New York: Routledge, 1999.

Butler, Paula. *Colonial Extractions: Race and Canadian Mining in Contempo-rary Africa*. Toronto: University of Toronto Press, 2015.

"Canadian Pro-Ferguson Rally Organizers Ask 'Whites' to Stay in Background." *Globe and Mail*, November 25, 2014. http:// www.theglobeandmail.com/news/national/canadian-pro-

ferguson-rally-organizers-ask-whites-to-stay-in-background/
article21781408.

Capps, Kriston. "Why City Fees Keep Rising Instead of Taxes." *City-Lab*, June 4, 2015. http://www.citylab.com/work/2015/06/
why-city-fees-keep-rising-instead-of-taxes/394844/.

Carmody, Pádraig. *The New Scramble for Africa*. Malden, MA: Polity
Press, 2011.

Condon, Patrick. "Passengers May Be Sued in Imams' Removal."
Washington Post, March 30, 2007. http://www.washing-
tonpost.com/wp-dyn/content/article/2007/03/30/
AR2007033001266_pf.html.

"Core Values of Librarianship." *American Library Association*, June 29,
2004. www.ala.org/advocacy/intfreedom/statementspols/
corevalues.

Danius, Sara, Stefan Jonsson, and Gayatri Chakravorty Spivak. "An
Interview with Gayatri Chakravorty Spivak." *boundary 2* 20,
no. 2 (1993): 24–50.

"Discovering Librarianship: The Future is Overdue." *American Library
Association*, accessed June 22, 2016. http://www.ala.org/of-
fices/diversity/imls.

Dyer, Richard. *White*. New York: Routledge, 1997.

Forman, James. *The Making of Black Revolutionaries: A Personal Account*.
New York: Macmillan, 1972.

Gambino, Lauren. "Southwest Airlines Criticized after Incidents
Involving Middle Eastern Passengers." *The Guardian*, November 21, 2015. https://www.theguardian.com/us-news/2015/
nov/21/southwest-airlines-muslim-middle-eastern-passen-
gers.

Garner, Steve. *Whiteness: An Introduction*. New York: Routledge, 2007.

Gates, Bill, Nathan Myhrvold, and Peter Rinearson. *The Road Ahead*.
New York: Viking, 1995.

Giroux, Henry. "Public Intellectuals, the Politics of Clarity, and the Crisis of Language." *State of Nature: An Online Journal of Radical Ideas* (April 2010). http://www.stateofnature. org/?p=5795.

"Grant Proposal." *IRDL: Institute for Research Design in Librarianship.* Accessed June 22, 2016. http://irdlonline.org/project-info/ grant-proposal.

"Guide for Authors [for *The Journal of Academic Librarianship*]." *Elsevier*, accessed June 15, 2016. https://www.elsevier.com/ journals/the-journal-of-academic-librarianship/0099-1333/ guide-for-authors.

Hampton, Henry, and Steve Fayer. *Voices of Freedom: An Oral History of the Civil Rights Movement from the 1950s through the 1980s.* New York: Bantam Books, 1991.

hooks, bell. *Teaching to Transgress.* New York: Routledge, 1994.

Hudson, David James. "On 'Diversity' as Anti-Racism in Library and Information Studies: A Critique." *Journal of Critical Library and Information Studies* 1, no. 1 (2017).

"Instructions for Authors." *College & Research Libraries.* Accessed June 15, 2016. http://crl.acrl.org/site/misc/author.xhtml.

Jimenez, Marina. "Mayan Families' Quest for Justice against Cana- dian Mining Company HudBay." *Toronto Star*, June 20, 2016. https://www.thestar.com/news/world/2016/06/20/the- mayans-vs-the-mine.html.

LaDuke, Winona. *All Our Relations: Native Struggles for Land and Life.* Cambridge, MA: South End Press; Minneapolis: Honor the Earth, 1999.

Lather, Patti. "Troubling Clarity: The Politics of Accessible Lan- guage." *Harvard Educational Review* 66, no. 3 (1996): 525–45. doi:10.17763/haer.66.3.6qxv1p081102560g.

Leake, Christopher, and Andrew Chapman, "Mutiny as Passengers Refuse to Fly until Asians are Removed," *Mail Online*, August 20, 2006. http://www.dailymail.co.uk/news/article-401419/Mutiny-passengers-refuse-fly-Asians-removed.html.

Leckie, Gloria, and John Buschman. "Introduction: The Necessity for Theoretically Informed Critique in Library and Information Science." In *Critical Theory for Library and Information Science: Exploring the Social from Across the Disciplines*, edited by Gloria E. Leckie, Lisa M. Given, and John E. Buschman, vii–xxii. Santa Barbara, CA: Libraries Unlimited, 2010.

Lorde, Audre. "Age, Race, Class, and Sex: Women Redefining Difference." In *Sister Outsider: Essays and Speeches*, 114–23. Trumansburg, NY: Crossing Press, 1984.

Macedo, Donaldo. "Introduction." In *Pedagogy of the Oppressed*, by Paulo Freire, 11-27. 30th Anniversary ed. New York: Continuum, 2005.

Maxey-Harris, Charlene, and Toni Anaya. *SPEC Kit 319: Diversity Plans and Programs*. Washington, DC: Association of Research Libraries, 2010. http://publications.arl.org/Diversity-Plans-and-Programs-SPEC-Kit-319.

Melamed, Jodi. *Represent and Destroy: Rationalizing Violence in the New Racial Capitalis*m. Minneapolis, MN: University of Minnesota Press, 2011.

Minter, Adam. "The Burning Truth behind an E-Waste Dump in Africa." *Smithsonian.com*, January 13, 2016. http://www.smithsonianmag.com/science-nature/burning-truth-behind-e-waste-dump-africa-180957597/?no-ist.

Neal, James G., and Anja Smit. "Charleston Conference 2016 Thursday Plenary." Ustream video, 1:45:00. Posted by "Charleston Conference," November 3, 2016. http://www.ustream.tv/recorded/92596956.

"New Review of Academic Librarianship—Instructions for Authors." *Taylor & Francis Online*, accessed June 15, 2016 http://www.tandfonline.com/action/authorSubmission?journalCode=racl20&page=instructions.

Parrie, Lizzie. "Security Scare Delays EasyJet Flight for Two Hours because Schoolboy Saw Another Passenger 'Writing in Arabic.'" *Daily Mail*, February 19, 2014. http://www.dailymail.co.uk/news/article-2563194/Security-scare-delays-EasyJet-flight-two-hours-schoolboy-saw-passenger-writing-Arabic.html.

Pawley, Christine. "Information Literacy: A Contradictory Coupling." *Library Quarterly* 73, No. 4 (2003): 422–52. doi:10.1086/603440.

Pearson, Hugh. *The Shadow of the Panther: Huey Newton and the Price of Black Power in America.* Cambridge, MA: Perseus Publishing, 1994.

"Plane Brought Back to Gate at Logan Airport." *FOX25*, April 16, 2013. http://www.fox25boston.com/news/plane-brought-back-to-gate-at-logan-airport/140056602.

"*portal: Libraries and the Academy*: Author Guidelines." *The Johns Hopkins University Press*, accessed February 17, 2016. https://www.press.jhu.edu/journals/portal_libraries_and_the_academy/guidelines.html.

Porter, Jody. "Mercury Levels Still Rising Near Grassy Narrows First Nation, Report Says." *CBC News*, June 15, 2015. http://www.cbc.ca/news/canada/thunder-bay/mercury-levels-still-rising-near-grassy-narrows-first-nation-report-says-1.3109261.

"ProQuest Broadens Commitment to Spectrum Scholarship Program." *ProQuest*, June 25, 2014. http://www.proquest.com/about/news/2014/ProQuest-Broadens-Commitment-to-Spectrum-Scholarship-Program.html.

Rampell, Catherine. "Ivy League Economist Ethnically Profiled, Interrogated for Doing Math on American Airlines Flight."

Washington Post, May 7, 2016. https://www.washingtonpost.com/news/rampage/wp/2016/05/07/ivy-league-economist-interrogated-for-doing-math-on-american-airlines-flight.

Ranganathan, S. R. *The Five Laws of Library Science*. 1931. Reprint, New Delhi: Ess Ess Publications, 2006. http://hdl.handle.net/2027/mdp.39015073883822.

Reese, Gregory L., and Ernestine L. Hawkins. *Stop Talking, Start Doing! Attracting People of Color to the Library Profession*. Chicago: American Library Association, 1999.

Revesz, Rachael. "Muslim Couple Kicked Off Delta Flight for 'Sweating', Saying 'Allah' and Texting." *The Independent*, August 4, 2016. http://www.independent.co.uk/news/world/americas/muslim-couple-kicked-off-delta-air-lines-plane-flight-attendant-uncomfortable-allah-sweating-texting-a7172591.html.

———. "Southwest Airlines Kicks Muslim Off a Plane for Saying 'Inshallah', Meaning 'God Willing' in Arabic." *The Independent*, October 6, 2016. http://www.independent.co.uk/news/world/americas/muslim-passenger-southwest-airlines-khairuldeen-makhzoom-arabic-phone-uncle-baghdad-cair-statement-a7347311.html.

Rogoschewsky, Tanya Lisa. "Developing a Conference Presentation: A Primer for New Library Professionals." *Partnership: The Canadian Journal of Library and Information Practice and Research* 6, no. 2, (2011). https://journal.lib.uoguelph.ca/index.php/perj/article/view/1573/2284.

The Simpsons, season 7, episode no. 8. First broadcast November 19, 1995 on Fox. Directed by David Silverman and written by Richard Appel and Dan Greaney.

Smith-Woodard, Marcia. "The Importance of Achieving Diversity in Libraries." *Indiana Libraries* 31, no 1 (2012): 50–53. https://journals.iupui.edu/index.php/IndianaLibraries/article/viewFile/2067/1946.

Stack, Liam. "College Student is Removed from Flight after Speaking Arabic on Plane." *New York Times*, April 17, 2016. http://www.nytimes.com/2016/04/17/us/student-speaking-arabic-removed-southwest-airlines-plane.html.

"Submission Guidelines." *In the Library with the Lead Pipe*. Accessed February 17, 2016. http://www.inthelibrarywiththeleadpipe.org/submission-guidelines.

"Submissions." *Journal of Librarianship and Scholarly Communication.* Accessed June 13, 2016. http://jlsc-pub.org/about/submissions.

Temper, Leah. "Unistoten Camp v. the PTP Pipeline, BC, Canada." *Environmental Justice Atlas*, May 9, 2016. https://ejatlas.org/conflict/unistoten-camp-v-the-ptp-pipeline-bc-canada.

Thobani, Sunera. *Exalted Subjects: Studies in the Making of Race and Nation in Canada.* Toronto: University of Toronto Press, 2007.

Trinh, Minh-ha T. *Woman, Native, Other: Writing Postcoloniality and Feminism.* Bloomington, IN: Indiana University Press, 1989.

Voyles, Traci Brynne. *Wastelanding Legacies of Uranium Mining in Navajo Country.* Minneapolis, MN: University of Minnesota Press, 2015.

Wolfe, Patrick. *Traces of History: Elementary Structures of Race.* New York: Verso, 2016.

PART THREE:

FISSURES:

IMAGINING NEW CARTOGRAPHIES

Chapter 10

MAPPING TOPOGRAPHIES FROM THE CLASSROOM: ADDRESSING WHITENESS IN THE LIS CURRICULUM

Nicole A. Cooke, Katrina Spencer, Jennifer Margolis Jacobs, Cass Mabbott, Chloe Collins, and Rebekah M. Loyd

> First, whiteness is a location of structural advantage, of race privilege. Second, it is a "standpoint," a place from which white people look at [themselves], at others, and at society. Third, "whiteness" refers to a set of cultural practices that are usually unmarked and unnamed.
> –Ruth Frankenberg, *White Women, Race Matters*

Whiteness is multifaceted and complicated, as are many definitions and concepts related to race, power, privilege, and oppression. And whiteness is no less complicated in the context of library and information science (LIS), a field that is notoriously and historically comprised of white women,[1] yet consistently serves populations and communities that are "increasingly pluralistic and intersectional."[2] Lorna Peterson, Isabel Espinal, Jody Nyasha Warner, Christine Pawley, Todd Honma, and

---

1. U.S. Department of Labor, Bureau of Labor Statistics, Current Population Survey, 2015, Table 11, "Employed persons by detailed occupation, sex, race, and Hispanic or Latino ethnicity," http://www.bls.gov/cps/cpsaat11.pdf. The Bureau of Labor Statistics stated that in 2014, the librarian workforce was approximately 86 percent non-Hispanic white, and 84.8 percent female.

2. Michael W. Apple, *Educating the "Right" Way: Markets, Standards, God, and Inequality* (New York: Routledge, 2006), 61-62.

other LIS educators and scholars have lamented that there is a dearth of
acknowledgement and implementation when it comes to race, racism,
and related topics, not only in the literature but in the field at large and
in the LIS classroom.[3] These laments are echoed in more recent addi-
tions to the literature,[4] but the complexity and impact of whiteness in
LIS remains acute. This dearth of awareness and understanding greatly
influences the education and preparation of effective and empathetic
information professionals who are charged with serving and interacting
with diverse community members and stakeholders.

How do library school educators attempt to take on the challenge of
discussing and educating future information professionals about these
potentially uncomfortable, but vitally important, concepts? Monica
Foderingham-Brown states, "all library school students should be able,
through library school curriculums, to learn how an ethnic group's history, language, culture, race and socioeconomic conditions influence their

---

3. Lorna Peterson, "Multiculturalism: Affirmative or Negative Action?"
Library Journal 120, no. 12 (1995): 30-31; Lorna Peterson, "Alternative Perspectives in Library and Information Science: Issues of Race," *Journal
of Education for Library and Information Science* 37, no. 2 (1996): 163-74, doi:
10.2307/40324271; Lorna Peterson, "The Definition of Diversity: Two
views. A More Specific Definition," *Journal of Library Administration* 27, no. 1-2
(1999): 17-26, doi: 10.1300/J111v27n01_03; Isabel Espinal, "A New Vocabulary for Inclusive Librarianship," in *The Power of Language/El Poder de la Palabra:
Selected Papers from the Second REFORMA National Conference*, ed. Lillian Castillo-Speed (Englewood, CO: Libraries Unlimited, 2001), 131-49; Jody Nyasha
Warner, "Moving Beyond Whiteness in North American Academic Libraries," *Libri* 51, no. 3 (2001): 167-72, doi: 10.1515/LIBR.2001.167; Christine
Pawley, "Unequal Legacies: Race and Multiculturalism in the LIS Curriculum," *Library Quarterly* 76, no. 2 (2006): 149-68, doi: 10.1086/506955; Todd
Honma, "Trippin' Over the Color Line: The Invisibility of Race in Library
and Information Studies," *InterActions: UCLA Journal of Education and Information Studies* 1, no. 2 (2005): 1-26, http://escholarship.org/uc/item/4nj0w1mp.

4. Freeda Brook, Dave Ellenwood, and Althea Eannace Lazzaro, "In Pur-
suit of Antiracist Social Justice: Denaturalizing Whiteness in the Academic
Library," *Library Trends* 64, no. 2 (2015): 246-84, doi: 10.1353/lib.2015.0048;
Angela Galvan, "Soliciting Performance, Hiding Bias: Whiteness and
Librarianship," *In the Library with the Lead Pipe* (June 2015), http://www.
inthelibrarywiththeleadpipe.org/2015/soliciting-performance-hiding-bias-
whiteness-and-librarianship/; April Hathcock, "White Librarianship in
Blackface: Diversity Initiatives in LIS," *In the Library with the Lead Pipe* (Octo-
ber 2015), http://www.inthelibrarywiththeleadpipe.org/2015/lis-diversity/.

information needs."[5] Vanessa Morris concurs stating that "because the profession is basically white and female, it behooves library schools to ensure that students are taught competencies that create librarians that are culturally aware of their own social and cultural privilege as well as aware of the social and cultural realities of the underprivileged."[6] Part of this learning and understanding needs to include conversations about whiteness, its inherent role in racism, power, privilege, and oppression, and how all of these things manifest in libraries and information organizations. I [first author Nicole A. Cooke] have the goal to actually implement the suggestions made by Foderingham-Brown, Morris, and others, and ensure that students have opportunities to examine their culture and privilege in a formal classroom setting, as well as learn about the disadvantages experienced by others. This is a difficult task, and this difficulty is one of the reasons this call to action appears cyclically in the literature. LIS curricula should provide opportunities for concentrated learning experiences (i.e., a dedicated class on diversity or social justice), but it is also crucial to work towards infusing an entire curriculum with these opportunities and sensibilities.

I have the luxury and privilege to teach a suite of courses related to diversity and social justice, one of which is entitled *Race, Gender, and Sexuality in the Information Professions* (RGS). The majority of my students are aspiring librarians; they come from various backgrounds and have differing thoughts about the impact they would like to make on the profession. They also enter my classroom with varying levels of knowledge and understanding about whiteness and other issues of race. To learn about these concepts and then explicitly attempt to apply

---

5. Monica Foderingham-Brown, "Education for Multicultural Librarianship: The State of the Art and Recommendations for the Future," *Acquisitions Librarian* 5, no. 9-10 (1993), 143, doi: 10.1300/J101v05n09_13.

6. Vanessa Irvin Morris, "A Seat at the Table: Seeking Culturally Competent Pedagogy in Librarian Education" (presentation, Association of Library and Information Educators Conference, Seattle, Washington, January 2007) 10-11, https://www.academia.edu/13724910/A_Seat_At_the_Table_Seeking_Culturally_Competent_Pedagogy_in_Librarian_Education.

them to LIS can be a challenging task, but I always invite students to
(1) help me co-create the learning experience, (2) take risks with me in
the classroom, and (3) embrace the idea of being uncomfortable. The
resulting journey can be intense, but is typically very rewarding. These
young information professionals may work in different types of libraries and in different capacities but they are all committed to recognizing
their own intersectionality and working with diverse communities in an
empathetic and humble manner. This reckoning of intersectionalities
includes checking their points of privilege and recognizing and working
against whiteness and its manifestations in the profession.

My classes, particularly the RGS course, are designed to encourage critical discussion and examination of challenging topics, and they
require students to participate in hands-on learning whenever possible.
I am committed to educating LIS students in a new way—my teaching
approach focuses on the development of empathy and cultural competence in students. The development, and subsequent maintenance,
of empathy and cultural competence requires intense self-reflection,
which is key—self-reflection opens minds and hearts in a way that allows
people to recognize whiteness and lose their defensiveness. Whiteness,
racism, privilege, and marginalization are hard, complicated, and emotional topics, and we can't combat them if we allow feelings of guilt,
inadequacy, anger, embarrassment, and helplessness to define our actions
(or lack thereof). Cultural competence and empathy permit us to take
the next steps forward, which include working towards inclusiveness
and equity in our communities and in our organizations.

In this way, I feel I can prepare LIS students of *all* races and creeds
to be more effective, understanding, and enthusiastic in their service
to diverse populations. Students engage in structured critical reflection,
and read and watch an interdisciplinary collection of articles, chapters, and videos designed to allow them to draw connections between
librarianship, race, gender, and sexuality. In doing so, many conversations
revolve around whiteness and its influence on the library world. Whiteness and privilege influence how students interact with the world and
how the world interacts with them. These discussions are enlightening,

particularly for those previously unfamiliar with their own privilege and who are now seeing it through the eyes of others.

In this reflective chapter, former students (many of whom have taken the RGS course) will offer their reflections on this learning experience and discuss the ways in which they are newly aware of intersectionality and whiteness in their personal and professional lives, and how this awareness will enable them to incorporate anti-racist approaches into their critical practices as information professionals who will serve and teach diverse populations. Such classes are an example of how LIS programs can consider and incorporate critical pedagogy and discussions into the graduate classroom. Leading by example can have a profound and lasting impact on how aspiring librarians learn new content, as well as how to teach and interact with others.

Katrina Spencer

The RGS course was richer than I could have anticipated. This was apparent from the first day when our instructor chose to use Chimamanda Ngozi Adichie's "The Danger of a Single Story" to shape the conversations students would have about disrupting preconceived notions about groups of people and recognizing and respecting both multifaceted and fluid identities.[7] What made this course unique was having an instructor who was *not* white and male who systematically prioritized the study of works authored by people who were also neither white nor male. As an African American, the opportunity to see someone who looks like me leading a course and mindfully incorporating works by authors outside of the hegemony was novel, worthwhile, and frankly groundbreaking.

In the United States, whiteness is regularly interpreted as default, normal, invisible, and unquestioned. It is also frequently implicit code for male, Christian, heteronormative, cisgender, US born, and able-bodied.

---

7. Chimamanda Ngozi Adichie, "The Danger of a Single Story," filmed July 2009, TED video, 18:49, https://www.ted.com/talks/chimamanda_adichie_the_danger_of_a_single_story?language=en.

Moreover, to our dismay, it is functionally synonymous with dominant, central, essential, privileged, educated, and socioeconomically stable, as well as the morally sound, logical standard for the fiber and fabric of America. Dr. Cooke unceremoniously interrupted these flawed false-hoods, as all educators should, with a great deal of scrutiny, a talent for exposing historically cloaked narratives, and a challenge for her students to search out truth. She showed the ways in which LIS has room for color, difference, social justice, and creativity, too. For example, it is rare to encounter an LIS course that discusses how progressive cataloging has reshaped the classification of various sexualities. It is also, perhaps, unique for a curriculum to provide a crash course on sensitively navi-gating mental illness in the workplace. I have also only seen one other course introduce zines as cultural tools that can power feminist mes-sages. All of these topics were central content in our course. Clearly, Dr. Cooke's pedagogy is both potent and pioneering. Hopefully, it will provide a model for reshaping LIS curricula beyond our course and beyond our campus.

Our culminating assignment was equally stimulating. Students used the Story Corps app to interview one another and reflect on how we would intentionally incorporate what we learned into our LIS practice.[8] It was at this time that I understood the importance of keeping critical practice at the front of my mind when I enter the professional field, allowing it to inform how I shape collection development policies, design exhibits, and seek training to better serve diverse populations. The RGS course was a sensitizing experience. It is far too easy for people of all colors and creeds to fall into a pattern of replicating whiteness and reproducing the hegemony—the status quo—and to do things as they have always been done. This course shook me awake and reminded me that there can be another, more conscientious way, a less-trodden path with a new trajectory that is richer because of the diversity it acknowledges. This contagious confidence, boldness, and optimism are the treasures I take away as I move ever closer to establishing my career.

---

8. "StoryCorps.me "Record and Share the Stories that are All Around You," *StoryCorps,* last accessed December 30, 2016, https://storycorps.me/.

Jennifer Margolis Jacobs

I thought I was very culturally aware before taking the *Social Justice in the Information Professions* course. As a college instructor of pre-service and current teachers, I incorporated multiculturalism into my courses, and as a former special education teacher, modifying materials and accommodating students had always come naturally to me. Furthermore, my mother is a Holocaust survivor, and I grew up learning about how anti-Semitism had affected our family. While I recognized the discrimination I encountered as a Jew, I had not thought about privileges I had just by having white skin. *Social Justice* rocked me to the core, as it caused me to reevaluate my cultural competence, and in turn, my white privilege.

During the *Social Justice* course, Dr. Cooke delivered a presentation about the steps required to develop cultural competence. I was shocked and somewhat embarrassed when I realized I was only about halfway there. My eyes were further opened after reading Peggy McIntosh's important piece on the benefits of white privilege.[9] Additionally, I realized I had much to learn after listening to a guest speaker (a social justice educator and social worker) who challenged us with an activity about privilege. Students analyzed different areas in our lives, such as gender, educational background, socioeconomic standing, and religion to determine our levels of privilege. I recognized that while I have faced discrimination for being Jewish, I also enjoy many privileges that are not available to other marginalized groups. I decided I wanted to do the work it takes to develop cultural competence and use my newly-recognized white privilege to inform my practice. After finishing *Social Justice*, I enrolled in Dr. Cooke's *Information Services to Diverse Users* course. The course assignments helped me to move forward in this process. Over the semester, I created a Wikipedia site based on my synagogue's library and hoped it would bring more attention to culturally diverse organizations. An editor who did not believe a synagogue library was

---

9. Peggy McIntosh, "White Privilege: Unpacking the Invisible Knapsack. Excerpt from White Privilege and Male Privilege: A Personal Account of Coming to See Correspondences through Work in Women's Studies," *Wellesley College Center for Research on Women*, 1988, http://www.collegeart.org/pdf/diversity/white-privilege-and-male-privilege.pdf.

"notable" enough subsequently removed the site; his rash and uninformed decision further empowered me to move forward and made me want to advocate even more for diversity. Soon after, I was asked to teach a *Diversity in Education* course for a teacher education program at another institution and was able to pass on what I had learned to my own students.

Most recently, I had the opportunity to take RGS with Dr. Cooke. As it was a small course, we delved into deep discussions, many of which revolved around privilege and how every professional's intersectionality influences their practice. I learned that several of my classmates were scared to drive long distances due to fear of police brutality. Others had to decide if they could attend social events in towns that might not be safe, or with people who were not accepting of cultural and racial differences. Their personal experiences further reinforced what I have been learning about in Dr. Cooke's courses.

As a school librarian, I want all of my students to feel safe. I want to have a library that includes materials representative of their cultural backgrounds and the communities in which they live. I want to reach out to cultural institutions, public libraries, and local organizations to support youth via collaboration. Diversifying can also apply to electronic resources that include features such as translation, reading level, and images. Equally important, I want to incorporate different formats of technology so that twenty-first century skills are accessible to all of my students. I am committed to welcoming all learners and therefore will continue developing my cultural competence.

Cass Mabbott

The concept of privilege is not new to me. I am white, cisgender, heterosexual, able-bodied, and aware of being middle class. My mother, being differently-abled, made sure I was never passive about my privilege. She instilled in me the sense to keep my privilege in check and to make sure I contemplated these factors before interacting with others. As a children's librarian and manager at a public library, my work with diverse populations made me further examine my privilege in order to meet the information needs of my young patrons. Initially, Dr. Cooke's classes appealed to me because of my experiences with, and my research on, serving diverse youth populations in public libraries. I registered because I expected to be exposed to authors and research that is pertinent to my interests and to improve my cultural competencies. While all of this did occur, my classroom experience was unexpectedly profound. Although I have spent most of my public library career extolling social justice and trying to make a difference, I was never able to have the types of frank conversations that were facilitated by our readings, lectures, and group work. It is very unlikely that I would have been afforded the chance to interact with people at such an intimate level at the public library, either with patrons or with colleagues.

However, it was not until I heard a guest lecturer (a social justice educator and social worker) speak on the aspects of white privilege that I was hit by the enormity of what privilege truly means. I was angered that up to this point, my LIS education had not addressed this necessary aspect of cultural competency, let alone social justice. I was angered that for the length of my tenure, my public library struggled to create meaningful diversity initiatives for its patrons and employees.

As a future LIS professor who will educate aspiring librarians, I can make a difference. It will be my mission to infuse concepts of intersectionality and challenge white privilege in my curricula, and to expose how white privilege is embedded in all aspects of our society. I want my students to be ready to interact with their patrons, customers, and colleagues as inclusively as possible. My white students will learn to speak up and act as an *ally* to nonwhites, making sure not to speak *for* them. As a way of combating my own white privilege and the complacency that often comes with it, I will be a social justice advocate no matter what the topic is that I am teaching.

Chloe Collins

As a woman of color who attended a women's college where I majored in Gender Studies, I have an understanding of the fundamentals of anti-racist, feminist thought; however, learning and implementing cultural competence is a process, and there is always work to be done. The RGS class was a welcome refresher as well as an invaluable learning experience. Readings such as Todd Honma's "Trippin' over the Color Line: The Invisibility of Race in Library and Information Studies," excerpts from *Women of Color in Librarianship: An Oral History,* Hope Olson's "The Power to Name: Representation in Library Catalogs," and Suzanne Hildenbrand's "Library Feminism and Library Women's History: Activism and Scholarship, Equity and Culture," informed our discussions of how librarians and information professionals can incorporate anti-racist, feminist(s), and queer theory into our work in order to create spaces that are not complicit in perpetuating racist, misogynist, ableist, and classist attitudes and policies.[10]

In my daily life and as a library student who aspires to work in museums, I prioritize incorporating anti-racist and queer approaches into my critical practice because I believe that we cannot adequately serve all of our users and patrons if we alienate them. This means that our collections must reflect our broader society. Even if the patrons we are serving appear to be somewhat homogeneous, it is our job to provide access to a range of information. We cannot make assumptions about the needs of our patrons based solely on their appearances or our own perceptions, and representing a multitude of groups, viewpoints, and experiences is imperative to building strong collections.

---

10. Honma, "Trippin' Over the Color Line;" Kathleen de la Peña McCook, *Women of Color in Librarianship: An Oral History* (Chicago: American Library Association, 1998); Hope A. Olson, "The Power to Name: Representation in Library Catalogs," Signs 26, no. 3 (2001): 639-68; Suzanne Hildenbrand, "Library Feminism and Library Women's History: Activism and Scholarship, Equity and Culture," *Libraries & Culture* 35, no. 1 (2000): 51-65.

Acknowledging the humanity of all of my patrons is something that I hope is inherent in the way I work, but I also know that we are all unwittingly guilty of committing microaggressions at times. For me, practicing cultural competence is largely informed by recognizing nuance, which manifests as an understanding of intersectionality, a recognition of whiteness and privilege, and an awareness of how systems of oppression operate, as well as a willingness to unlearn harmful thoughts and behaviors. It is important for us to know and hear our communities so that we can understand and meet the needs of the people coming to our institutions. I hope to implement the aforementioned frameworks in the fields of special collections and museum studies by reinterpreting what is considered canon and incorporating the voices of marginalized peoples into exhibitions, collections, and programs.

Rebekah M. Loyd

After taking Dr. Cooke's RGS, I am more conscious of my whiteness and its influence on the world around me. I had been introduced to cultural competence during my undergraduate studies, but this course taught me to incorporate intersectionality into the framework of ethical social justice. We learned to consider the intersecting influence of race, gender, and sexuality on a person's experience and point of view so we could approach library patrons with greater empathy and fewer assumptions. Since the class took place in the summer of 2015 when racial profiling and the Black Lives Matter movement were regularly in the news, discussion frequently focused on race and the assumptions people may make about racial identity.[11] During group conversations, I heard about the microaggressions and unjust assumptions my classmates had faced, and our guest speakers showed us the everyday racism and sexism embedded in current library practice.

---

11. Patrisse Cullors, Opal Tometi, and Alicia Garza, *Black Lives Matter*, December 2016, http://blacklivesmatter.com.

Since becoming aware of the power and privilege that my whiteness gives me, I try to correct for that privilege as much as I am able. For instance, I watch myself for common microaggressions. All of us instinctually make assumptions based on someone's appearance, background, or other readily-apparent features, but we must be self-aware and critique our assumptions for ingrained prejudice. I also do my best to educate others about cultural competence and privilege. We are all shaped by this sexist, racist, ableist, transphobic world, and cultural competence is about identifying and thereby unlearning offensive assumptions. By seeing the pitfalls that these automatic assumptions create, we can have mutually respectful interactions, both in the library and in the wider world. For instance, I know that my position at the reference desk gives me power in an interaction with a patron, so I can take steps to dismantle that power structure and approach the patron on equal footing. As a library worker and representative of my institution, I try to make patrons feel comfortable and safe in their community library.

The goal of cultural competence is to help patrons feel like the library understands and meets their needs. In the library, cultural competence includes hiring a truly diverse staff that reflects the community, staffing the reference desk with librarians who are empathetic and want to meet patrons' needs, and developing foreign language collections. In my work as an archivist, it also means valuing voices and collections from marginalized groups. We are responsible for listening to our community and providing the services our patrons need and want, even in the face of diverse collections' relative scarcity, undervaluation, and potentially unusual format or genre, as well as the special knowledge that might be needed for their arrangement and description. In short, cultural competence is a lifelong learning process of valuing other people's voices and meeting their needs, and no library or archive will ever adequately serve all its patrons without culturally competent staff.

Final Thoughts

Considering and mapping whiteness in LIS classrooms is of the utmost importance, as is infusing discussions of racism and other demanding concepts and conversations into the LIS curriculum.[12] These are concrete ways to address the holistic development of empathetic, aware, and socially just information professionals. Having these conversations and activities early and often in LIS classrooms allows students to become more engaged and to reflect on themselves and others. Ideally, the result is substantive personal growth and a transformation of thinking. These students are better prepared and more successful in their roles as information professionals and will hopefully further infuse and change the profession from within. Innovating, problematizing, and disrupting current LIS standards and assumptions can be demanding and sometimes arduous, but ultimately it can be empowering for both LIS students and instructors as we attempt to change the landscape and narrative of our profession. I am grateful for my brave students, both online and on campus, who elect to take these courses and voluntarily engage in a critically reflective journey in order to become their best possible selves. It is hoped that future iterations of these courses will reach even more students and impact the curriculum in such a way that discussions of whiteness, racism, and privilege become normalized.

---

12. Nicole A. Cooke and Miriam E. Sweeney, *Teaching for Justice: Implementing Social Justice in the LIS Classroom* (Sacramento, CA: Library Juice Press, 2017); Nicole A. Cooke, "Counter-Storytelling in the LIS Curriculum," in *Perspectives on Libraries as Institutions of Human Rights and Social Justice*, eds. Ursula Gorham, Natalie Greene Taylor, and Paul T. Jaeger (Bingley, UK: Emerald Group Publishing Limited, 2016), 331-48; Nicole A. Cooke and Joseph P. Minarik, "Linking LIS Graduate Study and Social Justice Education: Preparing Students for Critically Conscious Practice," in *Progressive Community Action: Critical Theory and Social Justice in Library and Information Science*, eds. Bharat Mehra and Kevin Rioux (Sacramento, CA: Library Juice Press, 2016) 181-214; Nicole A. Cooke, Miriam E. Sweeney, and Safiya Umoja Noble, "Social Justice as Topic and Tool: An Attempt to Transform an LIS Curriculum and Culture," *Library Quarterly* 86, no. 1 (2016): 107-24, doi: 10.1086/684147.

Bibliography

Adichie, Chimamanda Ngozi. "The Danger of a Single Story." Filmed July 2009. TED video, 18:49. https://www.ted.com/talks/chimamanda_adichie_the_danger_of_a_single_story?language=en.

Apple, Michael W. *Educating the "Right" Way: Markets, Standards, God, and Inequality.* New York: Routledge, 2006.

Brook, Freeda, Dave Ellenwood, and Althea Eannace Lazzaro. "In Pursuit of Antiracist Social Justice: Denaturalizing Whiteness in the Academic Library." *Library Trends* 64, no. 2 (2015): 246-84. doi: 10.1353/lib.2015.0048.

Cooke, Nicole A. "Counter-Storytelling in the LIS Curriculum." In *Perspectives on Libraries as Institutions of Human Rights and Social Justice,* edited by Ursula Gorham, Natalie Greene Taylor, and Paul T. Jaeger, 331-48. Bingley, UK: Emerald Group Publishing Limited, 2016.

Cooke, Nicole A., and Joseph P. Minarik. "Linking LIS Graduate Study and Social Justice Education: Preparing Students for Critically Conscious Practice," In *Progressive Community Action: Critical Theory and Social Justice in Library and Information Science,* edited by Bharat Mehra and Kevin Rioux, 181-214. Sacramento, CA: Library Juice Press, 2016.

Cooke, Nicole A., and Miriam E. Sweeney. *Teaching for Justice: Implementing Social Justice in the LIS Classroom.* Sacramento, CA: Library Juice Press, 2017.

Cooke, Nicole A., Miriam E. Sweeney, and Safiya Umoja Noble. "Social Justice as Topic and Tool: An Attempt to Transform an LIS Curriculum and Culture." *Library Quarterly* 86, no. 1 (2016): 107-24. doi: 10.1086/684147.

Cullors, Patrisse, Opal Tometi, and Alicia Garza. *Black Lives Matter,* December 2016. http://blacklivesmatter.com.

Espinal, Isabel. "A New Vocabulary for Inclusive Librarianship." In *The Power of Language/El Poder De La Palabra: Selected Papers from the Second REFORMA National Conference*, edited by Lillian Castillo-Speed, 131-49. Englewood, CO: Libraries Unlimited, 2001.

Foderingham-Brown, Monica. "Education for Multicultural Librarianship: The State of the Art and Recommendations for the Future." *Acquisitions Librarian* 5, no. 9-10 (1993): 131-48. doi: 10.1300/J101v05n09_13.

Frankenberg, Ruth. *White Women, Race Matters*. Minneapolis, MN: University of Minnesota Press, 1993.

Galvan, Angela. "Soliciting Performance, Hiding Bias: Whiteness and Librarianship." *In the Library with the Lead Pipe* (June 2015). http://www.inthelibrarywiththeleadpipe.org/2015/soliciting-performance-hiding-bias-Whiteness-and-librarianship/.

Hathcock, April. "White Librarianship in Blackface: Diversity Initiatives in LIS." *In the Library with the Lead Pipe* (October 2015). http://www.inthelibrarywiththeleadpipe.org/2015/lis-diversity/.

Hildenbrand, Suzanne. "Library Feminism and Library Women's History: Activism and Scholarship, Equity and Culture." *Libraries & Culture* 35, no. 1 (2000): 51-65.

Honma, Todd. "Trippin' Over the Color Line: The Invisibility of Race in Library and Information Studies." *InterActions: UCLA Journal of Education and Information Studies* 1, no. 2 (2005): 1-26. http://escholarship.org/uc/item/4nj0w1mp.

McIntosh, Peggy. "White privilege: Unpacking the Invisible Knapsack. Excerpt from White Privilege and Male Privilege: A Personal Account of Coming to See Correspondences through Work in Women's Studies." *Wellesley College Center for Research on Women* (1988). http://www.collegeart.org/pdf/diversity/white-privilege-and-male-privilege.pdf.

Morris, Vanessa Irvin. "A Seat at the Table: Seeking Culturally Competent Pedagogy in Librarian Education." Presentation, Association of Library and Information Educators Conference, Seattle, Washington, January 2007. https://www.academia.edu/13724910/A_Seat_At_the_Table_Seeking_Culturally_Competent_Pedagogy_in_Librarian_Education.

Olson, Hope A. "The Power to Name: Representation in Library Catalogs." *Signs* 26, no. 3 (2001): 639-68.

Pawley, Christine. "Unequal Legacies: Race and Multiculturalism in the LIS Curriculum." *Library Quarterly* 76, no. 2 (2006): 149-68. doi: 10.1086/506955.

de la Peña McCook, Kathleen, ed. *Women of Color in Librarianship: An Oral History*. Chicago: American Library Association, 1998.

Peterson, Lorna. "Multiculturalism: Affirmative or Negative Action?" *Library Journal* 120, no. 12 (1995): 30.

———. "Alternative Perspectives in Library and Information Science: Issues of Race." *Journal of Education for Library and Information Science* 37, no. 2 (1996): 163-74. doi: 10.2307/40324271.

———. "The Definition of Diversity: Two Views. A More Specific Definition." *Journal of Library Administration* 27, no. 1-2 (1999): 17-26. doi: 10.1300/J111v27n01_03.

StoryCorps.me. "Record and Share the Stories that are All Around You." *StoryCorps*. Accessed December 20, 2016. https://storycorps.me/.

U.S. Department of Labor, Bureau of Labor Statistics, Current Population Survey, 2015, Table 11, "Employed persons by detailed occupation, sex, race, and Hispanic or Latino ethnicity." http://www.bls.gov/cps/cpsaat11.pdf.

Warner, Jody Nyasha. "Moving Beyond Whiteness in North American Academic Libraries." *Libri* 51, no. 3 (2001): 167-72. doi: 10.1515/LIBR.2001.167.

Chapter 11

MAPPING WHITENESS AT THE REFERENCE DESK

April M. Hathcock and Stephanie Sendaula

Whiteness in Librarianship

There are several factors that influence librarians of color, which either contribute to their success or lead to their attrition. These factors include whether or not they are the sole librarian of color on staff; their relationship to and with support staff, who often reflect a greater ethnic diversity than credentialed librarians; how much support they receive from administration or groups, such as a Board of Trustees; and whether or not they encounter racism from either patrons or staff. In exploring the social construct of race in librarianship, the concept of whiteness can also be evaluated:

> Most of the time white people don't notice or question our whiteness and the benefit it brings. Racism keeps people of color in the limelight and makes whiteness invisible. To change this, we must take whiteness itself, hold it up to the light and see that it is a color too. Whiteness is a concept, and ideology, which holds tremendous power over our lives and, in turn, over the lives of people of color.[1]

This power can take the form of an ingrained belief that only white people can hold positions of authority, and an assumption that people

---

1. Paul Kivel, *Uprooting Racism: How White People Can Work for Racial Justice* (Gabriola Island, BC, Canada: New Society Publishers, 2011), 10-11.

of color solely hold support positions. These ingrained beliefs can lead to uncomfortable interactions between white patrons and librarians of color, especially at the reference desk.

Perhaps one question that reference librarians of color, including the authors of this chapter, dread more than others is, "Can I speak to a real librarian?" This seven-word question suggests more than it lets on. It implies that these librarians aren't real. It questions whether they should exist at all. It suggests that their knowledge isn't recognized by those in positions of privilege. It states that many white patrons still prefer and expect to be assisted by someone who looks like them, still prefer and expect to see someone who looks like them behind a reference desk. It's a seemingly polite way of refusing help without directly saying, "I'm refusing your help." Other variations of this question include, "I'd like to speak to the person in charge," when that person may very well be the person of color behind the reference desk.

The history of public resistance towards African Americans and other people of color inside the library, as both patrons and employees, is rooted in the segregation laws of the early twentieth century. In *Part of Our Lives: A People's History of the American Public Library*, Wayne Wiegand explains that black-only branches were the norm in southern cities such as Houston, Texas, and Louisville, Kentucky, where segregation was the law.[2] Meanwhile, "[b]lacks also experienced obstacles to integrated library services in the north, where real estate redlining and complicit city governments all but guaranteed ghettoized neighborhoods in which branches, like Chicago's Hall and [New York City]'s 135th Street librar- ies, served almost entirely black populations."[3] Today, this unofficial redistricting continues to occur in black and brown communities, and is a contributing factor to why white communities may see few patrons of color in their local libraries, let alone librarians of color. This poses a challenge for a country in which minorities are becoming, and in some

---

2. Wayne A. Wiegand, *Part of Our Lives: A People's History of the American Public Library* (New York: Oxford University Press, 2015), 155.

3. Ibid., 174.

areas already are, the majority. This also creates a significant challenge for a profession that is actively seeking to recruit and retain people who are diverse in terms of race and ethnicity, as well as other forms of identity, including gender expression, sexual orientation, and disability.

Microaggressions on the Reference Desk

"[T]he idea of a black head librarian is still an oxymoron for some. After 22 years of serving as a library leader, I still get asked the question from white colleagues: 'Is this [head librarian] a new role for you?'"[4] With this statement, Theresa S. Byrd, contributor to *The 21st-Century Black Librarian in America: Issues and Challenges*, touches upon an underlying reality that presumably all people of color in service fields face: the assumption that their skills are elementary and may not compare to those of their white colleagues. The unspoken question is whether or not they obtained this position because of their race, especially if they are in a position of authority. This question of qualifications, ability, or competency has been posed to the authors in a number of variations, such as, "Is this your first job?" and "Have you worked in a library before?" These questions are particularly telling when new white colleagues are often simply asked, "Which library did you work at before?" The underlying assumption is that the white person is already a skilled information professional.

For the nonwhite librarian, coming up against whiteness on the reference desk is nothing new, and while endlessly frustrating, rarely comes as a surprise. In a profession in which eighty-eight percent of credentialed members are white,[5] it is not a wonder that librarians of color are faced

4. Theresa S. Byrd, "Managing the Academic Library: The Role of the Black Librarian Leader in Three Different Institutional Environments," in *The 21st-Century Black Librarian in America: Issues and Challenges,* ed. Andrew P. Jackson, Julius Jefferson, Jr., and Akilah Nosakhere (Lanham, MD: The Scarecrow Press, 2012), 108.

5. American Library Association, *Diversity Counts 2009-2010 Update,* last accessed April 25, 2016, http://www.ala.org/offices/diversity/diversitycounts/2009-2010update.

with bias and racialized judgments in the midst of their day-to-day work. Librarians of color are continually questioned about their qualifications, challenged regarding their authority and intellect, and forced to perform above and beyond the requirements of their white colleagues.[6] These often subtle verbal and behavioral slights based on race, or *racial microaggressions*,[7] occur frequently and their negative effects can add up.

One of the authors recalls a particularly trying shift doing legal reference, when a white student approached the desk and asked that she "go get the librarian for a question." Despite her best efforts to assure the student that she was in fact a librarian and fully capable of helping with his request, he insisted on waiting until she fetched her white colleague for assistance. Such an experience was humiliating for the author, an accomplished practitioner and teacher with two law degrees and full library credentials to her name. The idea that a black woman could be qualified to work as a librarian and respond adequately to a legal reference question was beyond the student's imagination.

Unfortunately, the barriers erected by whiteness on the reference desk, while incredibly isolating for the librarian of color, are in no way rare or unique experiences. Librarians of color are constantly beset by perceptions from patrons and even colleagues that they are paraprofessionals rather than credentialed librarians, that they do not fit the embodied expectation of a research librarian, or that they are not a "cultural fit" for the library institution and needs of the patrons. When one of the authors tried to change this perception by dressing above the dress code—from business casual to business professional—she found that white patrons still perceived her as support staff, while patrons of color,

---

6. Juleah Swanson, Isabel Gonzalez-Smith, and Azusa Tanaka, "Unpacking Identity: Racial, Ethnic, and Professional Identity and Academic Librarians of Color," in *The Librarian Stereotype: Deconstructing Perceptions and Presentations of Information Work*, ed. Nicole Pagowsky and Miriam Rigby (Chicago: Association of College and Research Libraries, 2014), 160-61.

7. Ibid., 160; Jaena Alabi, "Racial Microaggressions in Academic Libraries: Results of a Study of Minority and Non-Minority Librarians," *Journal of Academic Librarianship* 41, no. 1 (2014): 47-48, doi: 10.1016/j.acalib.2014.10.008.

on the other hand, rightly assumed she was a credentialed librarian or even a branch manager.

This assumption that nonwhite librarians are not in fact librarians is further exacerbated by the fact that, in many libraries, people of color are often in positions of support (e.g. library assistant) while white personnel hold credentialed librarian positions. According to the American Library Association's *Diversity Counts* report:

> Credentialed librarians are predominantly women, ages 45–54, and white. Non-credentialed librarians represent approximately 43% of those reporting for the industry "library" and have a slightly more balanced ethnic and racial distribution than do credentialed librarians. Sixteen-point-eight (16.8) percent of non-credentialed librarians selected non-white race/ethnicity categories, whereas only 11% of credentialed librarians did so.[8]

Additionally, being the sole librarian of color among support staff who have a balanced racial distribution can lead to isolation and insecurity—either the feeling that one doesn't belong or is "too good" for members of their own race.

While some of these perceptions are overtly racialized—such as when a patron approaches the reference desk and comments that a librarian of color doesn't "look like a librarian"—many of these biased perceptions can be coded in the seemingly neutral language of professional standards or organizational expectations. Nonwhite librarians doing reference work can often find themselves called out by supervisors for a lack of "approachability" or "niceness," standards that are steeped in racialized expectations and constructs.[9] This kind of race-based marginalization can take a physical, mental, and emotional toll on librarians

8. American Library Association, *Diversity Counts Report* (Chicago: Office for Research and Statistics, Office for Diversity, 2007), 5, http://www.ala.org/offices/sites/ala.org.offices/files/content/diversity/diversitycounts/diversitycounts_rev0.pdf.

9. Freeda Brook, Dave Ellenwood, and Althea Eannace Lazzaro, "In Pursuit of Antiracist Social Justice: Denaturalizing Whiteness in the Academic Library," *Library Trends* 64, no. 2 (2016): 270, doi: 10.1353/lib.2015.0048.

of color and can result in feelings of isolation and a sense of loss of professional identity.[10]

Moreover, these types of racial microaggressions can come not only from white patrons, but from patrons of color as well. Whiteness on the reference desk is a phenomenon that affects all library users, just as whiteness in general stands rooted in the whole of American society.[11] However, those moments of surprise when patrons of color discover that the person who looks like them behind the desk is in fact a credentialed librarian can be great moments of connection. On one such occasion, one of the authors found herself developing an almost instant rapport with a black female student in a predominantly white institution who had approached the desk for help. She approached the desk tentatively and said, "I'm not sure if you can help me, but I could really use some assistance." When the student realized that she could actually be assisted by a black librarian, her face lit up in surprise and joy. The student proceeded to sit in front of the reference desk to chat, not only about her research question but to receive advice on navigating school and hairstyling tips as well.

That student could have easily bypassed the reference desk because of an assumption, rooted in whiteness, that reference help can only be provided by, for, and to white people. Instead, she sought help with her academic question and was able to connect with a librarian who looked and lived like her. She was able to break through the barrier that whiteness imposes on the reference desk and made a connection that ended up being advantageous to her throughout the year. The author heard from that student on numerous occasions after this encounter and even met other students of color who had been referred to the author for research help. Indeed, research has shown that this kind

---

10. Swanson, Gonzalez-Smith, and Tanaka, "Unpacking Identity," 161.

11. Todd Honma, "Trippin' Over the Color Line: The Invisibility of Race in Library and Information Studies," *InterActions: UCLA Journal of Education and Information Studies* 1, no. 2 (2005): 3-9, https://escholarship.org/uc/item/4nj0w1mp.

of ethnic identity sharing can enhance librarian-student interactions.[12] Overall, interactions like this and comments from patrons, such as "I never realized this was a career available to us," demonstrate the problem librarianship has in both performing outreach to communities of color, as well as working effectively toward the recruitment and retention of credentialed librarians of color.

Moving Forward

What can librarians do to combat these frequent microaggressions and help dismantle whiteness at the reference desk? More particularly, what role can and should white librarians play in providing support to their colleagues of color? Fighting against racism and whiteness at the reference desk cannot and should not be the burden of librarians of color alone.

One specific strategy that white librarians can adopt is *bystander intervention*.[13] Bystander intervention requires that white librarians step up and get involved to interrupt microaggressions and other forms of racist action as they witness it happening. For many, this can be a very uncomfortable prospect, but this kind of unabashed action is essential to developing a truly diverse and inclusive workplace.

One of the authors distinctly remembers a particularly encouraging moment when a supervisor engaged in this kind of upfront intervention. A patron demanded to speak with a white supervisor because he did not believe that the author had the skills to help with his request. When the supervisor arrived, she immediately told the patron, "This librarian is very talented, and we are lucky to have her. If you need help, she is the one to help you. I will leave you in her very capable hands." The supervisor then left the reference desk and returned to her office. The patron grudgingly agreed to the author's help and was surprised

12. Swanson, Gonzalez-Smith, and Tanaka, "Unpacking Identity," 163-64.

13. Eric Anthony Grollman, "A Call for Bystander Intervention to End Racism," *Eric Anthony Grollman, Ph.D.* (blog), February 27, 2013, https://egrollman.com/2013/02/27/bystander-intervention-racism/.

to find that she was able to get him exactly what he was searching for. Most important to her, however, was the knowledge that her supervisor, by intervening without hesitation, "had her back."

Another effective strategy involves using frequent *micro-affirmations* to counteract the negative effect of microaggressions. Micro-affirmations are small verbal and behavioral acts of encouragement, support, and confidence, most often done publicly, to show that a marginalized colleague is a valued and integral part of the team.[14] By engaging in micro-affirmations around colleagues of color, especially in front of patrons and other colleagues, white librarians can counteract, and even help to curtail, future racial microaggressions. Simple acts like openly deferring to a librarian of color's expertise in a particular area or actively soliciting a colleague of color's opinion on an important matter can make a significant difference.

In addition to this kind of proactive anti-racist practice on the part of white librarians, the library profession as a whole can work to dismantle whiteness at the reference desk by increasing the diversity of the librarians working at the desk. This kind of increased diversity in the profession can only be achieved by focusing on the development of effective strategies for both recruitment and retention. Unfortunately, studies show that "despite recent diversity recruitment measures, some racial and ethnic minority groups, notably African Americans and Latinos, are actually seeing a decrease in the number of credentialed librarians under age 45."[15] Therefore, besides increasing representation in the workforce, measures must be taken to promote and advance diversity long term to ensure that librarians of color, as they enter the profession, have meaningful opportunities for professional growth and advancement. Without this dual focus on recruitment and retention, libraries will continue to serve as no more than revolving doors for the

14. Mary Rowe, "Micro-Affirmations & Micro-Inequities," *Journal of the International Ombudsman Association* 1, no. 1 (2008): 46, http://www.ombudsassociation.org/Resources/IOA-Publications/IOA-Journal/Journal-PDFs/Volume1Journal.aspx.

15. American Library Association, *Diversity Counts Report*, 11.

members of those communities that our organizations will increasingly depend upon for survival.

For the sake of the future of the profession and the important work we do as librarians, we must all work together to dismantle whiteness at the reference desk. Our patrons should be able to seek help from and work with librarians who reflect the diversity of their own communities. Our colleagues of color should be able to work in environments in which they are safe from victimization. The reference desk should not be marked by whiteness, but by diversity and inclusion for all—both in front of and behind the desk.

Bibliography

Alabi, Jaena. "Racial Microaggressions in Academic Libraries: Results of a Study of Minority and Non-Minority Librarians." *Journal of Academic Librarianship* 41, no. 1 (2014): 47-53. doi: 10.1016/j.acalib.2014.10.008.

American Library Association. *Diversity Counts 2009-2010 Update*. Accessed April 25, 2016. http://www.ala.org/offices/diversity/diversitycounts/2009-2010update.

———. *Diversity Counts Report*. Chicago: Office for Research and Statistics, Office for Diversity, 2007. http://www.ala.org/offices/sites/ala.org.offices/files/content/diversity/diversitycounts/diversitycounts_rev0.pdf.

Brook, Freeda, Dave Ellenwood, and Althea Eannace Lazzaro. "In Pursuit of Antiracist Social Justice: Denaturalizing Whiteness in the Academic Library." *Library Trends* 64, no. 2 (2016): 246-84. doi: 10.1353/lib.2015.0048.

Byrd, Theresa S. "Managing the Academic Library: The Role of the Black Librarian Leader in Three Different Institutional Environments." In *The 21st-Century Black Librarian in America: Issues and Challenges*, edited by Andrew P. Jackson, Julius Jefferson, Jr., and Akilah Nosakhere, 105-09. Lanham, MD: The Scarecrow Press, 2012.

Grollman, Eric Anthony. "A Call for Bystander Intervention to End Racism." *Eric Anthony Grollman, Ph.D.* (blog). February 27, 2013. https://egrollman.com/2013/02/27/bystander-intervention-racism/.

Honma, Todd. "Trippin' Over the Color Line: The Invisibility of Race in Library and Information Studies." *InterActions: UCLA Journal of Education and Information Studies* 1, no. 2 (2005): 1-26. https://escholarship.org/uc/item/4nj0w1mp.

Kivel, Paul. *Uprooting Racism: How White People Can Work for Racial Justice.* Gabriola Island, BC, Canada: New Society Publishers, 2011.

Rowe, Mary. "Micro-Affirmations & Micro-Inequities." *Journal of the International Ombudsman Association* 1, no. 1 (2008): 45-48. http://www.ombudsassociation.org/Resources/IOA-Publications/IOA-Journal/Journal-PDFs/Volume1Journal.aspx.

Swanson, Juleah, Isabel Gonzalez-Smith, and Azusa Tanaka. "Unpacking Identity: Racial, Ethnic, and Professional Identity and Academic Librarians of Color." In *The Librarian Stereotype: Deconstructing Perceptions and Presentations of Information Work,* edited by Nicole Pagowsky and Miriam Rigby, 149-73. Chicago: Association of College and Research Libraries, 2014.

Wiegand, Wayne A. *Part of Our Lives: A People's History of the American Public Library.* New York: Oxford University Press, 2015.

Chapter 12

MY LIBRARIANSHIP IS NOT FOR YOU

Jorge R. López-McKnight

> Communication, the key to social change, lies in the realm of voicing
> our needs in the political arena.
> –Gloria López McKnight, "Communication: The Key to Social Change"

I am a learner. I am an educator.

I have stood in an empty library classroom and closed my eyes; I
have sat in my home, eyes closed, and imagined *who* is with me in that
space. Here is what I see:

*Communities of Color—smiling, serious, powerful, curious, quiet, loud, and
beautiful, of course.*

The sides of my mouth rise up, pushing my cheeks to touch the
bottom of my eyelids that struggle under the weight of water, and what
becomes crucial is that I ask myself this question:

Who is my librarianship for?

Understand that my librarianship is not for White folks.

I am regularly engaged in the reflective process of my experiences in
learning spaces, and this essay is a counterstory to identify acts and states
of whiteness taking place in those spaces between and among learners.

whiteness

What are we talking about when we talk about whiteness? Let's start from this definition by the scholar Zeus Leonardo: "'Whiteness' is a racial discourse [and] it can be said that whiteness is also a racial perspective or a world-view. Furthermore, whiteness is supported by material practices and institutions. That said, white people are often the subjects of whiteness because it benefits and privileges them."[1] Leonardo argues that structures are in place to ensure whiteness is center and dominant, and he tells us that the evasiveness of the concept contributes to its widespread nature and changing meaning. Additionally, I think it is important to note that whiteness is not strictly enabled by White folks. Nonwhites can participate in and maintain the racial discourse and practices upheld by institutions. Also worth acknowledging is that some White folks are involved in critical processes, both internal and external, that are focused on confronting and deconstructing whiteness.

In discussing how whiteness is positioned, Woody Doane points out how whiteness was "constructed as a claim to superiority and privilege in contradistinction to a racial 'other'—groups defined as inferior in an emerging racialized social system."[2] Presently, White is good, normal, and correct; thus, a positive value is placed on what Communities of Color are not. Value given to whiteness maintains white supremacy—its power, control, and importance. This has had, and continues to have, serious structural and material implications. In "The Color of Supremacy: Beyond the Discourse Of 'White Privilege,'" Leonardo lists twenty-nine examples of policies and laws ranging from the one-drop rule and

---

1. Zeus Leonardo, "The Souls of White Folk: Critical Pedagogy, Whiteness Studies, and Globalization Discourse," *Race Ethnicity and Education* 5, no. 1 (2002): 31-32, doi: 10.1080/13613320120117180.

2. Woody Doane, "Rethinking Whiteness Studies," in *White Out: The Continuing Significance of Racism*, ed. Ashley W. Doane and Eduardo Bonilla-Silva (New York: Routledge, 2003), 10.

anti-immigration laws to the genocide of Indigenous peoples. These examples show the explicit connections between historical and current violence—be it physical, emotional, and/or psychological—that plays out on the bodies and minds of Communities of Color.[3]

Whiteness is socially constructed, but has grown roots in the institutions, laws, and policies that support and maintain its value. The lens of critical race theory (CRT) has the potential to change and disrupt that structural domination.

Critical Race Theory

CRT was introduced in the 1970s, having developed from critical legal studies (CLS). CRT's framework was derived from the work of Derrick Bell, Alan Freeman, Kimberlé Crenshaw, and Richard Delgado, who were frustrated with the slow gains in the post-civil rights era and with new indirect forms of racism that were taking shape during that time period.[4]

The CRT framework has several important elements:

1. Race is central: race is always present, always real, and always alive, that is to say, it "is ordinary, not aberrational."[5]

2. Interest convergence: racism continues because it supports the material interests of the dominant culture. Advances only occur when it is beneficial to elite Whites and the psychological interests of poor and working-class Whites.[6]

---

3. Zeus Leonardo, "The Color of Supremacy: Beyond the Discourse of 'White Privilege'," *Education Philosophy and Theory* 36, no. 2 (2004): 146-48, doi: 10.1111/j.1469-5812.2004.00057.x.

4. Richard Delgado and Jean Stefancic, *Critical Race Theory: An Introduction* (New York: New York University Press, 2001), 3-4.

5. Ibid., 7.

6. Ibid., 16-19.

3. Race is a social construction: race is not based on biology or genetics, but rather outcomes of societal thinking and relationships.[7]

4. Critique of liberalism: challenging the traditional framework that has been in place in reaction to America's racial struggles; focuses on "color-blindness" and objectivity.[8]

5. Storytelling: narratives that center the experiences, understandings, and knowledges of Peoples of Color and the injustices and violence they encounter.[9]

Though I have outlined some of the major themes of CRT, most relevant to this essay's exploration is the last element mentioned: storytelling. Counterstories, as a way to provide a particular perspective, have been employed in library literature on various issues, though not in abundance. For example, on recruitment, retention, and promotion, Shaundra Walker provides us with a vital, necessary counterstory related to those processes and experiences.[10] In "The Black Body at the Reference Desk: Critical Race Theory and Black Librarianship," Tracie D. Hall states, "the library is one of many stages in the larger racial theater," and calls for the "continued mining of critical race theory as a means of linking individual anecdotes of racialized, personal experiences to a larger structural and systemic phenomenology of racism."[11]

We need to see and we need to hear our counterstories. These narratives have complex effects—they center our histories, normalize our

---

7. Ibid., 7.

8. Ibid., 21.

9. Ibid., 38.

10. Shaundra Walker, "Critical Race Theory and the Recruitment, Retention and Promotion of a Librarian of Color: A Counterstory," in *Where Are All the Librarians of Color? The Experiences of People of Color in Academia*, ed. Rebecca Hankins and Miguel Juárez (Sacramento, CA: Library Juice Press, 2015), 148-56.

11. Tracie D. Hall, "The Black Body at the Reference Desk: Critical Race Theory and Black Librarianship," in *The 21st-Century Black Librarian in America: Issues and Challenges*, ed. Andrew P. Jackson, Julius C. Jefferson Jr., and Akilah S. Nosakhere (Lanham, MD: Scarecrow Press, 2012), 198-99.

experiences, and function as acts of resistance. Additionally, I believe our counterstories—the writing and telling of them—are a necessary step in our healing process(es) against racialized violence. They are efforts that contain the potential for transformation and learning.

For me, personally, they are actions of power and liberation. However painful, they must be confronted, if possible. Otherwise, as the author and educator Junot Díaz points out, "there is nothing like trying to run away from all that stuff to guarantee their supremacy."[12] So in joining our community, I humbly speak up.

Bloomington, Indiana

Indiana University Bloomington (IU) is a large, research-focused public university and a predominantly white institution (PWI).[13] Having attended a PWI as an undergraduate, I was familiar, though not comfortable, with surviving in those spaces that were dominated by whiteness. Although I still saw myself as a student at IU, my position as a graduate student added to my identities. IU is also the site where my educator identity began to take shape. As an instruction assistant, I was tasked with leading information literacy seminars, primarily for lower-level undergraduate students in English Composition or Public Speaking courses.

When I think back on that time, I remember the classes full of White students, the instability of my voice, and being on display. Most of all, I remember the yearning I had (and still do) to see, and hopefully connect with, Students of Color. I remember how whiteness played out in those teaching and learning spaces.

---

12. Junot Díaz, "Celebrated Writer Junot Diaz Talks Openly with the New Yorker's Hilton Als," YouTube video, 1:10:02, posted by "Strand Bookstore," April 15, 2013, https://www.youtube.com/watch?v=fLhpASeC9JI.

13. Predominantly White Institutions (PWI) are higher educational spaces where White students make up the majority, more than 50%, of the student body. M. Christopher Brown II and T. Elon Dancy II, "Predominately White Institutions" in *The Encyclopedia of African American Education*, ed. by Kofi Lomotey (Thousand Oaks, CA: Sage Publications, 2010), 524-26, doi: h 10.4135/9781412971966.n193.

Always aware of my existence as a Person of Color, my identities were amplified because I was the authority in the classroom, up front and center. In those days, before class started, I used to write my full name on the board. I didn't write my name just so that students would know it; I wrote it as an act of resistance. The names that many of those students see are never our names. I could see and feel the doubt in their eyes, and as expected, their disengagement in the educational process would follow.

My instruction, at least in the beginning of my time there, was lecture-based, and though I now tend to favor group work, I think it was important (then and still now) for those White students to have a Person of Color in a position of authority in the classroom. I think back to one of my first information literacy seminars—I was nervous and sweating. To relax myself and the class, I made a casual comment about the tank top a White male student was wearing. He took offense and under his breath expressed a threat of physical violence. The class went terribly, and what I remember most from that unfortunate experience was the power of whiteness—specifically, the advantages it afforded some individuals to behave in systems that centered their existence, especially when their power was threatened.

In my position there, we also gave library tours to prospective and/or incoming students and their parents or guardians. Most, if not all, were White. I would expend a lot of energy to put them at ease. I was quick to smile with a professional appearance, both my dress and grooming in line with dominant ideas of professionalism, or whiteness. I would say my first name without an accent. Still, their questions were coded: "You're a graduate student here?" "You're going to be a librarian?"

Tiffany, José R., Madelyn, Enrique, and Emilie, I will forever be indebted to your support and understanding. Without our love, I would not have been able to heal; without our silences, I would not have been able to speak.

Boulder, Colorado

The University of Colorado Boulder is another large, research-focused PWI and has a liberal and open reputation. Arriving there after IU, I was excited to continue my professional path in the library and was grateful to be employed. The focus of my efforts there were again primarily teaching and learning activities, including numerous hours on the reference desk, a heavy instruction load, and outreach and engagement with the academic community. I was so eager to be involved, to be included, to belong.

For many hours, my brown body would be at the reference desk, working with the young learners, answering their questions. I was highly (in)visible. I remember asking one of my coworkers how many People of Color had occupied those teaching and learning spaces, to which they responded one or two, maybe none. It was in the classrooms—those highly vulnerable open spaces of potential transformation—where I had to contend with whiteness most often. Students were amused by the way I would speak, possibly due to the casualness I have with language or my matter-of-fact delivery. How I phrased something in my instruction might elicit a chuckle, which I could understand, but never enjoyed or accepted. I often felt, and saw, a lack of effort and engagement from many of the White students.

Many of my interactions with the young learners in these teaching and learning spaces were nice. They seemed appreciative of my assistance and my intelligence. However, especially with some of the White male students, my capability was questioned.

In outreach activities with Whites, much like my experience at IU, the energy to engage people was burdensome. The smiling and dressing in a professional way—really the performance to put them at ease—was emotionally taxing, and their line of questions: "You're a librarian here?" "Where did you go to school?" seemed to oscillate between surprise and suspicion.

But it was there, in those spaces and on those stages, both at IU and CU Boulder, in and among those instances of violence, where I was able to fully grasp who my librarianship is for. To be clear it is not for White people. Those folks are not who I am educating. They are not who I am trying to reach. They are not who I center.

Cebe and AH, it was not your words but your actions that made me feel safe, cared for, and important. Tiffany, Dr. López, Dr. Sanchez, and Valerie, I needed you, and it would have been cruel if you were not there. Though it was painful, we had each other and that meant everything.

Implications and Calling

Critical race theory, in particular storytelling, has helped me to begin to understand the intricacies of whiteness and its domination. It has helped me trace my understanding of its destruction that plays out on the minds and bodies of Peoples of Color. I have been able to name it and see it—its dominance is acted out in those academic library spaces.

We can learn, if we are willing, from our counterstories. They can be sites of liberation and powerful expressions that disrupt the dominant narrative, standing in opposition to commonly held beliefs about us, our histories, and our experiences. They can challenge and deconstruct whiteness in an authentic, accessible form. They can heal.

In my dreams, we all write our stories. They're so critically necessary and exceptionally beautiful; they can powerfully voice the systemic nature of whiteness. They can resurrect. I will continue to believe in them because they can be one map, of many, and "can show us the way out of the trap of unjustified exclusion. They can help us understand when it is time to reallocate power."[14]

---

14. Richard Delgado, "Storytelling for Oppositionists and Others," in The Latino/a Condition: A Critical Reader, ed. Richard Delgado and Jean Stefancic (New York: New York University Press, 1998), 260.

Bibliography

Brown II, M. Christopher, and T. Elon Dancy II. "Predominately White Institutions." In *The Encyclopedia of African American Education,* edited by Kofi Lomotey, 524-26. Thousand Oaks, CA: SAGE Publications, 2010. doi: 10.4135/9781412971966. n193.

Delgado, Richard. "Storytelling for Oppositionists and Others." In *The Latino/a Condition: A Critical Reader,* edited by Richard Delgado and Jean Stefancic, 259-70. New York: New York University Press, 1998.

Delgado, Richard, and Jean Stefancic. *Critical Race Theory: An Introduction.* New York: New York University Press, 2001.

Díaz, Junot. "Celebrated Writer Junot Diaz Talks Openly with the New Yorker's Hilton Als." YouTube video, 1:10:02. Posted by "Strand Bookstore," April 15, 2013. https://www.youtube.com/watch?v=fLhpASeC9JI.

Doane, Woody. "Rethinking Whiteness Studies." In *White Out: The Continuing Significance of Racism,* edited by Ashley W. Doane and Eduardo Bonilla-Silva, 4-18. New York: Routledge, 2003.

Hall, Tracie D. "The Black Body at the Reference Desk: Critical Race Theory and Black Librarianship." In *The 21st-Century Black Librarian in America: Issues and Challenges,* edited by Andrew P. Jackson, Julius C. Jefferson Jr., and Akilah S. Nosakhere, 197-202. Lanham, MD: Scarecrow Press, 2012.

Leonardo, Zeus. "The Color of Supremacy: Beyond the Discourse of 'White Privilege.'" *Education Philosophy and Theory* 36, no. 2 (2004): 137-52. doi: 10.1111/j.1469-5812.2004.00057.x.

———. "The Souls of White Folk: Critical Pedagogy, Whiteness Studies, and Globalization Discourse." *Race Ethnicity and Education* 5, no.1 (2002): 29-50. doi:10.1080/13613320120117180.

Walker, Shaundra. "Critical Race Theory and the Recruitment, Retention and Promotion of a Librarian of Color: A Counter-story." In *Where Are All the Librarians of Color? The Experiences of People of Color in Academia*, edited by Rebecca Hankins and Miguel Juárez, 135-60. Sacramento, CA: Library Juice Press, 2015.

Chapter 13

BREAKING DOWN BORDERS: DISMANTLING WHITENESS THROUGH INTERNATIONAL BRIDGES

Natalie Baur, Margarita Vargas-Betancourt, and George Apodaca

Introduction

In its development as a nation, the United States followed the pattern set in Western Europe: members of a nation state were expected to share the same language, culture, and values. In the United States, Anglo-Saxons used such expectations to exclude other races, especially nonwhites.[1] Eventually, the different white ethnicities constituted a majority group that instituted an exclusive "privileged social status" for whites and their dominance over nonwhites.[2] Ronald W. Walters refers to such system as *white nationalism*.[3]

---

1. Ronald W. Walters, *White Nationalism, Black Interests: Conservative Public Policy and the Black Community* (Detroit: Wayne State University Press, 2003), 14-15. Two examples of the official exclusion of nonwhites are the 1790 Immigration and Naturalization Act, which stated that citizenship was reserved for whites, and Chief Justice Roger B. Taney's 1857 ruling that black people had no rights. See Robert Newby, "The 'New Majority' Defeats White Nationalism? Assessing Issues of Race and Class in the Obama Presidency," *Critical Sociology* 36, no. 3 (2010): 371. doi: 10.1177/0896920510365205.

2. Walters, *White Nationalism, Black Interests*, 15.

3. Ibid., 14-15.

Although the Latino population has increased in the United States, Latinos continue to be underrepresented in mainstream society and in the library science profession.[4] Libraries and archives, from public to academic, have not been able to significantly increase the number of Latinos in the profession or develop outreach and training policies that can help Latino communities overcome the dominance of whiteness and white nationalism.[5] In an employment survey conducted by the Society of American Archivists (SAA) in 2015, only 2.34 percent of archivists identified as "Hispanic, Latino, or Spanish."[6] At the same time, Latinos continue to be underrepresented in US archival repositories. For fifty years, both the SAA and the Rare Books Manuscript Section (RBMS) of the Association of College and Research Libraries (ACRL)

---

4. Although the terms "Latino" and "Hispanic" have been used indiscriminately to refer to people from Latin America and the Spanish-speaking Caribbean, there is a difference in meaning between them. "Hispanic" has a racial connotation, for it refers to the descendants of Spanish settlers, whereas "Latino" represents "people of mixed ethnicities (i.e., of Spanish, Indian, African, and also Asian heritage) who share some similarities, including ancestors who spoke Spanish, but have unique places of origin, customs, foods, histories, and dialects." It is estimated that the population of Hispanics and Latinos in the United States increased "from 500,000 in 1900 to 50.5 million in 2010." See Patricia Montiel-Overall, Annabelle Villaescusa Nuñez, and Verónica Reyes-Escudero, *Latinos in Libraries, Museums, and Archives: Cultural Competence in Action! An Asset-Based Approach* (Lanham, MD: Rowman & Littlefield, 2016), xi, 1, 3. For statistics on the Latino population including educational attainment, income, poverty, work, etc., see Renee Stepler and Anna Brown, "Statistical Portrait of Hispanics in the United States," *Pew Research Center*, April 19, 2016, http://www.pewhispanic.org/2016/04/19/statistical-portrait-of-hispanics-in-the-united-states/.

5. Jennifer Vinopal, "The Quest for Diversity in Library Staffing: From Awareness to Action," *In the Library with the Lead Pipe* (January 2016), http://www.inthelibrarywiththeleadpipe.org/2016/quest-for-diversity/.

6. 86.08 percent identified as White or Caucasian. Society of American Archivists, "SAA Employment Survey," 2015, 31, http://files.archivists.org/membership/surveys/employment2015/SAA-EmploymentSurvey2015-summary_0615.pdf. A 2013 survey suggests the same trend among librarians: "In 2013, 3,661 of 118,666 credentialed librarians in the United States were Latino." Montiel-Overall, Villaescusa Nuñez, and Reyes-Escudero, *Latinos in Libraries*, 45.

have urged archivists and librarians to document Latino populations.[7] Yet their histories—especially those whose past is indispensable to understanding the history of the United States, such as Latino communities in the Southwest or Puerto Rican, Cuban, Dominican, and other immigrants—continue to be missing or incomplete.[8]

This chapter will examine the relationship between the history of Latin American and US relations, Latin American collections in the United States, and the lack of Latino library and information science (LIS) professionals. It will analyze the development and continuity of systemic racism or whiteness as the underlying thread. It will then consider the way in which the webinar series *Desmantelando Fronteras/Breaking Down Borders,* organized by the SAA's Latin American and Caribbean Cultural Heritage Archives (LACCHA) roundtable, contests this paradigm of whiteness. The authors propose the webinar series as an example of how the asset-based cultural competence framework can create bridges with Latin American repositories and result in the promotion of diversity, social inclusion, equity, and democracy, particularly in the US library and archives profession.

Whiteness, US Hegemony, and Archives

Peggy McIntosh defines white privilege or whiteness as an invisible system that conveys dominance to a group of people—i.e., whites—at the expense of other groups—nonwhites or minorities.[9] The exclu-

---

7. The concept of "symbolic annihilation" has been used "to describe the ways in which mainstream media ignore, misrepresent, or malign minoritized groups." The same concept can be applied to the underrepresentation of such communities in LIS collections. See Michelle Caswell, Marika Cifor, and Mario H. Ramirez, "To Suddenly Discover Yourself Existing: Uncovering the Impact of Community Archives," *The American Archivist* 79, no.1 (2016): 57, 59, doi: 10.17723/0360-9081.79.1.56.

8. Montiel-Overall, Villaescusa Nuñez, and Reyes-Escudero, *Latinos in Libraries,* 175-76.

9. Peggy McIntosh, "White Privilege: Unpacking the Invisible Knapsack," 1989, http://nationalseedproject.org/images/documents/Knapsack_plus_Notes-Peggy_McIntosh.pdf.

sion of minorities originates from an economic, social, cultural, and political system that produces an artificial racial difference.[10] This system differentiates between those who have the right to own and control (whites) and those who can be owned and/or controlled (nonwhites).[11] The system is invisible because neither group is taught to recognize that the privileges of whites are unearned assets legitimized by the "myth of meritocracy."[12] The result is hidden bias against and, surprisingly, within minorities.[13]

White nationalism continued even after the abolition of slavery and the Civil War. The concept of white American nationalism was used to legitimize systematic attacks on the establishment and protection of the civil rights of African Americans.[14] In the international arena, the same white American nationalism can be traced to the Monroe Doctrine, which ushered in a policy of US domination in the Americas.[15] In 1823, President James Monroe declared that the United States would take action against European powers that attempted to colonize any country in the Americas. As the economic, political, and military interests of the United States in Latin America and the Caribbean expanded, the Monroe Doctrine developed into a policy of US political hegemony. The interference of the United States in the region has led to a legacy of complicated relationships with Latin American and Caribbean countries;

---

10. Mario H. Ramirez, "Being Assumed Not to Be: A Critique of Whiteness as an Archival Imperative," *The American Archivist* 78, no. 2 (2015): 341-42, doi: 10.17723/0360-9081.78.2.339.

11. Ibid., 342.

12. McIntosh, "White Privilege."

13. Those who developed the organization Project Implicit and the Implicit Association Test "think that this is because stigmatized group members develop negative associations about their group from their cultural environments." Project Implicit, "Frequently Asked Questions," last accessed September 1, 2016, https://implicit.harvard.edu/implicit/faqs.html#faq10.

14. David W. Blight, *Race and Reunion: The Civil War in American Memory*, (Cambridge: Belknap Press, 2003), 272; Ussama Makdisi, "Diminished Sovereignty and the Impossibility of 'Civil War' in the Modern Middle East," *American Historical Review* 120, no. 5 (2015): 1750, doi: 10.1093/ahr/120.5.1739.

15. *Dictionary of World History* (Oxford: Oxford University Press, 2015), s.v. "Monroe Doctrine."

the Spanish-American War (1898) is one example.[16] Here, "racial differentiation" served to legitimize war. The American press depicted the Spaniards and their "dark-skinned" subjects as barbarians and justified American expansionism against Puerto Ricans, Cubans, and Filipinos based on the alleged superiority of the Anglo-Saxon civilization over "inferior races."[17]

The interests of US intellectuals paralleled US policy and positioned the United States to become a hegemonic intellectual power in Latin America. For this reason, a great part of Latin America's cultural heritage was removed from the countries of origin and transferred to US institutions in the nineteenth and early twentieth centuries. This practice conflicted with the 1815 Convention of Vienna, which stated that nations had rights over their intellectual and cultural heritage. Although the ideas behind the convention became popular in the mid-nineteenth century, collectors in the United States continued to acquire archival and cultural items from Latin America and deposited them in US private and public institutions.[18]

After World War II, the flow of cultural property from the "underdeveloped" world to the United States continued. In 1948, US librarians established the Farmington Plan, a collaborative agreement among select US libraries in which each would be asked to specialize in a specific region of the world.[19] At the height of the Cold War, when Latin America became a battlefield between the United States and the Soviet Union, the interest in archives, rare books, and artifacts continued. For this reason, in 1953, the Farmington Plan recognized Latin America as one

---

16. Another is the Mexican-American War (1846-1848), in which Mexico lost half of its territory to the United States. J. M. Callahan, "Mexican-American War," in *Dictionary of American History*, vol. 5, ed. Stanley I. Kutler (New York: Charles Scribner's Sons, 2003): 339-42.

17. Blight, *Race and Reunion*, 347; Makdisi, "Diminished Sovereignty," 1750.

18. Bruce Montgomery, "Reconciling the Inalienability Doctrine with the Conventions of War," *American Archivist* 78, no. 2 (2015): 297, doi: 10.17723/0360-9081.78.2.288.

19. Ralph D. Wagner, *A History of the Farmington Plan* (Lanham, MD: Scarecrow Press, 2002), 86.

of the regions from which materials should be collected.[20] Collaboration was essential for the success of the mission, as it was acknowledged early on that it was impossible for the Library of Congress to collect everything. The restitution of cultural property, however, was not written into the equation.[21]

Although the Farmington Plan was cancelled in 1972, the uneven relationship between Latin American and US repositories continues to this day, as evidenced by the sale of the Gabriel García Márquez archive to the University of Texas at Austin's Harry Ransom Center in November 2014.[22] The sale of the archives to an institution outside of Colombia, the author's country of birth, generated a great deal of debate around the issue of cultural patrimony. The National Library of Colombia voiced regret that a collection as important as the García Márquez archive did not remain in its country of origin.[23] The transference of the collection also caused debate among members of the SAA, especially the membership of the LACCHA roundtable. The controversy reached a climax when the university refused to release the purchase price for the collection even after the Associated Press filed a Freedom of Information Act request. After much consideration, the SAA issued a statement encouraging the Harry Ransom Center to release the information. In February 2015, the center revealed the price paid

---

20. Wagner, *A History of the Farmington Plan*, 210.

21. Even though the original scope of the Farmington Plan was the collection of published material, it was extended to special collections materials, such as archives and manuscripts.

22. Wagner, *A History of the Farmington Plan*, 383; Harry Ransom Center at The University of Texas at Austin, "Nobel Prize-Winning Author Gabriel García Márquez's Archive Acquired by The University of Texas at Austin's Harry Ransom Center," November 24, 2014, http://www.hrc.utexas.edu/press/releases/2014/ggm.html.

23. Joanna Scutts and Ashifa Kassam, "Archive of Colombian Literary Great Gabriel García Márquez Goes to Texas," *The Guardian*, November 24, 2014, http://www.theguardian.com/books/2014/nov/24/colombian-writer-gabriel-garcia-marquezs-archive-goes-to-texas.

for the materials: 2.2 million US dollars.[24] This story highlights, once more, the uneven relationship between Latin American and American repositories regarding the cultural heritage of the former. It is unlikely that Latin American institutions had enough funds readily available to purchase a collection that they considered part of their cultural heritage.

The eagerness of US repositories to acquire preeminent collections from Latin America contrasts not only with the lack of outreach programs meant to provide Latinos access to archival materials, but also with the scarcity of records that document the history of Latinos in the United States.[25] The subsequent disconnect has driven Latino communities away from resources—information and knowledge—that, we argue, could help improve their quality of life through access to documentation about their own histories and experiences. It has also resulted in few Latinos pursuing LIS careers. US repositories need to address such challenges in order to overcome whiteness in mainstream culture and in the LIS profession.

Deficit Model Versus Asset-Based Approach

Whiteness in the LIS profession reflects mainstream culture's underrepresentation and undervaluation of Latino and Latin American language and culture.[26] One of the approaches that library science professionals have used in their attempts to better serve Latinos is what has been defined as the "deficit model," an approach that focuses on the needs and perceived failures of Latinos, such as poor school performance

---

24. Society of American Archivists, "SAA Response to Member Request re University of Texas Acquisition of García Márquez Archive," last accessed February 2, 2016, http://www2.archivists.org/news/2015/saa-response-to-member-request-re-university-of-texas-acquisition-of-garcia-marquez-archiv.

25. For repositories that constitute exceptions, see Montiel-Overall, Villaescusa Nuñez, and Reyes-Escudero, *Latinos in Libraries,* 176.

26. Although tenuous, the distinction between the terms "Latino" and "Latin American" is that the former refers to people in the United States whose family comes from Latin American countries, whereas the latter refers to people who live or grew up in Latin America.

due to poverty or parents with low educational levels.[27] However, this kind of model is inadequate. Instead of promoting cultural competence among library science professionals, it has reinforced the white American nationalist idea of nonwhites as inferior.

In *Latinos in Libraries, Museums, and Archives: Cultural Competence in Action! An Asset-Based Approach,* Patricia Montiel-Overall, Annabelle Villaescusa Nuñez, and Verónica Reyes-Escudero define cultural competence as "the capacity to recognize the significance of culture in one's own life and in the lives of others; to acquire and respectfully use knowledge of diverse ethnic and cultural groups' beliefs, values, attitudes, practices, communication patterns, and assets to strengthen LIS programs and services through increased community participation."[28]

Instead of the deficit model, these authors propose an "asset-based approach." Indeed, their culture is one of the greatest assets of Latino communities.[29] To this day, US LIS professionals have not done a good job of representing these cultures, or of providing these communities access to existing resources. Learning from Latinos and Latin Americans, especially from LIS professionals from both the US and Latin America, can foster cultural competence among US librarians and archivists. This in turn can improve the services that US institutions provide to Latinos and increase the representation of Latino and Latin American cultures, both in the LIS profession and in mainstream culture, as a strategy for overcoming whiteness.

Development of the *Desmantelando Fronteras/Breaking Down Borders* Project with a Critical Eye

In 2012, through the US Department of State, Natalie Baur and Margarita Vargas-Betancourt developed two webinars on basic principles

27. Montiel-Overall, Villaescusa Nuñez, and Reyes-Escudero, *Latinos in Libraries,* 27, 31, 51.

28. Ibid., 23.

29. Ibid., 27, 28.

of archiving for a Latin American audience of library science professionals.[30] The size of the first webinar's audience, their expertise, and also their thirst for information impressed and surprised the authors. It also revealed that Latin American librarians and archivists were not necessarily in need of basic training, but could instead share their own knowledge and experiences with one another and with US audiences. Through this experience, Baur and Vargas-Betancourt recognized that an asset-based approach had to replace the predominant deficit-model approach. In the spring of 2015, during their tenures as co-chairs of LACCHA, they decided to apply the asset model to the development of a series of online webinars featuring archival projects and initiatives from Latin America and the Caribbean. They hoped that the series would promote a better understanding of the library science profession globally and would give way to collaborative projects among archivists in the Americas. Furthermore, they believed that exposure to the experience and knowledge of Latin American and Caribbean colleagues could foster cultural competence among US archivists and librarians, which in turn could improve library services, with an emphasis on the Latino community in the United States.

In the initial stage of the webinar series *Desmantelando Fronteras/ Breaking Down Borders*, Baur, Vargas-Betancourt, and George Apodaca, LACCHA's online communication liaison, developed a mission statement for the series in both English and Spanish. The announcement expressed the goal of creating a more inclusive space for bi-directional sharing of professional experiences between US, Canadian, and Latin American and Caribbean colleagues:

> La mesa redonda de los Archivos de Patrimonio Cultural de Latinoamérica y el Caribe (LACCHA) de la Sociedad de Archivistas Americanos (SAA), en asociación con la Biblioteca Digital del Caribe (dLOC) y la Asociación de Bibliotecas Universitarias, de Investigación e Institucionales del Caribe (ACURIL), ha organizado Desmantelando Fronteras/

---

30. Natalie Baur and Margarita Vargas-Betancourt, *Herramientas para Desarrollar Bibliotecas y Colecciones Especiales,* October 24 and November 20, 2012, http://ufdc.ufl.edu/IR00001560/00001.

Breaking Down Borders, una serie de seminarios por Internet recalcando proyectos archivísticos de Latinoamérica y el Caribe. Esta serie provee un espacio colaborativo para archivistas de Latinoamérica y el Caribe donde se pueden compartir proyectos, experiencias y mensajes principales y a la vez fomentar comunicación bidireccional entre profesionales a lo largo de las Américas.

The Latin American and Caribbean Cultural Heritage Archives round-table (LACCHA) of the Society of American Archivists (SAA), in partnership with the Digital Library of the Caribbean (dLOC) and the Association of Caribbean University, Research and Institutional Librar-ies (ACURIL), has organized a series of online events, Desmantelando Fronteras/Breaking Down Borders, a webinar series showcasing archival projects of Latin America and the Caribbean. This series provides a col-laborative space for Latin American and Caribbean archivists to share their projects, experiences, and takeaways and fostering a two-way com-munication between professionals throughout the Americas.[31]

After establishing the mission statement and scope of the project, the team then established formal partnerships with several regional professional organizations in order to facilitate networking and trust building with potential webinar speakers and participants from Latin America and the Caribbean. The LACCHA co-chairs solidified agree-ments for partnerships with the Association of Caribbean University, Research and Institutional Libraries (ACURIL) and the Digital Library of the Caribbean (dLOC) in order to attract participation from members and partners associated with those allied organizations. Because many colleagues from the Caribbean had already had positive experiences working and sharing with ACURIL and dLOC, having those organiza-tions onboard for the webinar series was crucial for attracting potential presenters. These partnerships built the necessary trust in the project that presenters from outside the United States who were unfamiliar with the

---

31. For information on the launching of the webinar series, see George Apodaca, Natalie Baur, and Margarita Vargas-Betancourt, "Breaking Down Borders. LACCHA Launches New Webinar Series with Colleagues in the Carib-bean and Latin America," *Archival Outlook* (May/June 2015): 14, 27, http:// www.bluetoad.com/article/Breaking_Down_Borders%3A_LACCHA _Launches_New_Webinar_Series_with_Colleagues_in_the_Caribbean_and_ Latin_America/2012787/259343/article.html.

SAA needed in order to buy into the project. The webinar organizers also established contact with the *Asociación Latinoamericana de Archivos* (Latin American Association of Archives, with the acronym ALA) in order to be more inclusive of Mexico, Central America, and the Southern Cone. An underlying assumption of the project is the belief that an ongoing dialog can counteract uneven relationships between US and Latin American and Caribbean institutions due to cultural patrimony by developing cultural competence in US librarians and archivists. In this way, the webinar series can serve as a valuable example of a proactive way to challenge whiteness in the LIS profession.

Establishing partnerships with professional organizations that have a scope beyond the United States and Canada has also had benefits beyond recruiting presenters and building peer-to-peer trust for the project. The SAA has not historically had many formal ties with other professional organizations beyond those in the United States, Canada, Australia, and Europe. Although the core goal of the *Desmantelando Fronteras/Breaking Down Borders* project is to break down borders to cooperation and flow of information and professional experiences, primarily through peer-to-peer interaction, involving regional organizations has been an important part of the equation in the hope that efforts like these will better position organizations like the SAA within the Americas. It is also an effort to create at least one pathway to overcoming the US/Canada and English-language isolation of an organization that already has serious issues with diversity in the cultural, linguistic, and racial representation of its membership.[32]

Although the strategies outlined above helped overcome potential cultural and political obstacles, the project also had to directly address technological challenges. The webinar organizers had worked extensively in Latin American and Caribbean countries and with colleagues in the region, and were acutely aware of both the social and technological factors that would go into planning an innovative, successful, and sustainable project. For the technological side of the project, organizers

---

32. Society of American Archivists, "SAA Employment Survey," 31.

knew ahead of time that Internet connectivity and reliability would be
a major defining factor. The organizers decided to preempt connectivity
issues by having presenters pre-record their presentations. This solved
two issues. First, it resolved the problem of unreliable Internet connections for video streaming. Second, it was a way to continue building
trust with presenters, allowing them to be in total control of the presentation experience and alleviating any anxiety related to connectivity
issues on the day of the live event. Pre-recording the presentations
does involve more planning and coordination, but it has already proven
to be worthwhile. During the event in March 2015 featuring speakers
from Curaçao and Guyana, the speaker from Guyana was unable to
connect to the live webinar event, despite previous successful connections during the practice sessions in the preceding weeks. Because the
presentation was pre-recorded, it was broadcasted as originally planned,
and the speaker answered questions via e-mail during the live question
and answer session.

To promote the webinars, announcements are written in both English
and Spanish, regardless of the language in which the webinar will be
presented. The multilingual announcements also reflect the commitment
to a multilingual balance of the projects, as the team strives to balance
presentations in English, Spanish, and, in the future, additional Latin
American and Caribbean languages such as French and Portuguese.

Finally, significant planning went into ensuring long-term sustain-
ability and access to the project, as well as allowing presenters to have
control over the copyright of their materials. All webinars are recorded,
and the recording and the webinar announcements are deposited in
the online scholarly repository at the University of Miami Libraries.[33]
The team made the decision to archive the presentation materials in
this way to provide an open access platform, which in turn creates

33. Latin American and Caribbean Cultural Heritage Archives (LACCHA)
Society of American Archivists (SAA), Desmantelando Fronteras/Breaking
Down Borders, last accessed September 20, 2016, http://scholarlyrepository.
miami.edu/laccha_saa/.

equitable access to materials. Equity is needed to overcome the potential distrust that Latin American and Caribbean institutions have towards US repositories, a result of the uneven, and for many years unregulated, flow of Latin American and Caribbean cultural artifacts to the United States, and of the "deficit model" followed by US LIS institutions. This model has reinforced the idea of US superiority instead of promoting the acknowledgement of Latin American and Caribbean institutions as partners. In addition, the open access movement has been very strong in Latin America, and the emergence of institutional repositories and open access publishing formats rivals the state of similar efforts in the United States. Therefore, depositing the recordings and announcements in an open platform has been a familiar and supported strategy for many of the Latin American participants.

Summaries and Reflections on Webinar Events

The first webinar took place in March 2015 and featured two dLOC partners: the University of Curaçao's digital repository project and the Caribbean Information Resource Network (IRN). The University of Curaçao has contributed their extensive archives, made up of primary source documents and other materials which are part of the Dutch Caribbean Digital Platform, and which constitute a collection of national importance to the history and culture of the island. The Caribbean IRN is concerned with connecting activists, researchers, artists, and teachers who research and work in areas of sexual diversity in the Caribbean. The Caribbean IRN today includes newspaper and magazine articles, essays, activist organization reports, interviews, photographs, and other materials, all of which offer research material on the complexity of the lives and experiences of LGBTQ persons in the Caribbean. As part of dLOC, both collections are open access and offer a variety of personal, political, and community perspectives, all of which are available for consultation online.

The second webinar was presented in conjunction with institutions in Honduras and Ecuador and highlighted the experiences the presenters had in managing major archival recovery projects in public institutions. The first presentation described the work that independent conservator Nelly Peralta has done in Ecuadorian libraries and archives through her consultation firm, Papiro Studios. Peralta spoke specifically about the major recovery, preservation, and conservation project she led at the *Biblioteca Municipal Juan Montalvo Vinces* (Municipal Library Juan Montalvo Vinces) in the coastal region of Ecuador. Presenters from Honduras shared their experiences recovering the severely damaged and neglected archives at the Honduran National Archives, and work at the Secretariat of Foreign Relations and International Cooperation which focused heavily on the major recovery efforts following the catastrophic 2009 flooding of the Foreign Relations' archives. The three presentations described problems that many archives throughout the world have in common: technical issues, limited resources, and the lack of proper planning for environmental disasters and other unexpected events. The three presentations together highlighted a universal need for national and institutional support for maintaining archival and library programs, issues that are shared across borders and languages.

During the third webinar, presenters spoke about the Florida-Puerto Rico Newspaper Project, a mass digitization program undertaken by the University of Florida George A. Smathers Libraries and the University of Puerto Rico in Río Piedras. The goals of the project were to digitize historically important newspapers published in Florida and Puerto Rico between 1836 and 1922 in order to include them in a searchable online database. The project was made possible by a grant from the National Endowment for the Humanities and the Library of Congress. The inclusion of the newspaper materials from both Florida and Puerto Rico has encouraged more institutions to create projects that include materials from all US states and territories.

Due to recent transparency and open government legislation in the United States and many Latin American countries, the organizers planned the fourth webinar to focus on the role of archives in ensuring transparency and access in Ecuador and Colombia.[34] Continuing in the tradition of highlighting cooperative projects and themes, the fifth webinar was in English and shared the challenges and successes of two US-Latin American archival initiatives: the Itinerant Archivists pilot project and delegation trip to Ecuador in September 2015, and the history and development of the newly-inaugurated Latin American Digital Initiatives project at the Teresa Lozano Long Institute of Latin American Studies' Benson Latin American Studies and Collections (LLILAS Benson) at the University of Texas at Austin.

The sixth and most recent webinar featured the recent activities of the Mexican organization, *Apoyo al Desarrollo de Archivos y Bibliotecas de México* (Support of the Development of Archives and Libraries in Mexico, with the acronym ADABI), whose mission is to rescue and recover the documentary patrimony of Mexico.

The six webinars that have been presented during the 2015-2016 cycle have touched on many emerging archival themes in the Americas, such as transparency, collaborative projects and cooperatives, archival recovery projects, and the development of shared digital platforms and resources. None of these trends and initiatives exist in a vacuum, and the *Desmantelando Fronteras/Breaking Down Borders* project has successfully

---

34. For additional information on the legislation of governmental and archival transparency in Latin America, see Red de Transparencia y Acceso a la Información, "Quiénes Somos," last accessed September 19, 2016, https://redrta.org/quienes-somos/. For additional information on the legislation in Colombia and Ecuador, see Secretaría de Transparencia Presidencia de la República, "La Secretaría," last accessed September 19, 2016, http://www.secretariatransparencia.gov.co/secretaria/Paginas/funciones-secretaria.aspx and Instituto Ecuatoriano de la Propiedad Intelectual, "Transparencia," last accessed September 19, 2016, http://www.propiedadintelectual.gob.ec/transparencia/.

served as a vehicle for the asset-based approach, amplifying the voices of those undertaking these major projects and sharing their successes, failures, challenges, and experiences across borders and languages.

Program Feedback and Takeaways

The webinar series founders and organizers believe that the project has enough momentum to effectively sustain itself, an indication that the archival profession will not be satisfied until diverse and multifaceted developments across the field are afforded the serious attention they merit.

One way the organizers were able to evaluate the performance of the webinars was through an online survey that participants were asked to fill out at the completion of each webinar. A link to the voluntary feedback survey was offered following the live question-and-answer session and on average drew about six responses per webinar. The average webinar drew twenty-five attendees from countries representing almost every corner of the Western hemisphere. Responses were overwhelmingly positive; they applauded the utility of information, resources, and news made available from peers across borders who shared information about their ongoing and completed projects. In addition, some participants offered ideas to further facilitate the webinar experience for all. For example, they expressed a desire for English-translated transcripts for the Spanish-only webinars so participants could follow along and review the information at their leisure. Conversely, this led to the idea of providing Spanish-translated transcripts for the English-only portions of future webinars on a more regular basis, in order to be as inclusive as possible.

As became apparent from the feedback received, as well as from the existence of professional library and archives associations around the Western hemisphere, the thirst for this type of collaboration had always existed. Unfortunately, there was no focused strategy or plan to take it from a conceptual stage to actual implementation, until now.[35]

---

35. The advent of digital humanities, however, is giving rise to global collaborative projects such as that of Global Outlook, last accessed September 15, 2016, http://www.globaloutlookdh.org.

The balance struck between an honest multilingual platform, relevant content, a delivery system anchored in a strong online presence, and the legitimization provided by reciprocally-beneficial partnerships proves how far a "home-grown" endeavor can go.

The goal of the webinar series is first to show the profession that projects of this caliber can be done well and sustainably, and second, that partnerships with Latin American and Caribbean colleagues and institutions provide room for cultural competence and a successful asset-based approach to overcome the stronghold of whiteness in the library and archives profession. LACCHA's webinar series was an effective way to kick-start these collaborations and to tap into a reservoir full of potential.

Finally, because we live in an increasingly globalized and technologically-advanced society, a hemispheric understanding is needed within the archival world to adequately address the issues faced by the populations we document and serve. When migrations separate citizens from their countries of origin and diasporic communities form in lieu of the support networks they had back home, it becomes vital for archivists and librarians to be fully aware of the situation at hand in order to be better able to document it as well as possible. Many of the collections hosted in US institutions contain a heavy legacy of colonialism: the materials were sacked from the original country without permission or under questionable circumstances, adequate access is not provided, and/or there are people arranging and describing these collections who do not have the necessary understanding of the cultural and historical contexts surrounding the materials. LIS professionals must recognize that in order to connect effectively with Latino communities, it is necessary to acknowledge the legacy of white nationalism in the United States present in libraries and archives and its impact in the marginalization of Latinos.

It is the expectation of the organizers that the development of this webinar series helps dispel the antiquated notion that Latinos, Latin Americans, and people from the Caribbean are at a deficit in relation to the library science profession in the United States, and that it instead inspires collaboration amongst equal peers. In this way, they hope to contribute to an increased development of cultural competence among

US archivists and librarians, which in turn will help them empower the Latino, Latin American, and Caribbean communities they serve. By doing so, LIS professionals can have a major role in dismantling the topographies of whiteness.

Bibliography

Apodaca, George, Natalie Baur, and Margarita Vargas-Betancourt. "Breaking Down Borders. LACCHA Launches New Webinar Series with Colleagues in the Caribbean and Latin America." *Archival Outlook* (May/June 2015): 14, 27. http://www. bluetoad.com/article/Breaking_Down_Borders%3A_LAC-CHA_Launches_New_Webinar_Series_with_Colleagues_ in_the_Caribbean_and_Latin_America/2012787/259343/ article.html.

Baur, Natalie, and Margarita Vargas-Betancourt. *Herramientas para Desarrollar Bibliotecas y Colecciones Especiales.* October 24 and November 20, 2012. http://ufdc.ufl.edu/IR00001560/00001.

Blight, David W. *Race and Reunion: The Civil War in American Memory.* Cambridge, MA: Belknap Press, 2003.

Callahan, J. M. "Mexican-American War." In *Dictionary of American History*, vol. 5, edited by Stanley I. Kutler, 339-42. New York: Charles Scribner's Sons, 2003.

Caswell, Michelle, Marika Cifor, and Mario H. Ramirez. "To Suddenly Discover Yourself Existing: Uncovering the Impact of Community Archives." *The American Archivist* 79, no.1 (2016): 56-81. doi: 10.17723/0360-9081.79.1.56.

Global Outlook. Accessed September 23, 2016. http://www.globaloutlookdh.org/.

Harry Ransom Center at The University of Texas at Austin. "Nobel Prize-Winning Author Gabriel García Márquez's Archive Acquired by The University of Texas at Austin's Harry Ransom Center," November 24, 2014. http://www.hrc.utexas.edu/ press/releases/2014/ggm.html.

Instituto Ecuatoriano de la Propiedad Intelectual. "Transparencia."
Accessed September 19, 2016. http://www.propiedadintelec-
tual.gob.ec/transparencia/.

Latin American and Caribbean Cultural Heritage Archives (LAC-
CHA) Society of American Archivists (SAA). *Desmantelando
Fronteras/Breaking Down Borders.* Accessed September 20,
2016. http://scholarlyrepository.miami.edu/laccha_saa/.

Makdisi, Ussama. "Diminished Sovereignty and the Impossibility of 'Civil War' in the Modern Middle East." *American
Historical Review* 120, no. 5 (2015): 1739-52. doi: 10.1093/
ahr/120.5.1739.

Marable, Manning. *How Capitalism Underdeveloped Black America:
Problems in Race, Political Economy, and Society.* Cambridge, MA:
South End Press, 2000.

McIntosh, Peggy. "White Privilege: Unpacking the Invisible Knapsack." 1989. http://nationalseedproject.org/images/docu-
ments/Knapsack_plus_Notes-Peggy_McIntosh.pdf.

"Monroe Doctrine." In *Dictionary of World History.* Oxford: Oxford
University Press, 2015.

Montgomery, Bruce. "Reconciling the Inalienability Doctrine with
the Conventions of War." *The American Archivist* 78, no. 2
(2015): 288-316. doi: 10.17723/0360-9081.78.2.288.

Montiel-Overall, Patricia, Annabelle Villaescusa Nuñez, and Verónica
Reyes-Escudero. *Latinos in Libraries, Museums, and Archives:
Cultural Competence in Action! An Asset-Based Approach.* Lan-
ham, MD: Rowman & Littlefield, 2016.

Newby, Robert. "The 'New Majority' Defeats White Nationalism? Assessing Issues of Race and Class in the Obama
Presidency." *Critical Sociology* 36, no.3 (2010): 371-86. doi:
10.1177/0896920510365205.

Project Implicit. "Frequently Asked Questions." Accessed September 23, 2016. https://implicit.harvard.edu/implicit/faqs.
html#faq10.

Ramirez, Mario H. "Being Assumed Not to Be: A Critique of Whiteness as an Archival Imperative." *The American Archivist* 78, no. 2 (2015): 339-56. doi: 10.17723/0360-9081.78.2.339.

Red de Transparencia y Acceso a la Información. "Quiénes somos." Accessed September 19, 2016.   https://redrta.org/quienes-somos/.

Scutts, Joanna, and Ashifa Kassam. "Archive of Colombian Literary Great Gabriel García Márquez Goes to Texas." *The Guardian,* November 24, 2014. http://www.theguardian.com/books/2014/nov/24/colombian-writer-gabriel-garcia-marquezs-archive-goes-to-texas.

Secretaría de Transparencia Presidencia de la República. "La Secretaría." Accessed September 19, 2016. http://www.secretariatransparencia.gov.co/secretaria/Paginas/funciones-secretaria.aspx.

Society of American Archivists. "SAA Employment Survey." 2015. http://files.archivists.org/membership/surveys/employment2015/SAA-EmploymentSurvey2015-summary_0615.pdf.

———. "SAA Response to Member Request re University of Texas Acquisition of García Márquez Archive." Accessed February 2, 2016. http://www2.archivists.org/news/2015/saa-response-to-member-request-re-university-of-texas-acquisition-of-garcia-marquez-archiv.

Stepler, Renee, and Anna Brown. "Statistical Portrait of Hispanics in the United States." *Pew Research Center.* April 19, 2016. http://www.pewhispanic.org/2016/04/19/statistical-portrait-of-hispanics-in-the-united-states/.

Vinopal, Jennifer. "The Quest for Diversity in Library Staffing: From Awareness to Action." *In the Library with the Lead Pipe* (January 2016). http://www.inthelibrarywiththeleadpipe.org/2016/quest-for-diversity/.

Wagner, Ralph D. *A History of the Farmington Plan.* Lanham, MD: Scarecrow Press, 2002.

Walters, Ronald W. *White Nationalism Black Interests: Conservative Public Policy and the Black Community.* Detroit: Wayne State University Press, 2003.

Chapter 14

DISRUPTING WHITENESS: THREE PERSPECTIVES ON WHITE ANTI-RACIST LIBRARIANSHIP

Melissa Kalpin Prescott, Kristyn Caragher, Katie Dover-Taylor

Introduction

In this chapter, we will focus on the work that white librarians must do to disrupt and dismantle racism and white supremacy in ourselves, our institutions, and our communities. We will explore three examples of white anti-racist library work at different levels, using Chris Bourg's proposed framework for enacting diversity, inclusion, and social justice in libraries and library work as a guide (see **Figure 1**).[1]

Bourg's framework reminds us to consider the various communities we belong to, including our workplaces, our local communities, the library and information science (LIS) community, the global community, and ourselves as potential sites for transformation. Each of us has a role to play in ensuring diversity, inclusion, and social justice in libraries, and we interact with those circles of community in different ways depending on the various privileges we hold. Our contributions are as follows:

---

1. Chris Bourg, "Talking at Harvard About Libraries and Social Justice," *Feral Librarian* (blog), September 17, 2016, https://chrisbourg.wordpress.com/2016/09/17/talking-at-harvard-about-libraries-and-social-justice/.

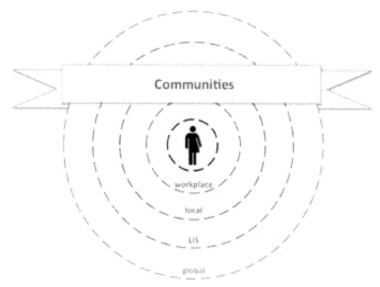

Figure 1. Framework for Diversity, Inclusion, and Social Justice in Libraries
(courtesy of Chris Bourg)

- Melissa Kalpin Prescott will discuss the work of anti-racist white allies at the personal and interpersonal level, discussing what white librarians can do to move beyond "checking their privilege" to engage in meaningful anti-racist work.

- Kristyn Caragher will discuss anti-racist librarianship in action at the workplace level, describing the experience of designing, implementing, and facilitating the Anti-Oppression Workshop Series for library staff at the University Library at the University of Illinois at Urbana-Champaign.

- Katie Dover-Taylor will discuss anti-racist work at the local, LIS, and global levels, covering anti-racist public library practice, the need for discussions of anti-racism in LIS to be more inclusive of perspectives outside the academy, and the potential to connect with social justice organizers and activists engaged in anti-racist efforts beyond libraries.

Toward Anti-Racist Librarianship: The Work of White Allies

Melissa Kalpin Prescott

Important conversations about the lack of diversity in librarianship are occurring that call attention to the "invisible normativity of whiteness."[2] At the same time, recent interest in critical librarianship is sparking discussions on social media that are creating awareness of the oppressive structures within which librarianship was developed and continues to operate.[3] Librarians are beginning to organize efforts to address systemic oppression in the hopes of creating a truly inclusive culture that benefits everyone. In a profession that continues to be overwhelmingly white despite concerted efforts to increase diversity, I assert that we need to confront the issue directly by using an anti-racist approach. Specifically, white librarians need to develop an anti-racist analysis and apply it to librarianship, confront white privilege in its multiple manifestations, and work in alliance with librarians of color to dismantle institutional racism.

Anti-racism stems from critical race theory and requires us to develop a critical consciousness of our racialization and racial identity that leads us to dismantle racist systems through activism. It requires us to uncover how internalized racial superiority and internalized racial oppression necessarily work together to maintain and perpetuate institutional racism. Anti-racism also addresses the ways that intersectionality compounds

---

2. April Hathcock, "White Librarianship in Blackface: Diversity Initiatives in LIS," *In the Library with the Lead Pipe* (October 2015), http://www.inthelibrarywiththeleadpipe.org/2015/lis-diversity/. See also Chris Bourg, "The Unbearable Whiteness of Librarianship," *Feral Librarian* (blog), March 3, 2014, https://chrisbourg.wordpress.com/2014/03/03/the-unbearable-whiteness-of-librarianship/, and Angela Galvan, "Soliciting Performance, Hiding Bias: Whiteness and Librarianship," *In the Library with the Lead Pipe* (April 2015), http://www.inthelibrarywiththeleadpipe.org/2015/soliciting-performance-hiding-bias-whiteness-and-librarianship/.

3. For examples, see Twitter hashtags #critlib, #radlibchat, and #libleadgender.

the effects of power differentials in society. For example, as a woman, I experience oppression based on gender, but as a white woman, I experience unearned advantages in many aspects of my life. When, for example, I compare my experience of gender oppression to that of my female colleague of color, I minimize her experience of multiple oppressions. Focusing on how we as white people are also oppressed allows us to deny our white guilt and personal responsibility for racism. To avoid derailing our work, Rachel Luft cautions us against the "flattening of difference" that can happen when we begin anti-racist work through an intersectional approach rather than one that focuses on race.[4] Establishing a critical racial lens first is especially important in light of "new racism," defined by Robin DiAngelo as "[t]he ways in which racism has adapted over time so that modern norms, policies, and practices result in similar racial outcomes as those in the past, while not appearing to be explicitly racist."[5] We see new racism today in "post-racial" and "colorblind" rhetoric.

An anti-racist analysis requires us to develop a critical consciousness of how racism is embedded into social systems and institutions to maintain power and privilege for whites. Both whites and people of color are socialized into their racial roles through persistent messages from institutions, including family, media, schools, churches, health care, government, and others. These messages result in the internalization of racial superiority or racial inferiority, depending on the racial group to which we are assigned. For whites, it can be difficult to acknowledge the privileges we are afforded solely because of the color of our skin. We internalize ubiquitous messages that tell us we have worked hard to earn the social and economic privileges we possess. To challenge our merit in this way can be devastating. However, once we recognize how

---

4. Rachel E. Luft, "Intersectionality and the Risk of Flattening Difference," in *The Intersectional Approach: Transforming the Academy through Race, Class and Gender*, ed. Michele Tracy Berger and Kathleen Guidroz (Chapel Hill: University of North Carolina Press, 2009), 101.

5. Robin DiAngelo, *What Does It Mean to Be White? Developing White Racial Literacy* (New York: Peter Lang, 2012), 106.

systemic racism hurts all of society, both whites and people of color, it is possible to look past our initial discomfort and guilt and to focus our agency toward positive social change.

As a white librarian in a profession that is eighty-eight percent white,[6] I have an essential role to work as an ally with my colleagues of color in order to disrupt power structures that privilege white people and disadvantage people of color. Andrea Ayvazian describes the behavior of allies as "clear action aimed at dismantling the oppression of others in areas where you yourself benefit—it is proactive, intentional, and often involves taking a risk."[7] For anti-racist white allies, recognizing our unearned privilege is only the beginning. We must commit to the difficult personal work that forces us to address ways in which we perpetuate systems of white supremacy. This work begins with critical self-reflection on our social positions (i.e., the intersection of race, ethnicity, class, gender, sexual orientation, ability, religion, national origin, etc.) and the contextualization of our experience within the constructs of society. Janet Helms' white racial identity development theory is the first to delineate a process whereby whites move along a continuum from having no white identity to internalizing "a positive [w]hite racial identity [that] is evidenced by a lived commitment to anti-racist activity, ongoing self-examination and increased interpersonal effectiveness in multiracial settings."[8] The model gives us a framework to talk about

---

6. American Library Association, "Diversity Counts 2009-2010 Update," last accessed January 13, 2017, http://www.ala.org/offices/diversity/diversitycounts/2009-2010update.

7. Andrea Ayvazian, "Interrupting the Cycle of Oppression: The Role of Allies as Agents of Change," in *Readings for Diversity and Social Justice*, ed. Maurianne Adams et al., 2nd ed. (New York: Routledge, 2010), 625.

8. Sandra M. Lawrence and Beverly Daniel Tatum, "White Racial Identity and Anti-Racist Education: A Catalyst for Change," in *Beyond Heroes and Holidays: A Practical Guide to K-12 Anti-Racist, Multicultural Education and Staff Development*, ed. Enid Lee, Deborah Menkart, and Margo Okazawa-Rey, 2nd ed. (Washington, DC: Teaching for Change, 2002), 46. For more information on racial identity development, see Janet E. Helms, *Black and White Racial Identity: Theory, Research, and Practice* (New York: Greenwood Press, 1990); Janet E. Helms, "An Update of Helms's White and People of Color Racial Identity Models," in *Handbook of Multicultural Counseling*, ed. Joseph G. Ponterotto

and understand the complex and continuous work of unlearning racism while operating within inherently racist systems and institutions.

Even when we're committed to anti-racism, our internalized racial superiority can undermine our work, alienate others, and hinder our progress toward a positive white racial identity. We may unknowingly invalidate the experiences of people of color by adopting a "white savior" mentality, presuming that people of color need and want us to fix racial inequities for them and that they "lack the agency necessary to enact positive changes in their own lives."[9]

Alternatively, we may dissociate ourselves, as "good white people," from other whites who demonstrate overt racial prejudices or who don't share an anti-racist analysis.[10] This distancing behavior is also highly problematic in our role as allies. As a member of white society, we are privy to in-group exchanges that exclude people of color. As anti-racist white allies, it is our responsibility in these situations to engage in critical conversations with other white people, "to speak up against systems of oppression, and to challenge other whites to do the same."[11]

Engaging in meaningful anti-racist librarianship requires us to question the "presumed and oppressive 'neutrality' of [w]hiteness" and its embeddedness in the services and spaces we provide for our library users.[12] Beverly Tatum tells us that we each have a "sphere of influence" within which we can effect change.[13] As librarians, we teach, serve on

et al. (Thousand Oaks, CA: Sage, 1995), 181-98; and Beverly Daniel Tatum, "Teaching White Students about Racism: The Search for White Allies and the Restoration of Hope," *Teachers College Record* 95, no. 4 (1994): 462-76.

9. Julio Cammarota, "Blindsided by the Avatar: White Saviors and Allies Out of Hollywood and in Education," *Review of Education, Pedagogy, & Cultural Studies* 33, no. 3 (2011): 245.

10. Shannon Sullivan, *Good White People: The Problem with Middle-Class White Anti-Racism* (Albany, NY: State University of New York Press, 2014), 5.

11. Tatum, "Teaching White Students about Racism," 474.

12. Freeda Brook, Dave Ellenwood, and Althea Eannace Lazzaro, "In Pursuit of Antiracist Social Justice: Denaturalizing Whiteness in the Academic Library," *Library Trends* 64, no. 2 (2015): 248.

13. Beverly Daniel Tatum, *"Why Are All the Black Kids Sitting Together in the Cafeteria?" And Other Conversations About Race* (New York: Basic Books, 2003), 105.

committees, create policies and procedures, and engage with the community. All of these activities create opportunities for us to disrupt, resist, and dismantle the status quo. We have significant power in determining whose voices we validate, what ideologies we support (both overtly and implicitly), and how we adapt as a social institution to reorient our practices in inclusive and anti-racist ways. If we are to reflect authentic diversity within librarianship, not only in our demographics but also in our professional values and standards, we must work as allies to our colleagues of color to decenter whiteness and enact inclusivity. Through an anti-racist approach, we can work toward this vision.

Anti-Oppression Workshop Series at the University Library

Kristyn Caragher

After the death of Sandra Bland in July 2015, I was talking with Siri Nelson, a black queer woman and good friend of mine, about racism and police brutality. She said that while she appreciated having this conversation with me, a white queer woman, what I really needed to do was have conversations about racism in predominantly white spaces and communities. Her comment inspired and pushed me to center anti-racist and anti-oppressive work in both my personal and professional lives in a more sustained and dedicated way than I had done previously.

A few months later, in fall 2015, I conceived the idea of the Anti-Oppression Workshop Series as several workshops dedicated to addressing oppression and racism in library practice and culture. I deliberately used the word *anti-oppression* rather than *diversity* because I wanted to name the systems of oppression that contribute to hostile work environments for librarians and staff of color. As Cheryl L. Branche points out, "diversity and multiculturalism suggest inclusiveness of diverse and many cultures; the obverse racism and race consciousness are rarely used, acknowledged or studied. The need for diversity cannot be investigated effectively without addressing the origins of the diversity deficit."[14] It was in the interest of addressing the origins of this deficit that the series was conceived.

Through institutional support from the University Library at the University of Illinois at Urbana-Champaign (UIUC), I was able to implement the Anti-Oppression Workshop Series in the spring of 2016. The series consisted of six one hour-long workshops on three distinct topics, with each workshop in the series offered twice. Workshops one and two focused on differentiating between "diversity" and "anti-oppression," since changes in both language and conversation are active steps that librarians can make towards dismantling structural inequality within librarianship and addressing related issues in the surrounding higher education landscape. Workshops three and four focused on intersectional librarianship,[15] and workshops five and six addressed practical solutions for creating an environment that is not hostile to librarians and staff of color.

One of the biggest hurdles I experienced throughout the process of developing and facilitating the series was wrestling with perfectionism. Perfectionism as a characteristic of white supremacy organizational culture manifests when "making a mistake is confused with being a mistake, doing wrong with being wrong."[16] I was afraid of making a mistake, of messing up, and being judged for it. The pressure to succeed and the added responsibility of having to propose, explain, and defend the series to people at varying levels of authority within the library's organizational structure, including presenting to the University Library Administrative Council, only exacerbated my fears.

---

14. Cheryl L. Branche, "Diversity in Librarianship: Is There a Color Line?" in *The 21st-Century Black Librarian in America*, eds. Andrew P. Jackson, Julius Jefferson, Jr., and Akilah Nosakhere. (Lanham, MD: The Scarecrow Press, Inc., 2012), 204.

15. Fobazi Ettarh, "Making a New Table: Intersectional Librarianship," *In the Library with the Lead Pipe* (July 2014), http://www.inthelibrarywiththeleadpipe. org/2014/making-a-new-table-intersectional-librarianship-3.

16. Kenneth Jones and Tema Okun, "White Supremacy Culture," Change-Work, 2001, http://www.cwsworkshop.org/PARC_site_B/dr-culture.html.

The knowledge that I was bound to mess up and say or do the wrong thing, which is the first truth April Hathcock presents in her blogpost, "You're Gonna Screw Up,"[17] also reminded me that I was capable of apologizing, learning from my mistakes, and doing better the next time. By working through the anxiety, resistance, and fear, it became clear to me that the only way we—and by *we* I mean white people—are going to develop the stamina to do anti-racist work *is by actually doing the work*. If we do not resist the oppressive institutional norm of perfectionism, we risk keeping white supremacy intact. We risk leaving the work to our fellow librarians and staff of color, who are already dealing with and coping with racism in the workplace on a daily basis. We risk not putting in the mental and emotional work and therefore diminishing our capacity to have the difficult conversations that are so necessary to dismantle white supremacy and transform our libraries into anti-oppressive spaces where racial diversity is actually possible.

The workshops were structured so that the roughly eighty participants, the majority of whom were white, were actively involved in reflecting, discussing, sharing, and strategizing together in order to figure out tangible ways to create an anti-racist and anti-oppressive library environment. Participation in small group discussions, as well as sharing with the entire group, was encouraged to help white people in particular strengthen their capacity and resolve to have conversations about race, racism, and white supremacy. In addition, it challenged them to do so in front of their peers of color, despite any perceived risk of getting it "wrong."

For example, during workshops one and two, when asked why the University Library was more or less homogenous—a question April Hathcock suggests that libraries struggling with lack of diversity ask[18]—

---

17. April Hathcock, "You're Gonna Screw Up," *At the Intersections* (blog), April 13, 2016, https://aprilhathcock.wordpress.com/2016/04/13/youre -gonna-screw-up/.

18. April Hathcock, "A Cure for the Common Whiteness: Diversity Recruitment," *At the Intersections* (blog), February 19, 2016, https://aprilhathcock. wordpress.com/2016/02/19/a-cure-for-the-common-whiteness-diversity-recruitment/.

several white participants responded with reasons for why people of color *choose* not to enter into the profession, such as low pay. They did not consider how discrimination, structural inequality, bias, and the whiteness of the profession could contribute to the lack of racial diversity in librarianship.[19] However, librarians and staff of color shared an alternative perspective. They said that when librarians or staff of color who were already working in the library attempted to address racism in the workplace, or to bring up issues about the lack of racial diversity, they were met with silence or, even worse, their livelihoods were potentially put at stake, including the risk of not having a reference to use later.

This example also demonstrates the ways in which white participants place the reason for the field's homogeneity on the shoulders of people of color rather than seeing themselves and inequitable practices as core reasons. In this instance, had the white participants been invested in perfectionism—again, when "making a mistake is confused with being a mistake, doing wrong with being wrong"[20]—they might have felt more hesitant to share. Instead, the workshops gave the white participants an opportunity to hear directly from the librarians and staff of color about their experiences, and they also had the opportunity to reevaluate what they had been taught were reasons why the field is overwhelmingly white.[21]

Bourg's framework for diversity, inclusion, social justice, and libraries demonstrates that there are many communities in which we can do

---

19. See Rebecca Hankins and Miguel Juárez, eds., *Where are All the Librarians of Color? The Experiences of People of Color in Academia* (Sacramento, CA: Library Juice Press, 2016); Andrew P. Jackson, Julius C. Jefferson, Jr., and Akilah S. Nosakhere, eds., *The 21st-Century Black Librarian in America: Issues and Challenges* (Lanham, MD: The Scarecrow Press, Inc., 2012); Kelly McElroy and Chris Diaz, "Residency Programs and Demonstrating Commitment to Diversity" (presentation, Association for College and Research Libraries Conference, Portland, Oregon, March 28, 2015), http://digitalcommons.nl.edu/faculty_publications/46; Galvan, "Soliciting Performance, Hiding Bias."

20. Kenneth Jones and Tema Okun, "White Supremacy Culture."

21. See footnote 19.

anti-oppression work, including the workplace.[22] The Anti-Oppression Workshop series highlighted the need not only for efforts that intentionally address oppression in the workplace, but also for honest spaces where participants are willing to speak up and where mistakes are permitted. In addition to allowing current professionals the time to examine their own biases, perfectionism, and the ways in which they uphold oppression, such spaces also support participants in figuring out tangible anti-oppressive strategies that they could implement in their places of work.

Anti-Racist Library Practice: Engaging with Local Communities, within LIS Circles, and Beyond

Katie Dover-Taylor

As David James Hudson points out, our diversity discourse at large tends to approach racism as an individual problem rather than a structural problem.[23] If we buy into the myth of racism as a purely personal failing or a failing of our individual institutions, we neglect the crucial collective work that is necessary if we are to imagine, design, and collaboratively build an anti-racist librarianship. Hudson also reminds us that critical work requires faith in community—that all of our work to illuminate or untangle injustice is incomplete and interdependent.[24] It is by acknowledging that we as individuals cannot "solve" racism that we free ourselves to become a small part of a larger movement that practices anti-racism and disrupts whiteness in our everyday lives.

---

22. Chris Bourg, "Diversity, Inclusion, Social Justice and Libraries: Proposing a Framework," *Feral Librarian* (blog), April 16, 2016, https://chrisbourg.wordpress.com/2016/04/16/diversity-inclusion-social-justice-and-libraries-proposing-a-framework/.

23. David James Hudson, "On Critical Librarianship and Pedagogies of the Practical" (presentation, Critical Librarianship and Pedagogy Symposium, Tucson, Arizona, February 25, 2016), https://arizona.hosted.panopto.com/Panopto/Pages/Viewer.aspx?id=38721a22-ed66-4904-bd93-f2953353e7ee.

24. Ibid.

Working effectively in community requires us to retrain ourselves to think of each person we work with as a complex individual rather than an identity category. Fobazi Ettarh's work explicitly connects critical librarianship with the black feminist concept of intersectionality. Our anti-racist librarianship must also be intersectional—we must consider how race, gender, sexuality, disability, and other axes of identity "contribute to unique experiences of oppression and privilege."[25]

So how do we embody anti-racist librarianship together, in community? In this section, I will discuss practices of anti-racist librarianship in the three outer rings of Bourg's framework:

- At the local level, exploring how libraries and librarians can bring an anti-racist lens to their work within communities;

- at the LIS level, considering the way we approach conversations about race and racism within our professional circles;

- and at the global level, discussing how we can engage in the Movement for Black Lives and other struggles for social justice.

Addressing Race and Racism Locally

At the local level, we find a variety of examples of librarians engaging with their communities to provide racial justice resources, organize discussions of race and racial equity, and support anti-racist work. In December 2014, librarians at the Oakland Public Library in California launched a #BlackLivesMatter resource series, which offered lists of books, articles, and videos to provoke action and discussion.[26] Their guides included:

---

25. Ettarh, "Making a New Table."

26. Amy Sonnie, "Listen, Learn, Participate: A #BlackLivesMatter Resource Series," *From the Main Library* (blog), December 22, 2014, http://oaklandlibrary.org/blogs/from-main-library/listen-learn-participate-blacklivesmatter-resource-series.

- Institutional Racism: History and Context

- Protest, Social Movements & Community Solutions

- Police Conduct, Race and the Justice System

- Talking to Kids About Racism and Justice[27]

In 2015, the Oakland Public Library followed up the launch of these resources with "a series of events on policing, prisons, racial justice and social change in the United States."[28]

The Skokie Public Library's 2015 Voices of Race series is another excellent example of the work that library staff members can do to facilitate difficult discussions of race and racism in the local community. Skokie is a diverse community in Illinois where over ninety languages are spoken and forty percent of the population is foreign born.[29] Voices of Race was created collaboratively by librarians of color, white librarians, and surrounding community organizations. The series spanned four months and culminated in the library staff's participation in Stand Against Racism, a national initiative of the YWCA. Related programs for patrons of all ages included theatrical performances, lectures, book discussions, and a patron-curated art exhibit. The library provided knapsacks to patrons inspired by Peggy McIntosh's 1988 essay, "White Privilege: Unpacking the Invisible Knapsack."[30] In 2016, Voices of

---

27. Ibid.

28. Amy Sonnie, "Listen, Learn, Participate: #BlackLivesMatter Event Series," *From the Main Library* (blog), February 28, 2015, http://oaklandlibrary.org/blogs/from-main-library/listen-learn-particiate-blacklivesmatter-event-series.

29. Amy Koester and Amita Lonial, "Skokie Library Tackles Race," *School Library Journal*, June 12, 2015, http://www.slj.com/2015/06/diversity/about-race-a-community-event-shifts-from-celebrating-diversity-to-discussing-race/.

30. Peggy McIntosh, "White Privilege: Unpacking the Invisible Knapsack," *Independent School* (Winter 1990): 31-33, http://www.wvu.edu/~lawfac/jscully/Race/documents/whiteprivilege.pdf.

Race received national recognition in the form of the American Library Association Excellence in Library Programming Award.[31]

The Madison Public Library maintains a list of racial equity and social justice resources tailored to their local community.[32] Madison, Wisconsin is one of several communities in the United States that participate in the Local and Regional Government Alliance on Racial Equity (GARE). GARE is a national network that provides resources and training for local governments that want to "proactively work to advance racial equity, focusing on eliminating inequities and increasing success for all."[33] Advocating for our local communities to consider joining GARE and using their toolkit to develop library policies that center racial equity are two ways we can support the development of new structures that are fundamentally anti-racist.

In order to bring these anti-racist library programs and resources into being, Oakland, Skokie, and Madison librarians required support and buy-in from their library administrations and local communities. Unfortunately, not all of us live or work in a place where our administrators and community leaders are supportive of social justice efforts. If our institutions actively discourage or silence discussions of race and social justice, we can still do our own work towards creating a welcoming, inclusive, and anti-racist environment. Microactivism consists of everyday ways we can center the narratives and truths of people of color and prioritize social justice in our communities.[34] Our own expressions of microactivism will depend on our local contexts, but might include

31. Cheryl Malden, "Skokie Public Library Winner of the ALA Excellence in Library Programming Award," *American Library Association News*, March 22, 2016, http://www.ala.org/news/press-releases/2016/03/skokie-public-library-winner-ala-excellence-library-programming-award.

32. Madison Public Library, "Racial Equity Resources," 2017, http://www.madisonpubliclibrary.org/racial-equity.

33. Local and Regional Government Alliance on Race and Equity, "Tools & Resources," last accessed September 8, 2016, http://racialequityalliance.org/tools-resources/.

34. Rachel Lockman, "Academic Librarians and Social Justice: A Call to Microactivism," *College & Research Libraries News* 76, no. 4 (2015): 193-94, http://crln.acrl.org/content/76/4/193.short.

reading and collecting the works of diverse authors, creating displays that highlight the lives and realities of people of color, or speaking out to counter the racism and microaggressions we witness against others in our everyday lives.

Organizing for Racial Justice within LIS

One of the most crucial first steps that white librarians can take in the LIS community is to acknowledge and address the harm that our racism and the "unbearable whiteness of librarianship" has done to colleagues and patrons of color in the past and present so that we don't perpetuate that harm in the future.[35] Anti-racist work requires white people to show a willingness to deal with painful truths that might make us feel discomfort. Our discomfort pales in comparison to the trauma caused in black communities denied access to public libraries or jailed for checking out books in the Jim Crow South, the daily sting of microaggressions that impact librarians and library staff of color and make them feel alienated at work, or the message we send with behavior policies that disproportionately target youth of color for "rowdy" behavior and ban them from the library.[36] To begin to listen and accept the testimony of librarians, library staff, and patrons of color is to discover the depths of our own willful ignorance and to see the enormity of the transformative work that lies ahead.

Libraries 4 Black Lives (L4BL) is a collective of librarians dedicated to that transformative work.[37] L4BL is a call to action, a gathering place for ideas, and a newly-forming network of librarians dedicated

35. Bourg, "The Unbearable Whiteness of Librarianship."

36. DeNeen L. Brown, "He Tried to Check Out a Robert E. Lee Book From the Library. He Got Jailed Instead," *Washington Post*, August 25, 2016, https://www.washingtonpost.com/local/he-tried-to-check-out-a-robert-e-lee-book-from-the-library-he-got-jailed-instead/2016/08/25/f0e7df6a-6805-11e6-8225-fbb8a6fc65bc_story.html.

37. Libraries 4 Black Lives, "Take the Pledge," last accessed November 1, 2016, http://libraries4blacklives.org/pledge.

to anti-racism.[38] L4BL provides a forum for librarians and library staff to become involved in anti-racist organizing within LIS and to connect with the Movement for Black Lives.

Organizing at the LIS level gives librarians stymied by their local setting an opportunity to find another outlet in which to do social justice work. For example, in 2016, I helped to coordinate and co-moderate a panel called "Librarians of Color Survival Guide: Truth and Self Care."[39] As a white librarian, I initially debated whether it made sense for me to be involved in a panel that was designed to center the lived experiences of librarians of color. After consulting with the panelists and my co-moderator, we decided it was important to find a way for me to participate and show my solidarity without centering myself or my whiteness, and I thus took on an assistant role, modeling what it means to listen to and support people of color.

Outside the Echo Chamber: Anti-Racist Library Practice Beyond LIS

Much of the scholarly discussion of anti-racist activities in libraries centers around work done in academic settings. Those of us who work in public libraries may be more likely to approach anti-racist work from personal experience or a community-oriented perspective, rather than by employing critical theory. My hope is that the discussion of critical librarianship happening within LIS will become more accessible to people outside the academy—by actively including public librarians, library staff, grassroots organizations that work to make media and information technology accessible to marginalized communities, people who do not consider themselves librarians but organize information resources and programs for community use, and members of the public who may find

---

38. Lisa Peet, "Public Librarians Launch Libraries4BlackLives," *Library Journal*, August 10, 2016, http://lj.libraryjournal.com/2016/08/people/public-librarians-launch-libraries4blacklives/#.

39. Allied Media Projects, "Allied Media Conference 2016: Librarians of Color Survival Guide: Truth and Self-Care," 2016, https://amc2016.sched.org/event/77SL/librarians-of-color-survival-guide-truth-and-self-care.

great value in resources that libraries can offer but for whatever reasons (including structural racism and unwelcoming institutional culture) do not consider libraries to be "for them." Our anti-racist organizing in LIS must tirelessly seek out perspectives far beyond academic libraries and library scholarship if we are to change the status quo in libraries.

One way to approach the disconnect between librarians and the global community is to begin to hold our conversations about privilege, anti-racism, and social justice in libraries beyond the echo chamber of library scholarship and library conferences. This was one of our primary goals for the Radical Librarianship Track at the Allied Media Conference (AMC), which I helped to organize in 2015 and 2016. The AMC is "a collaborative laboratory of media-based organizing strategies for trans-forming our world."[40] Formerly the Midwest Zine Conference, AMC is an annual gathering of a vibrant community of people using many kinds of media to incite social change. The conference centers the voices and solutions of queer and trans people of color. The Radical Librarianship Track is a series of sessions at AMC that hopes to introduce librarians, archivists, and museum workers to the diverse environment of AMC and to broaden our understanding of what constitutes library work. The value of hosting these conversations at AMC is that we get to involve three audiences that otherwise might rarely meet:

- Professional librarians, archivists, and museum workers who want to apply the principles of media-based organizing to their work in cultural institutions [41]

- People who organize grassroots or community libraries and want to learn more about how to structure their collections and programs

---

40. Allied Media Projects, "Allied Media Conference," 2016, https://www.alliedmedia.org/amc.

41. Allied Media Projects, "Media-based Organizing," 2016, https://www.alliedmedia.org/media-based-organizing.

- Diverse library users who want to engage in discussions of how all kinds of libraries, archives, and museums can best serve their communities in the present and future

In 2015, we hosted a session presented by Olaronke Akinmowo, the creator and operator of the Free Black Women's Library, a mobile, interactive, pop-up library that features over 400 books written by black women.[42] Originally funded by a Culture Push Fellowship for Utopian Practice intended to support boundary-pushing, interdisciplinary, and socially-engaged artwork, the library is of and for its community—centering black women's experiences of the world and transforming public spaces into places that explicitly celebrate blackness. The library pops up at parks and community gardens, on stoops in Akinwomo's Brooklyn neighborhood, and in barbershops and other local businesses and community organizations to share stories, conversations, music, performances, and books.[43] As a librarian without formal training who also identifies as a performer and artist, Akinmowo is not limited by the boundaries we place on professional librarians. In the Radical Librarianship Track at AMC, she found an opportunity to share the story of the Free Black Women's Library and to get suggestions on how to organize her collection. This is a strong example of anti-racist library practice that we could both learn from and support if we look beyond our established understanding of LIS.

There are plenty of opportunities for white librarians to become involved in the movement for racial justice locally, nationally, and within LIS. Join the call for Libraries 4 Black Lives. Find out if your area has a chapter of Black Lives Matter you can support or a chapter of Showing Up for Racial Justice (SURJ), a national network of groups and individuals organizing white people for racial justice, that you can

---

42. Culture Push, "Fall 2014 Fellow: Olaronke Akinmowo," 2014, http://www.culturepush.org/olaronke-akinmowo.

43. Emma Bracy, "The Free Black Women's Library Gives Away Books and Black Girl Magic," *Fusion*, October 5, 2016, http://fusion.net/story/354277/free-black-womens-library-books-black-girl-magic/.

join.[44] Find like-minded librarians and begin to assemble your personal toolkit of anti-racist practices. Whatever you decide to do to support social justice in your communities, showing up is the first step. As April Hathcock says, "you're gonna screw up."[45] Do not let that dissuade you. Do the work.[46]

Bibliography

Allied Media Projects. "Allied Media Conference." 2016. https://www.alliedmedia.org/amc.

————. "Allied Media Conference 2016: Librarians of Color Survival Guide: Truth and Self Care." Allied Media Conference. 2016. https://amc2016.sched.org/event/77SL/librarians-of-color-survival-guide-truth-and-self-care.

————. "Media-Based Organizing." 2016. https://www.alliedmedia.org/media-based-organizing.

American Library Association. "Diversity Counts 2009-2010 Update," accessed January 13, 2017. http://www.ala.org/offices/diversity/diversitycounts/2009-2010update.

Ayvazian, Andrea. "Interrupting the Cycle of Oppression: The Role of Allies as Agents of Change." In *Readings for Diversity and Social Justice*, 2nd ed., edited by Maurianne Adams, et al., 625-28. New York: Routledge, 2010.

Bourg, Chris. "Diversity, Inclusion, Social Justice and Libraries: Proposing a Framework." *Feral Librarian* (blog), April 16, 2016. https://chrisbourg.wordpress.com/2016/04/16/diversity-inclusion-social-justice-and-libraries-proposing-a-framework/.

---

44. Showing Up for Racial Justice, last accessed November 1, 2016, http://www.showingupforracialjustice.org/.

45. Hathcock, "You're Gonna Screw Up."

46. April Hathcock, "DO THE WORK!!! #libleadgender Chat March 9," *At the Intersection* (blog), March 4, 2016, https://aprilhathcock.wordpress.com/2016/03/04/do-the-work-libleadgender-chat-march-9/.

———. "Talking at Harvard About Libraries and Social Justice." *Feral Librarian* (blog), September 17, 2016. https://chrisbourg. wordpress.com/2016/09/17/talking-at-harvard-about-librar- ies-and-social-justice/.

———. "The Unbearable Whiteness of Librarianship." *Feral Librar- ian* (blog), March 3, 2014. https://chrisbourg.wordpress. com/2014/03/03/the-unbearable-whiteness-of-librarian- ship/.

Bracy, Emma. "The Free Black Women's Library Gives Away Books and Black Girl Magic." *Fusion.* October 5, 2016. http://fu- sion.net/story/354277/free-black-womens-library-books- black-girl-magic/.

Branche, Cheryl L. "Diversity in Librarianship: Is There a Color Line?" In *The 21st-Century Black Librarian in America,* edited by Andrew P. Jackson, Julius C. Jefferson Jr, and Akilah S. No- sakhere, 203-06. Lanham, MD: The Scarecrow Press, 2012.

Brook, Freeda, Dave Ellenwood, and Althea Eannace Lazzaro, "In Pursuit of Antiracist Social Justice: Denaturalizing Whiteness in the Academic Library." *Library Trends* 64, no. 2 (2015): 246-84. doi: 10.1353/lib.2015.0048.

Brown, DeNeen L. "He Tried to Check Out a Robert E. Lee Book from the Library. He Got Jailed Instead," *Washington Post,* August 25, 2016. https://www.washingtonpost.com/local/ he-tried-to-check-out-a-robert-e-lee-book-from-the-library- he-got-jailed-instead/2016/08/25/f0e7df6a-6805-11e6- 8225-fbb8a6fc65bc_story.html.

Cammarota, Julio. "Blindsided by the Avatar: White Saviors and Al- lies Out of Hollywood and in Education." *Review of Educa- tion, Pedagogy & Cultural Studies* 33, no. 3 (2011): 242-59. doi:1 0.1080/10714413.2011.585287.

Culture Push. "Fall 2014 Fellow: Olaronke Akinmowo." 2014. http:// www.culturepush.org/2014-fall-fellow-olaronke-akinmowo/.

DiAngelo, Robin. *What Does It Mean to Be White? Developing White Racial Literacy.* New York: Peter Lang, 2012.

Ettarh, Fobazi. "Making a New Table: Intersectional Librarianship." *In the Library with the Lead Pipe* (July 2014). http://www.inthelibrarywiththeleadpipe.org/2014/making-a-new-table-intersectional-librarianship-3.

Galvan, Angela. "Soliciting Performance, Hiding Bias: Whiteness and Librarianship." *In the Library with the Lead Pipe* (April 2015). http://www.inthelibrarywiththeleadpipe.org/2015/soliciting-performance-hiding-bias-whiteness-and-librarianship/.

Hankins, Rebecca, and Miguel Juárez, eds. *Where are all the Librarians of Color? The Experiences of People of Color in Academia.* Sacramento, CA: Library Juice Press, 2016.

Hathcock, April. "A Cure for the Common Whiteness: Diversity Recruitment." *At the Intersection* (blog), February 19, 2016. https://aprilhathcock.wordpress.com/2016/02/19/a-cure-for-the-common-whiteness-diversity-recruitment/.

———. "DO THE WORK!!!#libleadgender Chat March 9." *At the Intersection* (blog), March 4, 2016. https://aprilhathcock.wordpress.com/2016/03/04/do-the-work-libleadgender-chat-march-9/.

———. "White Librarianship in Blackface: Diversity Initiatives in LIS." *In the Library with the Lead Pipe* (October 2015). http://www.inthlibrarywiththeleadpipe.org/2015/lis-diversity/.

———. "You're Gonna Screw Up." *At the Intersection* (blog), April 13, 2016. https://aprilhathcock.wordpress.com/2016/04/13/youre-gonna-screw-up/.

Helms, Janet E. "An Update of Helms's White and People of Color Racial Identity Models." In *Handbook of Multicultural Counseling*, edited by Joseph G. Ponterotto et al., 181-98. Thousand Oaks, CA: Sage, 1995.

————. *Black and White Racial Identity: Theory, Research, and Practice.* New York: Greenwood Press, 1990.

Hudson, David James. *On Critical Librarianship and Pedagogies of the Practical.* Presentation, Critical Librarianship and Pedagogy Symposium, Tucson, AZ, February 25, 2016. https://arizona.hosted.panopto.com/Panopto/Pages/Viewer.aspx?id=38721a22-ed66-4904-bd93-f2953353e7ee.

Jackson, Andrew P., Julius C. Jefferson, Jr., and Akilah S. Nosakhere, eds. *The 21st-Century Black Librarian in America: Issues and Challenges.* Lanham, MD: The Scarecrow Press, 2012.

Jones, Kenneth, and Tema Okun, "White Supremacy Culture." ChangeWork, 2001. http://www.cwsworkshop.org/PARC_site_B/dr-culture.html.

Koester, Amy, and Amita Lonial. "Skokie Library Tackles Race." *School Library Journal,* June 12, 2015. http://www.slj.com/2015/06/diversity/about-race-a-community-event-shifts-from-celebrating-diversity-to-discussing-race/.

Lawrence, Sandra M., and Beverly Daniel Tatum. "White Racial Identity and Anti-Racist Education: A Catalyst for Change." In *Beyond Heroes and Holidays: A Practical Guide to K-12 Anti-racist, Multicultural Education and Staff Development,* 2nd ed., edited by Enid Lee, Deborah Menkart, and Margo Okazawa-Rey, 49-56. Washington, DC: Teaching for Change, 2002.

Libraries 4 Black Lives. "Take the Pledge." 2016. http://libraries-4blacklives.org/pledge.

Local and Regional Government Alliance on Race and Equity. "Tools & Resources." 2015. http://racialequityalliance.org/tools-resources/.

Lockman, Rachel. "Academic Librarians and Social Justice: A Call to Microactivism." *College & Research Libraries News* 76, no. 4 (2015): 193-94.

Luft, Rachel E. "Intersectionality and the Risk of Flattening Difference." In *The Intersectional Approach: Transforming the Academy through Race, Class and Gender*, edited by Michele Tracy Berger and Kathleen Guidroz, 100-17. Chapel Hill, NC: University of North Carolina Press, 2009.

Madison Public Library. "Racial Equity and Social Justice Resources." 2017. http://www.madisonpubliclibrary.org/racialequity.

Malden, Cheryl. "Skokie Public Library winner of the ALA Excellence in Library Programming Award." *ALA News*, March 22, 2016. http://www.ala.org/news/press-releases/2016/03/skokie-public-library-winner-ala-excellence-library-programming-award.

McElroy, Kelly, and Chris Diaz. "Residency Programs and Demonstrating Commitment to Diversity." Presentation, Association for College and Research Libraries Conference, Portland, OR, March 28, 2015. http://digitalcommons.nl.edu/faculty_publications/46.

McIntosh, Peggy. "White Privilege: Unpacking the Invisible Knapsack." *Independent School*, (Winter 1990): 31-36. http://www.wvu.edu/~lawfac/jscully/Race/documents/whiteprivilege.pdf.

Peet, Lisa. "Public Librarians Launch Libraries4BlackLives." *Library Journal*, August 2016.

Showing Up for Racial Justice (SURJ). 2016. http://www.showingupforracialjustice.org/.

Sonnie, Amy. "Listen, Learn, Participate: #BlackLivesMatter Event Series." *From the Main Library* (blog), February 28, 2015. http://oaklandlibrary.org/blogs/from-main-library/listen-learn-particiate-blacklivesmatter-event-series.

———. "Listen, Learn, Participate: a #BlackLivesMatter Resource Series." *From the Main Library* (blog), December 22, 2014. http://oaklandlibrary.org/blogs/from-main-library/listen-learn-participate-blacklivesmatter-resource-series.

Sullivan, Shannon. *Good White People: The Problem with Middle-Class Anti-Racism.* Albany, NY: State University of New York Press, 2014.

Tatum, Beverly Daniel. "Teaching White Students about Racism: The Search for White Allies and the Restoration of Hope." *Teachers College Record* 95, no. 4 (1994): 462-76.

———. *"Why Are All the Black Kids Sitting Together in the Cafeteria?" and Other Conversations About Race.* New York: Basic Books, 2003.

About the Contributors

George Apodaca is currently Administrative Fellow within Harvard's University Archives. He received his MLS from the University of Arizona in 2013, where he formed part of a select cohort of Knowledge River scholars whose aim has been to serve the information needs of Latino and Indigenous peoples, foster an understanding of information issues from the perspective of these communities, and advocate for culturally sensitive information services in both libraries and archives. Prior to his time in Cambridge, he worked in the Manuscripts and Archives Department at the University of Delaware Library as Pauline A. Young Resident and in Special Collections at the University of Arizona Libraries.

Natalie Baur is a member of the librarian faculty at the Biblioteca Daniel Cosío Villegas at El Colegio de México in Mexico City and formerly the Archivist for the Cuban Heritage Collection at the University of Miami Libraries. She holds an MA in History and a certificate in Museum Studies from the University of Delaware and an MLS with a concentration in Archives, Information and Records Management from the University of Maryland. Most recently, she was a Fulbright-Garcia Robles scholar at the Universidad Nacional Autónoma de México (UNAM) for the 2015-2016 academic year, researching transnational opportunities for sustainable digital preservation programs in the Americas.

Ian Beilin is Humanities Research Services Librarian at Columbia University. He has a PhD in European history from Columbia and an MSIS from the University at Albany. Previously he was Instruction and Outreach Librarian at New York City College of Technology (CUNY) where he taught the credit-bearing course "Research and Documentation for the Information Age." He has written and presented on topics in critical library instruction and critical information literacy, including "Beyond the Threshold: Conformity Resistance, and the ACRL Information Literacy Framework for Higher Education," and "Teaching the Skills to Question: A Credit-Course Approach to Critical Information Literacy." His current research projects are on the practice of critical information literacy in a research library environment, and a historical study looking at conformity and resistance among 20th century German academic librarians. He is also at work on a co-authored book on the cultural history of fin de siècle Europe, to be published by Bloomsbury.

Kristyn Caragher is a newly minted public librarian based in the Chicago area. She completed a Certificate of Advanced Study (CAS) in Library and Information Science at the University of Illinois at Urbana-Champaign in 2016, after successfully earning the Master of Science in Library and Information Science from the University of Illinois in 2014. When she is not busy trying to figure out how to implement anti-oppressive practices in the workplace, she can be found reading at the local feminist bookstore or socializing with other radical librarians. To learn more about her work, visit www.kristyncaragher.com.

Chloe Collins graduated from Smith College in 2013, where she studied Women and Gender Studies and Book Studies. Chloe strives to integrate critical practice into her studies at the University of Illinois' School of Information Sciences by incorporating intersectional feminism into Special Collections and Museum Studies. Chloe looks forward to bringing an intersectional feminist lens to her work as an aspiring academic art and design or museum librarian.

Nicole A. Cooke is an assistant professor at the School of Information Sciences at the University of Illinois at Urbana-Champaign and a faculty affiliate at the School's Center for Digital Inclusion. She holds an MEd in Adult Education from Penn State, and an MLS and a PhD in Communication, Information and Library Studies from Rutgers University, where she was one of the first twelve ALA Spectrum Doctoral Fellows. She was named a "Mover & Shaker" by *Library Journal* in 2007 and was the 2016 recipient of the ALA's Equality Award. Her research and teaching interests include human information behavior (particularly in the online context), critical cultural information studies, and diversity and social justice in librarianship (with an emphasis on infusing them into LIS education and pedagogy). Prior to joining the Illinois faculty, Nicole was an academic librarian, focusing on reference and instruction, for over twelve years.

Katherine M. Crowe is the Curator for Special Collections and Archives at the University of Denver. She oversees acquisition and curation of primary resource collections, permanent university records in all formats, and special and rare materials. Her work also includes facilitating in-person and online discovery, the creation of exhibits, and services to users of primary resources. She works with interested students, faculty, donors, and researchers at the University of Denver to collect records that fill the gaps in the University's historical record, and to encourage researchers and students to read existing archival records "against the grain" so that the voices of underrepresented and marginalized communities can be heard.

Katie Dover-Taylor is a white, queer ciswoman who was born and raised in the city of Detroit. She now works as a public librarian focused on technology training for adult patrons with a range of backgrounds and skill levels. She has presented on the topics of empathy and digital literacy at library conferences throughout Michigan. In 2015 and 2016, Katie served on the coordinating team for the Radical Librarianship

Track at the Allied Media Conference (AMC), bringing the first official gathering of library-centric content to an annual conference which draws a diverse spectrum of creative and technology-savvy people engaged in social justice work.

Sarah Hannah Gómez holds an MA in children's literature and MS in library and information science from the University of Arizona. She spent two years as a librarian at an independent school in Northern California. She is now a freelance writer, editor, and consultant, as well as an adjunct professor at Emporia State University. She is working towards a PhD in history and critical theory of children's literature at the University of Arizona. Find her online at shgmclicious.com.

April M. Hathcock is the Scholarly Communications Librarian at NYU where she educates the campus community on issues of ownership, access, and rights in the research lifecycle. She received her JD and LLM in International and Comparative Law from Duke University School of Law and her MLIS from the University of South Florida. Before entering librarianship, she practiced intellectual property and antitrust law for a global private firm. Her research interests include cultural creation and exchange, and the ways in which social and legal infrastructures benefit the works of certain groups over others.

Todd Honma is an assistant professor of Asian American Studies at Pitzer College. His research interests include race and social justice in LIS, zines and community engagement, and the cultural politics of body modification. His work has been published in journals such as *InterActions: UCLA Journal of Education and Information Studies*, *AAPI Nexus: Policy, Practice and Community*, *Amerasia*, *Radical Teacher*, and *In the Library with the Lead Pipe*.

David James Hudson is a critical race and information studies scholar, a poet and spoken word artist, and an associate librarian at University of Guelph in the traditional territory of Attawandaron/Neutral People (also known as Guelph, Ontario, Canada).

Nicole M. Joseph is an Assistant Professor of Mathematics and Science Education in the Department of Teaching and Learning at Vanderbilt University. Dr. Joseph was a 2014 National Academy of Education/Spencer Post-Doctoral Fellow and her research interests include mathematics education and equity from an intersectional perspective. She primarily studies Black women and girls, their identity development and their experiences in mathematics and mathematics education. She also studies the role of race, class, gender and other socially constructed identities in mathematics identity development as well as the history of mathematics education of African Americans (1837-1957).

Melissa Kalpin Prescott is an Associate Professor and Research and Instruction Librarian at St. Cloud State University. She is a member of the planning team for the Anti-Racist Pedagogy Across the Curriculum (ARPAC) project that consists of an annual workshop, follow-up support, and ongoing assessment and improvement. Melissa also teaches credit-bearing information literacy and critical reasoning courses.

Jorge R. López-McKnight is a First-Year Experience Librarian at the University of New Mexico. In his role, he participates in a numerous teaching and learning activities with freshman and transfer students to support their growth and educational processes. With his colleagues, he also teaches a credit-bearing course, OILS 101, Introduction to Information Studies. His research interests include critical race theory and LIS, educators of color identities and teaching practices, and university libraries-high school relationships. He holds an MLS from Indiana University.

Rebekah M. Loyd graduated from William Jewell College with a degree in history in 2014. Her abiding interest in cultural history and social justice have led her to pursue an MLIS with a concentration in Special

Collections from the University of Illinois' School of Information Sciences. Rebekah looks forward to continuously incorporating the principles of feminist pedagogy, diversity, and inclusion in her career and research in special libraries and archives.

Cass Mabbott is a doctoral student at the School of Information Sciences, University of Illinois, Urbana-Champaign. Before pursuing her doctorate, she was a youth services librarian and manager for seventeen years, mostly at the Seattle Public Library. She has been a lecturer at the University of Washington's iSchool for the past seven years. Her research includes social justice issues with youth in public libraries, information behavior of very young children, the history of youth services in public libraries, children's literature, and management of public libraries.

Jessica Macias is a graduate student in the MMLIS program at the University of Southern California. Her professional experience has been primarily in academic libraries, where she has grown as a Library Technician. While being acutely aware of the lack of diversity within the profession, the common bond shared over the love for the written word fuels her endless respect for libraries and those who work in them.

Janiece Mackey is a PhD student in Curriculum and Instruction at the University of Denver, where she was a graduate assistant for Dr. Nicole Joseph. She is also the Executive Director of Young Aspiring Americans for Social and Political Activism (YAASPA), which cultivates youth to be civically engaged in community and career. Her foundation and research interests focus on the nexus of critical race theory and career pathways at the K-12 education level. She has also centered her work and research on social science academic and career development to support the next generation of what she calls critical conscious-preneurs and praxticioners.

Jennifer Margolis Jacobs is an Information Specialist at Avon Center Elementary School (Round Lake Beach, Community Consolidated

School District 46 in Illinois). She is also an adjunct instructor for the School of Education at Dominican University and Southern Illinois University. A 2016 graduate from the Masters of Library and Information Science program at the University of Illinois at Urbana-Champaign, she plans on incorporating diversity and social justice into her practice as a school librarian. Jacobs also holds a dual BS from Western Michigan University, and a MA from Northeastern Illinois University (learning disabilities). She is also the proud mother of three children, Benji, Heloise, and Esther.

Rafia Mirza is currently the Digital Humanities Librarian and liaison to History, Disability Studies, and Women's and Gender Studies at the University of Texas at Arlington. She did graduate coursework in American studies at the University of Minnesota and received her MSI from the University of Michigan in 2008. Her research interests include digital humanities, digital pedagogy, project management, and mass culture. She welcomes comments at librarianrafia@gmail.com.

Vani Natarajan works as a Research and Instruction Librarian for the Humanities and Global Studies at Barnard College. She draws inspiration from, and gives thanks to, the creative resistance and capacious visions of feminist and queer writers, artists, and activists of color. Vani also writes fiction.

Gina Schlesselman-Tarango is an Instructional Services and Initiatives Librarian at California State University, San Bernardino. She facilitates critical information literacy opportunities for students and faculty, teaches a first-year seminar course, provides reference services, and is a collection development liaison to sociology, criminal justice, and gender and sexuality studies programs. She holds a BA in sociology/ anthropology, a master's of social sciences, and an MLIS. Her research interests include gender and race in LIS, critical information literacy, and feminist navigations of infertility. You can view more of her work at ginaschless.com.

Maura Seale is currently the collections, research, and instruction librarian for African American studies, American history and studies, European history, music, and women's and gender studies at Georgetown University. She received her MA in American studies from the University of Minnesota in 2005 and her MSI from the University of Michigan in 2007. Her research interests include critical theory and librarianship, information literacy, pedagogy, and mass culture. She welcomes comments at mauraseale@gmail.com.

Stephanie Sendaula is an Associate Editor at *Library Journal,* where she writes and edits reviews of non-fiction (and occasionally fiction) titles and contributes to features. She received her MLIS from Drexel University and her BA in journalism from Temple University, and was previously a public librarian in New Jersey handling reference, instruction, and collection development. As a public librarian, she became an advocate for comics and graphic novels as well as diversity in all forms of literature, all of which she is still passionate about today.

Katrina Spencer is a 2016 graduate from the Masters of Library and Information Science program at the University of Illinois at Urbana-Champaign, and will serve as the Diversity Resident Librarian at the University of Wisconsin at Madison. Her career will continue to examine international studies and collections, engage writing, and examine issues of otherness and subalternity. For more, visit katleespe.com.

Margarita Vargas-Betancourt is the Curator of Latin American and Caribbean Special Collections at the George A. Smathers Libraries of the University of Florida. She is in charge of processing and curating Latin American and Caribbean manuscripts and serving as liaison and reference librarian to faculty and students. She uses her background on colonialism, ethnohistory, and diversity to identify and highlight the hidden voices in archival collections and to serve and empower Latino students at the University of Florida.

Shaundra Walker serves as Assistant Professor and Associate Director for Instruction & Research Services at Georgia College in Milledgeville, Georgia. She holds a PhD in Educational Leadership, with a concentration in Higher Education Administration, from Mercer University. Her dissertation was entitled, "The Role of the HBCU Library Alliance Leadership Program in Developing Leaders." Walker's research focuses on leadership and organizational development within libraries at historically Black colleges and universities. She is a graduate of Spelman College, where she received the Bachelor of Arts degree in history, and Clark-Atlanta University, where she earned a master of science in library and information studies.

Megan Watson is currently Information Literacy Librarian at the University of Alaska Southeast Egan Library. She previously worked as Research & Instruction/Education Librarian at the University of Washington Bothell & Cascadia College Campus Library and was a founding member of the Library's Equity, Diversity, and Social Justice Team. Megan also serves on the ACRL Diversity Committee and earned an MLS and MA from Indiana University Bloomington.

INDEX

Voices of Race, 305

CPSIA information can be obtained
at www.ICGtesting.com
Printed in the USA
LVHW050007310820
664592LV00018B/2752

9 781634 000222